AS COMMUNICATION AND CULTURE:
The Essential Introduction

Third edition

Peter Bennett and Jerry Slater

Routledge
Taylor & Francis Group

LONDON AND NEW YORK

First published 2001 as *Communication Studies: The Essential Introduction*
Reprinted 2002, 2003

Second edition published 2005 as *AS Communication Studies: The Essential Introduction*

This edition published 2008
by Routledge
2 Park Square, Milton Park, Abingdon, Oxon, OX14 4RN

Simultaneously published in the USA and Canada
by Routledge
270 Madison Ave, New York, NY 10016

Routledge is an imprint of the Taylor & Francis Group, an informa business

© 2008 Peter Bennett and Jerry Slater

Reprinted 2009

Typeset in Folio and Bauhaus by
Keystroke, 28 High Street, Tettenhall, Wolverhampton
Printed and bound in Great Britain by Bell & Bain Ltd, Glasgow

British Library Cataloguing in Publication Data
A catalogue record for this book is available from the British Library

Library of Congress Cataloging-in-Publication Data
      Bennett, Peter, 1961–
      As communication & culture : the essential introduction /
      Peter Bennett & Jerry Slater. — 3rd ed.
          p. cm. — (The essentials series)
      AS communication studies / Andrew Beck, Peter Bennett, Peter Wall.
      2nd ed. 2005
      1. Communication. I. Slater, Jerry. II. Beck, Andrew, 1952– AS communication
      studies. III. Title.
      P90.B34 2008
      302.2—dc22
      2007049693

ISBN10: 0–415–45512–X
ISBN13: 978–0–415–45512–1

AS COMMUNICATION AND CULTURE:

The Essential Introduction

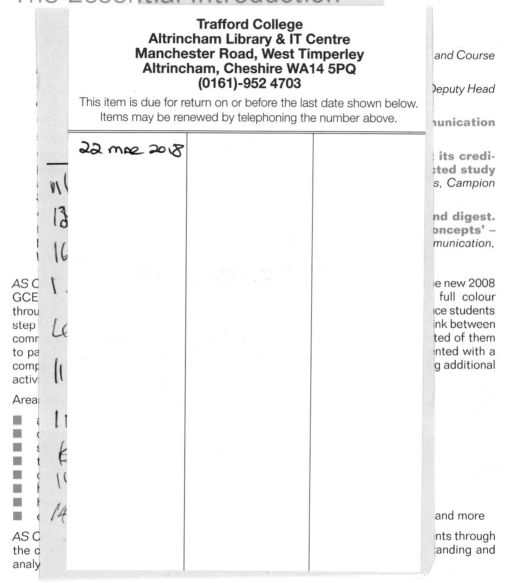

and Course

Deputy Head

munication

its credi-
cted study
s, Campion

nd digest.
oncepts' –
munication,

AS C   e new 2008
GCE   full colour
throu   ce students
step   nk between
comm   ted of them
to pa   nted with a
comp   g additional
activ

Area

- a
- c
- s
- t
- g
- h
- e

and more

AS C   nts through
the c   anding and
analy

Peter Bennett is Chief Examiner for GCE Communication and Culture, Senior Lecturer in the School of Education at the University of Wolverhampton, co-editor of *Communication Studies: The Essential Resource* (2003) and co-author of *Framework Media: Channels* (2003) and *A2 Media Studies: The Essential Introduction* (2005).

Jerry Slater is Principal Examiner for GCE Communication and Culture, teacher at Colchester Sixth Form College and co-author of *A2 Media Studies: The Essential Introduction* (2005).

The *Essentials* Series

This series of textbooks, resource books and revision guides covers everything you could need to know about taking exams in Media, Communication or Film Studies. Working together the series offers everything you need to move from AS level through to an undergraduate degree. Written by experts in their subjects, the series is clearly presented to aid understanding with the textbooks updated regularly to keep examples current.

Series Editor: Peter Wall

AS Communication and Culture: The Essential Introduction, Third Edition
Peter Bennett and Jerry Slater

Communication Studies: The Essential Resource
Andrew Beck, Peter Bennett and Peter Wall

AS Film Studies: The Essential Introduction, Second Edition
Sarah Casey Benyahia, Freddie Gaffney and John White

A2 Film Studies: The Essential Introduction, Second Edition
Sarah Casey Benyahia, Freddie Gaffney and John White

Film Studies: The Essential Resource
Peter Bennett, Andrew Hickman and Peter Wall

AS Media Studies: The Essential Introduction for AQA, Third Edition
Philip Rayner and Peter Wall

A2 Media Studies: The Essential Introduction for AQA, Second Edition
Peter Bennett, Jerry Slater and Peter Wall

AS Media Studies: The Essential Revision Guide for AQA
Jo Barker and Peter Wall

A2 Media Studies: The Essential Revision Guide for AQA
Jo Barker and Peter Wall

Media Studies: The Essential Resource
Philip Rayner, Peter Wall and Stephen Kruger

CONTENTS

Just how does communication vary in these different situations? In order to consider this question we must bring in the final element of our simple model: the *message*. If we focus for a moment on just one of the entries in Martha's log,

'text Lianne (best friend) to see if she's going to be late as usual'

we can identify two key elements of the message:

What is being said (the *content* of the message)
How it is being said (the *form* of the message).

This is a crucial distinction that will crop up time and time again in your study of communication, so it's important to make sure at this early stage that you have really got the hang of it. The content of Martha's message is an enquiry. The thought has crossed her mind as she sits on the bus that it may be a good time to find out if her friend will be late for college today. The content is taking shape in Martha's mind even before she reaches for her mobile to give the message a form. Martha's log doesn't tell us just what form the message takes, but we could guess that it would look like this:

R U on time 2day

To analyse the form of this message further we would note that it is based on a knowledge of both the written and the spoken versions of the English language. It is a sentence in English, but one which has the distinctive properties of 'text-speak'. Martha, of course, is very confident that her friend will recognise the form of the message and understand the content of the message in an instant.

To make sure that this distinction between form and content is quite clear, let's look at another of Martha's communication activities,

'I try to be a good listener and sympathise with him.'

The content of Martha's message here is pretty straightforward – she wants to express a feeling of sympathy and understanding to her friend. Once again, Martha doesn't describe the form of the message so we shall have to use some guess-work. She may very well use expressions of spoken English: such as:

'I'm really sorry about that'
'Don't let it get you down'
'Things are bound to get better.'

Taken at face value, these expressions say little, but if you take into account the way in which they are spoken they can become more meaningful. Tone of voice as well as variations in pitch and volume are all important in expressing our feelings. Martha does tell us that she tries to be 'a good listener' – but how could she give a form to this part of her message, the part that contains the idea that 'I'm interested in what you are saying, I'm concerned and I want to help'? Words alone have their limitations in the expression of feelings such as this so Martha will have accompanied her words with other forms of communication such as nodding, supporting sounds such as 'Mmm' and 'Oh', direct eye contact and, perhaps, a consoling hand on F's arm. All these are examples of non-verbal communication – types of communication other than language. If the content of a message involves emotions or feelings, it is often very effectively expressed in non-verbal forms.

ACTIVITY

Take two further examples from Martha's log and two examples from your own experience to show the difference between the form and the content of messages.

Now that we have successfully distinguished between the form and the content of a message we need to take the next step, which is to understand just how strongly form and content are linked together. In fact, the link is so strong that any change in the form of a message almost inevitably influences the content. Let's go back to the phone text example to demonstrate this. What if Martha had texted the following to her friend:

Are you on time today?

This is a perfectly well formed and correctly punctuated sentence of English but Leanne, the receiver, would probably do more than just raise her eyebrows if she received a text in this form. The sort of thoughts that might cross her mind would be, 'What's wrong with Martha?' or 'Has someone stolen Martha's phone?' Here we can see that the form of the message has actually become more important than the content; we could even go as far as to say that it *is* the content. You have probably heard the expression 'It's not what you say it's the way that you say it' to put across the same idea that the form of the message can have a very powerful influence over its content.

Let's recap now on the progress we have made so far in defining the term 'communication'.

1. Communication involves a sender, a message and a receiver.
2. Senders and receivers are not necessarily human beings.
3. We spend a lot of our time sending and receiving messages.
4. We engage in many different types of communication activity from mass communication to face-to-face interaction.

Figure 1.2 Does this toy train have anything to do with sending and receiving messages? Only if it reminds you of the railway model of communication

5. We communicate in different ways in different situations; for example, as our roles change.
6. Messages have both form and content. These two are different but closely connected.

The approach to communication we have adopted here is sometimes called the railway model because it sees communication proceeding in a straight line from the sender to the receiver, almost as if the message is a 'thing' to be transported from one location to another.

This kind of approach gives us a clear and simple model of communication as a process. (An alternative name is the *process* approach.) As we shall see later in the course, this model can be useful in helping us to plan our communication acts in order to make them as effective as possible. However, it is an approach that does have some serious limitations. For example, it seems to imply that the sender is somehow more important than the receiver and that the act of reception, particularly listening, is secondary to the act of transmitting a message. Also, the railway model is particularly unhelpful in considering the important area of *meaning*. In order to develop some more sophisticated approaches to communication which enable us to deal with the meanings of messages, we shall first need to explore the second of our key terms: culture.

Culture

We should acknowledge straight away that the term 'culture' is every bit as difficult as 'communication' because it is a word that has been used in many different ways by different people. Our job is to explore some of the most important interpretations. The dictionary provided a useful starting point for our discussion of communication, so perhaps it will be just as helpful as we begin to understand culture. My *Concise Oxford Dictionary* gives four definitions, the first of which is:

> *'noun. tillage of the soil; rearing, production (of bees, oysters, fish, silk, bacteria) quantity of bacteria thus produced.'*

Oh dear. At first glance this looks most unpromising. You may even be asking yourself if you are on the right course if you are going to be studying soil, bees and oysters – let alone bacteria! However, perhaps there is some value in looking a little more closely at this definition because it does point us in the direction of an important aspect of culture.

Let's start with 'tillage of soil'. A farmer or a gardener works on the soil to improve its quality and to make it more productive. Uncultivated land is transformed into cultivated land by agriculture. This process of preparing, developing, improving and enriching leads us towards a familiar way in which the term 'culture' is used. A person could be described as a cultivated individual, by which is meant someone whose manners are refined and who is well educated with an appreciation of art and beauty. As we leave behind the world of oysters, bees and bacteria, we can still hang on to the idea of culture as something that comes from a process of

Figure 1.3 What's ploughing got to do with culture?

enriching, refining, improving and striving for perfection, as well as the process itself. In this sense culture is often used to describe great works of art as well as their production and appreciation.

This view of culture is widely used today, particularly by people who like to measure cultural activities and works of art against 'the best'. It was even more influential in the nineteenth century. The poet and educationalist Matthew Arnold (1822–88) described culture as 'the best that has been thought and known', the crowning glory of civilisation. In his opinion, the study of culture and its appreciation could make the world a better place if everyone could come to share the values of intelligence, beauty and perfection. Arnold argued that it was the job of the education system to make sure that everybody was given access to 'the best' of culture or a 'passion for sweetness and light' as he termed it. Arnold thought that the work of certain writers (Homer, Dante, Shakespeare and Milton) should be used to measure all other literature. He called these writings 'the touchstones'.

ACTIVITY

You have almost certainly studied Shakespeare, but what about the other 'touchstone' writers?

Use the internet to make some brief notes on Homer, Dante and John Milton.

What do you think it is about their work that Arnold respected?

The Industrial Revolution

It is no coincidence that Arnold's views about culture were developed in the wake of Britain's Industrial Revolution. This was a time (roughly 1780–1830) of massive social and economic upheaval. Some important characteristics of the Industrial Revolution were:

- A rapid growth of urban areas as people moved from the countryside to towns and cities.
- A change in the pattern of employment as jobs in factories and mills replaced jobs on the land.
- Mechanisation of manufacturing production methods based on machines, particularly the steam engine.
- Rapid development of the railway system leading to greater mobility.
- An expansion of the British Empire opening up new markets for finished products (such as clothes) and guaranteed sources of raw materials (such as cotton).

You have probably studied the causes and consequences of the Industrial Revolution in history classes but further information on this important period can be found at www.bbc.co.uk/history/british/victorians/ and www.thehistory channel.co.uk/site//features/the_industrial_revolution.php.

Figure 1.4 *Coalbrookdale by Night* painted in 1801 by Philip James de Loutherbourg. Coalbrookdale, near Ironbridge in Shropshire, is the birthplace of the Industrial Revolution

This period of British history is also sometimes referred to as the Age of Empire. Although Britain abolished the slave trade in 1807, huge amounts of money had been made from slavery and these ill-gotten fortunes were important sources of the capital (money to invest) needed to fuel the early stages of the Industrial Revolution. The later stages of the nineteenth century were the heydays of empire. Britain, like other European countries, had brought lands in Asia, Africa and the Americas under direct rule through military conquest and the power of the navy. These colonies such as India, Nigeria and Jamaica supplied the factories and mills of Britain with raw materials.

What did all this mean for Arnold's idea of culture as 'the best that has been thought and said'? Matthew Arnold was certainly a staunch critic of what he saw as the negative consequences of the Industrial Revolution. In his view, materialism – the obsession with money, profits and possessions – was eroding the true values which he associated with art and beauty.

New social classes were developing in the nineteenth century. The industrial working class supplied all the labour power upon which Britain's prosperity was based. A new middle class of managers, clerks, shop owners and civil servants also emerged. For Arnold and other Victorian commentators these two classes needed the benefits of a culture supplied by the education system. Religion was in decline and Arnold had no faith in the ability of either of these classes to produce anything of any cultural value from their own resources. Culture was also seen as a way of 'rescuing' the working class and the middle class from all the harmful effects of the Industrial Revolution, such as immorality, selfishness and disobedience.

Arnold thought that a proper understanding of art and literature would unite the classes, prevent social disorder and fill the moral vacuum created by the weakness of organised religion. He was particularly worried that 'the populace', as he called them, had a tendency towards anarchy, riot and disorder. In other words, the majority of the population were uneducated brutes with no respect for authority. The education system could help to keep them in their place and reduce the threat of unrest or rebellion. Clearly, then, Arnold did not see the benefits of culture with its 'sweetness and light' simply for its own sake, he also saw it as a means of social control.

The Canon

INFORMATION BOX – THE CANON

A body of work in fields such as art, literature and music which represents Arnold's idea of 'the best'. These are then considered worthy of study because they have timeless values that are relevant to all people in all societies. Works in the canon are often called *classics*.

Figure 1.5
No! Not a cannon,
a canon!

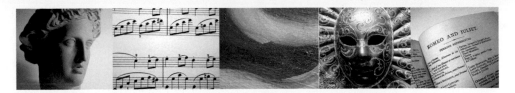

Figure 1.6 Canonical works – classical artworks, music and literature

ACTIVITY

List the writers, painters and composers who you think are qualified for membership of the canon.

The idea of the canon is controversial these days, though it still has its supporters. Two of its staunchest supporters in the 1930s and 1940s were the Leavises (Frank and Queenie). Matthew Arnold may have worried about the decline of morals in an industrial age, but the Leavises feared a different but equally powerful threat: the effects of mass communication.

It is certainly true that mass communication developed very rapidly in the period in question as the timeline shows.

1881	Education Act	Attendance at elementary school compulsory for 5–10 year olds
1887	Invention of the gramophone (record player)	
1895	Birth of cinema	Exhibition of films by the Lumière Brothers in Paris
1896	*Daily Mail* launched	The first newspaper designed for mass circulation. Price: a halfpenny (240 pennies to the pound)
1900	*Daily Express* launched	
1903	Founding of *John Bull* magazine	Soon to become Britain's best-selling magazine

1913	World's first motion picture palace opens	The Regent in New York with a capacity of 1800
1915	*Sunday Pictorial* (later *Sunday Mirror*) launched	
1915–26	US spending on advertising triples to $2,700m	
1918	Education Act	School leaving age raised to 14. State scholarships (financial support) made available for university education.
1919	First million-selling record	*Japanese Sandman/ Whispering* by the Paul Whiteman Orchestra
1920s	800 films a year produced in the US	In 2006, 480 feature films were produced in the US
1921	Sales of records decline as radio becomes more popular	
1923	*The Radio Times* launched	A best-selling magazine ever since
1924	1.5 million radio sets in use in the UK	
1926	*Melody Maker* launched	A weekly paper devoted to popular music
1927	Birth of the 'talkies', beginning of the end for silent films	First major talkie was *The Jazz Singer*
1931	*Woman's Own* launched	Now part of the IPC media group
1936	BBC begins regular television services	The service stopped during the war and resumed in 1946
1938	Launch of the *Beano*	Later to become home of Biffo the Bear, Dennis the Menace and The Bash Street Kids
1939	Sales of *Woman* reach 750,000	2007 circulation: 370,000
1947	School leaving age raised to 15	

1948	Sales of the *News of the World* reach 8 million	Still Britain's best-selling newspaper, current sales are around 3.5 million (2007)
1949	Introduction of 45 rpm records	The single became the staple of the best-selling charts (the 'hit parade') from 1952, replacing sheet music sales
1953	Nearly 20 million watch the coronation of Queen Elizabeth on television	Beginning of the 'television age'

Figure 1.7 The explosion of mass communication and mass literacy: a timeline

The steady development of a compulsory education system may have given more people access to the 'canon', but to the alarm of critics such as the Leavises, people did not choose to devote themselves to classical music and literature. They preferred pop music, American films and the *Beano*. Entertainment, glamour, excitement and fun were more likely to win mass audiences than so-called 'high art'.

The Leavises were not just in favour of the canon, they were very distinctly against popular culture – the sort of things that most people actually liked. Films, advertising, radio, popular fiction and newspapers all came under attack because they were considered to be:

- Lacking in 'taste'
- Sentimental (i.e. sloppy and overly emotional)
- Superficial (easy, lightweight and undemanding)
- Self-indulgent
- Addictive
- Dangerous, because they tempt us away from the more rewarding qualities of 'real' culture.

What was it about the works in the canon that made them so important? These are some of the qualities of the canon which the Leavises wanted to defend:

- **They reflect a 'golden age' which existed before the Industrial Revolution**
  This is the view that the Old England that existed before the Industrial Revolution was a much better place in many ways. People's values then were simple and pure and their language had not been ruined by mass communication.

- **They have qualities that will last for ever**
  Unlike 'here today, gone tomorrow', throwaway products of popular culture, works in the canon have stood the test of time. It is not particularly important how or why they were produced because the value lies inside the works themselves. This is called *intrinsic* value.

- **They have a humanising influence**
  This means that readers of classical works will be rewarded for putting in the extra effort needed to understand them. These works deal with complex and deep issues, for example, what it is that makes us human. Works in the canon may be more difficult, but by reading, studying and understanding a poem such as Shakespeare's Sonnet 29 (see box) we become more sensitive to the human condition; we learn more about ourselves and others

William Shakespeare Sonnet 29

When, in disgrace with fortune and men's eyes,
I all alone beweep my outcast state
And trouble deaf heaven with my bootless cries
And look upon myself and curse my fate,
Wishing me like to one more rich in hope,
Featured like him, like him with friends possess'd,
Desiring this man's art and that man's scope,
With what I most enjoy contented least;
Yet in these thoughts myself almost despising,
Haply I think on thee, and then my state,
Like to the lark at break of day arising
From sullen earth, sings hymns at heaven's gate;
For thy sweet love remember'd such wealth brings
That then I scorn to change my state with kings.

- **They need to be preserved by a minority**
  This one of the most controversial parts of the Leavises' approach to the canon. They felt that only an elite, educated minority could fully appreciate culture and that it was therefore their job to defend and promote the values of this culture. It led to them being accused of *elitism* – the idea that people who appreciate the canon are superior to those inferior people who like pop music, television, magazines and newspapers.

Challenging the canon

In many ways, most of this book is a challenge to the canon and the definition of culture associated with it. It has been, and remains, an influential idea with many university departments and even A-level courses looking no further than the canon when devising programmes of study. From the 1960s onwards, though, many critics have attacked the canon and its underlying assumptions. These are some of the questions posed by opponents of the traditional canon as put forward by the Leavises:

■ Why are dead white European men so heavily represented in the canon?
■ Who decides which works of art should be admitted to the canon and what gives them the right to decide?
■ Why should anything be excluded just because it is new?
■ Why are certain formats such as film, radio and television automatically excluded?

ACTIVITY

How do you think that defenders of the canon would respond to these critical questions?

Culture as everyday life

We shall now turn to a very different approach to the definition of 'culture' – one which goes someway towards addressing the questions posed immediately above. In a 1958 essay the Welsh writer Raymond Williams coined the phrase 'culture is ordinary'. Williams was not interested in establishing a hierarchy of culture with 'the best that has been thought and said' at the top and the *Beano* somewhere near the bottom. He wanted to get away from the idea of league tables of value in order to focus on the ordinary experiences or ordinary people. Culture, in this sense, is a whole way of life which may include the appreciation of opera, classical literature and the paintings of the Renaissance masters – but which also includes having breakfast, watching TV soaps or chatting with friends at the bus stop. Above all it is *your* culture; yes, you – the reader of this book. The study of culture is also the study of your life: your habits, your routines, your behaviour. The things you do because you like doing them and the things you do because you have to.

Figure 1.8 Some things we do for pleasure, others less so . . .

Sharing the 'rules' of culture

This is a particularly important concept in the understanding of culture as a way of life. Culture involves learning. From our earliest days we begin the process of learning all that we need to know in order to be members of our culture; a process that continues throughout our lives. We learn for example that our culture has certain rules about areas such as:

- How to behave as a girl or as a boy
- The 'manners' expected of us when we eat food
- How to relate to others, whether they are close friends or strangers
- When to speak and when to stay silent
- How to take part in games.

These are just a few instances of areas where our culture sets out 'rules'. The key point is that we must share an understanding of these rules. This *sharing of accepted rules* is another way of describing culture as a way of life.

Let's take just one of these rules to demonstrate this approach to culture. It is the rule which states:

When you see someone you know, you should offer them a greeting.

This may seem a simple and straightforward rule, something most of us have learned at an early age. However, once we start to delve a little deeper we can see that this is quite a complex area. In studying 'greeting' as part of culture as a way of life, we would want to examine the following questions:

■ What sort of greeting should we offer?

There are many possibilities; for example, a smile, raised eyebrows, a hand-shake, high fives, a nod, a hug, or a kiss on the cheek. Spoken greetings include 'Hi', 'Hello', 'Good morning', 'Hey', 'How do you do?'.

The greeting could combine several of these examples or other possibilities.

■ How do you decide which form of greeting to use?

There are all sorts of things to take into account here:

- ■ How well you know the other person
- ■ The nature of your relationship (e.g. close friends, co-worker or boss)
- ■ Your age and the age of the person you are greeting
- ■ The place and time of your meeting
- ■ The length of time since you last met each other
- ■ Your gender and the gender of the other person.

■ Are the rules the same everywhere?

No – far from it. Each culture has its own set of rules. In New Zealand a traditional Maori greeting is the *hongi*, a touching of noses to share the breath of life. In Thailand the *wai* is a greeting gesture in which the palms of the hand are put together and held upright just below the chin. This is followed by a slight bow of the head (see Jandt, 2007, pp. 114, 119). What is more there are many variations within a culture. Cultures are often subdivided into subcultures, each with its own slightly different set of rules.

■ Are the rules fixed?

Again, no. The rules change over time. The word 'Hi' and the slapped hand or high five are fairly recent but other forms of greeting such as going down on one knee or bowing with one arm swept upwards were much more common in the Britain of the Middle Ages. Cultural rules are *dynamic*. They change over time but the changes are likely to be fairly gradual.

■ What happens if you break the rules?

Few cultural rules carry the same status as laws, most of them are not even written down. So nobody is likely to call the police if you break the greetings rules. However, there may be consequences if you don't conform to expectations. If a friend sees you but offers no greeting at all, you are likely to feel annoyed or hurt. You may decide to retaliate by 'ignoring them back' or perhaps you would confront them and demand an explanation. You may even decide to re-evaluate a relationship because someone failed to greet you especially if they did it more than once.

There is also the possibility of breaking the rule by choosing the wrong sort of greeting for the situation – perhaps by being too formal or too informal. We also have to consider the possibility that someone may break or bend the rules deliberately because they want to achieve a particular effect. For example, a greeting which is a smile but a very quick tight smile or a 'hello' in a sarcastic tone of voice could make the person being greeted feel small and inferior. This example also raises another aspect of culture as a way of life: *power*.

As we shall see in future chapters the power to enforce cultural rules and the power to break them is not distributed equally. It is sometimes suggested that the whole complex network of rules which make up a culture is there to keep power in the hands some people and out of the hands of others.

It is now time to recap on the progress we have made so far with this definition of culture as 'ordinary', as 'everyday' or as 'a whole way of life'.

- Culture has a complex set of rules which we learn and share.
- There are different sets of rules for different cultures, though there might be large or small areas of overlap.
- There can be different sets of rules within a culture, usually to distinguish one subcultural group from another.
- Cultural rules change gradually over time.
- Cultural rules are influenced by factors such as time, place, age and gender.
- Power is an important factor in understanding cultural rules.
- Cultural rules can be very subtle and complex.
- It's easy to make mistakes!

We have used the expression 'set of rules' several times in this chapter. These are dealt with in more detail in Chapter 2 where we shall refer to them as Cultural Codes.

Cultural practices

Our definition of culture has so far considered rules or codes of behaviour. In studying these we are interested in the things people do in everyday life – such as greeting each other. It would be impossible to list all of these as the list would take up the rest of this book, but a few examples will give you some idea of the scope of 'culture as everyday life'.

- Greeting each other (yes, we've done that one)
- Going shopping

- Visiting a heritage centre
- Horse riding
- Worshipping
- Going to a festival
- Taking a holiday
- Celebrating a birthday
- Waiting for a bus
- Taking a walk in the countryside
- Following a band or a celebrity or a football club as a fan.

All of these are examples of *cultural practices* or activities. If we were to study any one of them, we would look for the rules, the codes which guide people's behaviour as they perform these activities. Just as we did in the case of greeting, we would look for variations of these codes both within and between cultures and their relationships with other variables such as age or gender. In our earlier example about greetings we noted that power may be an important factor in understanding the different ways in which people greet each other; perhaps to explain how certain greetings can make people seem inferior or superior, good about themselves or bad about themselves. In the same way, we would ask questions about power in relation to any cultural activity.

If the form of a greeting can have an influence on our feelings, greeting must have certain meanings that we can detect. These meanings are shared with other members of our culture. Raymond Williams used the expression 'structure of feeling' to describe the way in which members of a culture are united by shared interpretations of cultural practices. So, the most important question to ask about the cultural practice you choose to study is, 'What does it *mean* to go shopping, to celebrate a birthday or to follow Nottingham Forest?'

Cultural products

In addition to the Cultural Practices discussed above, our definition of culture as 'ordinary' or 'ways of life' also includes the *things* that we encounter in our daily lives. These things, or cultural products, are as many and as diverse as the cultural activities but once again a list of examples should help to explain the general idea.

- An MP3 player
- A pair of jeans
- This book
- The Ford Mondeo
- The Houses of Parliament
- A hairstyle
- Michelangelo's *David*.

In terms of our first definition of culture, some of these (like the statue of David) have high cultural value and some (like a pair of jeans) have little cultural value.

Figure 1.9 Cultural products

This time, though, we are not as interested in value as we are in meaning. Cultural products such as those listed above all have complex meanings, but the meanings do not reside inside the things themselves. Instead, the meanings come from the ways in which the objects are represented to us in words, pictures, moving images or any other form of communication. In this sense, to know what a thing means is to know what it is; the cultural product has no identity that is separate from the meanings we attach to it.

In order to explore the implications of these ideas, we'll use an example in the same way as we did for the cultural activity of greeting. Our case study for a cultural product is the Samsung Mini MP3 phone.

Figure 1.10 Samsung's mini MP3 phone, the X830

The Samsung is designed to compete in a huge global market; the estimated sales for mobile devices in 2008 is 1.6 billion (www.guardian.co.uk/business/2007/oct/27/technology.gadgets). In Britain, mobile phones are replaced after 18 months on average and we throw away 15 million of them a year. www.guardian.co.uk/news/2006/mar/26/mobilephones.theobserversuknewspages). It is a highly competitive market with large profits at stake, so it is important for manufacturers such as Samsung that their products are seen as desirable and that consumers

Case study

WHY IS THE SAMSUNG MINI MP3 PHONE A CULTURAL PRODUCT?

Like so many of the things we spend our money on, this device has meanings which, like the meanings of cultural activities discussed above, are shared and negotiated among large groups of people. The straightforward uses of the X830 include phoning and texting, storing and playing audio files and taking digital pictures – but even the ability to perform all these multiple tasks does not guarantee sales success. The device must also say something positive about its owner and give a sense of pride and satisfaction in ownership. This is made clear in the following extract from Samsung's press release to mark the launch of the X830.

> Samsung's latest mini music phone comes with an innovative MP3 player design. The unique swing-open form factor allows for a perfect combination of mobile phone and MP3 player function. When closed, the X830 functions like an MP3 player with a music player interface that horizontally displays the playlist, equalizer settings and song information. Swinging the phone open exposes the keypad and doubles its length for optimal mobile communication experience.
>
> The X830 attracts mobile users who prefer portability and an exceptional trendy design. Slim and narrow in size, the mobile phone measures an incredibly compressed 84×30×19.9mm and weighs in at a mere 75 grams for light mobility.
>
> This mini MP3 phone's portability and compactness does not compromise the ease of use for its various multimedia functions. The click wheel navigation gives users hassle free control of the music functions. The built-in 1GB memory allows for storage of 250 songs. Users can also download audio files from CNN or BBC websites by podcasting function. The USB 2.0 connection is fast enough to handle large data volumes, and the Music Library organizes downloaded music according to album name, song title, artist and genre for effortless search and playback. The phone also has Bluetooth(r) connectivity that allows users to talk or enjoy their music through a wireless stereo headset.
>
> Moreover, the 'Mini MP3 phone' comes in six different colour choices – black, pure white, oasis blue, candy pink, orange and lemon green – to truly be a fully functioning fashion accessory.

Note particularly the following phrases: 'an exceptional trendy design' and 'fully functional fashion accessory'. There is also the choice of six different colours with its implicit invitation to consumers to express themselves; are you an oasis blue kind of person or a candy pink person? Clearly, there are many links between the meanings of the product and the identity of the owner. This leads to two important aspects of the cultural product:

- Cultural products *communicate* with people who perceive them – people such as (potential) owners or users as well as casual observers
- Cultural products connect to individual *identity*. If I choose or admire or simply express an opinion about a cultural product, this says something about me.

So far, we have considered only the positive meanings which a manufacturer may seek to attach to a product. However, you will be very well aware that some products, including portable communication devices, may have other, less attractive meanings. Being 'cool' is probably the ultimate accolade for a mobile phone/MP3 player, but it is a notoriously difficult property to achieve. Moreover, the shifting sands of fashion and the rapid pace of technological change can soon reduce today's cool to tomorrow's tragically uncool. So is Samsung's X830 cool and desirable? That's for you to decide, because manufacturers and advertisers cannot enforce meanings onto us, they can only do their best to 'get it right'.

One of the ways in which the X830 attempts to get it right is by incorporating points of reference in the design to another product which has already established its cool credentials: the Apple iPod. Although the Samsung device does not slavishly copy the design of the iPod, there are certain similarities of proportion and style which help us to locate the product within a network of meanings established by the iPod.

Figure 1.11 iPod Nano

These are likely to be shared meanings, but we must also acknowledge that a cultural product such as the Samsung Mini MP3 phone has many meanings and that these meanings are different for different people. It is also worth pointing out the significant links between cultural products and cultural practices; there are certainly many cultural practices associated with a product such as the X830

perceive some qualities in their product which lead them to make a purchase. The design and marketing processes and advertising campaigns all make a powerful contribution as they seek to invest attractive meanings into the product.

ACTIVITY

List the cultural practices (activities) that you could engage in with the Mini MP3 phone. For each practice identify at least one 'rule'.

Practice	Rule
Make a phone call	Not in the cinema
Read text	Hold under the table if in class
*	
*	
*	
*	

Communication and culture: putting them together

This chapter has introduced you to communication and culture as separate concepts, but we are sure that the ties between them have become increasingly clear. This is especially the case in our second definition of culture: culture as ways of life. This approach stresses the significance of shared meanings in relation to both cultural practices and cultural products. How else could these meanings possibly be shared other than by communication? This is not to say that everyone accepts without question the meaning of every cultural practice and every cultural product. The communication of cultural meaning is rarely so straightforward. On the contrary, there are failures of communication, arguments and negotiations as well as attempts to impose or resist meanings. Culture communicates with us incessantly; it has a big role to play in making us who we are. But we are not just receivers of cultural messages, we are also senders as we communicate with others through our practices and products.

This is the reason why *your* personal experience is right at the heart of this fascinating subject.

References and further reading

Du Gay, Paul et al. (1997) *Doing Cultural Studies: The Story of the Sony Walkman*, Sage/The Open University

Jandt, Fred E. (2007) *An Introduction to Intercultural Communication: Identities in a Global Community*, 5th edn, Sage, Thousand Oaks, California

2 CODES

Now that you have completed the first chapter you will have a good idea of the territory covered by Communication and Culture. Our next task is to explore the ways in which culture is communicated. In order to do so we shall be looking closely at various codes, particularly the Codes of Language and Non-Verbal Communications.

What is a code?

A code is a system of communication which requires three elements:

- **Signs** Anything that expresses a meaning; for example, a written word, a gesture or a cultural object such the mini MP3 phone discussed in Chapter 1.
- **Rules** Signs are nearly always used in combination with other signs to create complex meanings. However, they are not put together randomly but in accordance with certain underlying principles. For a language such as English we would call the rules a grammar.
- **Shared understanding** A code only works if a group of people share the knowledge and understanding of rules and signs. We dealt with this idea in our discussion of culture because all cultures are based on a shared understanding of codes.

The concept of the code is further explored in Chapter 4 where you will be shown how to use codes in your analyses of cultural codes and cultural practices. For the time being, it is probably easiest to demonstrate the idea of a code using the English language as an example.

English as a code

The signs of English are words (or part of words) which may be spoken or written. Look at the following word fragments:

chew the the -ed carpet dog

Without breaking sweat you should be able to arrange these works into a meaningful sentence. You can do this because you understand the rules of English. Some of the rules you have applied are these:

■ English puts the Subject of a sentence before the Verb and the Verb before the Object. You have worked out that the dog must be the Subject because carpets cannot chew but they can be chewed, so *carpet* must be the Object.
■ There is only one Verb (a 'doing' word) – *chew* – so the word *chewed* must come between the Subject and the Object. (English is known as an SVO language because, unlike many other languages, it puts the Subject, the Verb and the Object in this order.)
■ Articles (or determiners) such as *a* or *the* come before nouns in English. There are two definite articles – *the* – so these must come before each of the two nouns.
■ The past tense of a verb adds the suffix *-ed* to the infinitive *chew* so *chew* and *-ed* must go together and the sentence must concern an event in the past.

It doesn't matter whether you could write these rules down or not. It doesn't even matter whether you can identify subjects, verbs, objects or infinitives. The point is that you must know these rules in order to be able to compose the sentence. You have effortlessly performed a task which could not have been done by anyone who does not share your knowledge of the English language. Most codes work via an *implicit* knowledge of rules. We don't really think about the rules, we just use them all the time as we create and understand the meanings of signs.

Lastly, your understanding of the rules and the signs must be shared with others, that is, those with knowledge of the English language. This is not a particularly exclusive club – there are about 11,000 million people who use English as their first or second language. As we shall see, there are many variations in the ways these people use English so, although we can identify an English-speaking culture of 11,000 million, we can also identify numerous cultural subgroups which use English in their own particular ways.

A detailed descriptive analysis of English as a code is well beyond the scope of this book but you will certainly need to explore the ways in which language works as a system of signs when you get to grips with the Semiotic toolkit in Chapter 4. As you will find, many of the tools of cultural analysis have been developed from the study of language. Here, though, our focus is on cultural aspects of communication so we are less concerned with the internal rules and structures of language, the *grammar*, than we are with the codes which relate to language in use. It was helpful (we hope) to pull apart the sentence about the dog and the carpet because it demonstrated the principles of a code. However, our analysis and your ability to put the words together into a sentence were based on grammatical rules. This did not really help us to make all that much progress in interpreting the meanings of the sentence. Let's assume that the sentence, *the dog chewed the carpet*, was spoken rather than written. To make some sense of this utterance we would need more information. For example:

- Who spoke and who did they address?
- What tone of voice was used?
- What was the relationship between the speaker and the addressee?
- Did the speaker accompany the sentence with any other act of communication such as a laugh or a frown or waving fists in the air?
- What was said before and after this particular sentence?
- Whose dog was it . . . and whose carpet?

Answers to these questions would help to provide the essential information about the two factors which are critical to the understanding of speech or any other act of communication:

- context
- form.

The context of a communication may involve one or more of a number of dimensions:

- The physical environment – for example, noisy or quiet, a mosque or a fast-food restaurant, a classroom or a bus.
- The relationship between communicators and their roles – intimate and friendly or a professional working relationship, such as brother/sister or doctor/patient.
- Shared experience – does the communication enable participants to make links with what is already known and (often) taken for granted?
- The event or cultural practice of which the communication is a part – a wedding or a funeral, relaxed, informal chat or a formal meeting at work.
- Wider culture – shared or different values and expectations

(see Maybin, 1996, p. 12)

We shall return frequently to the idea of context as we go on to deal with the different *forms* of language. The form of a spoken sentence can have a drastic influence on its meaning. Just by adjusting the volume and tone of what you say, many different meanings can be implied. Tender words in the ear of a lover will not have quite the same effect if they are shouted rather than whispered.

It's the same with written language. You are probably familiar with some of the rules of communication on the net (or netiquette) such as these:

We expect other drivers to observe the rules of the road. The same is true as we travel through cyberspace. That's where *netiquette*, a term coined for either *network etiquette* or *Internet etiquette* comes in handy. Here are a few pointers to guide you through your online communications:

continued

---

1. Avoid writing email or posting messages in newsgroups, forums, blogs and other online venues using all capital letters.

   IT LOOKS LIKE YOU'RE SHOUTING! Not only that, it's difficult to read.

2. When you talk with someone, your tone of voice conveys great meaning. To add personality and humour to your messages, use **smileys**, also known as **emoticons**, expressions you create from the characters on your keyboard. A few popular ones include:

:-)	Happy		**:-e**	Disappointed
:-(	Sad		**:-<**	Mad
:-o	Surprised		**:-D**	Laughing
:-@	Screaming		**;-)**	Winking
:-I	Indifferent			

   (Source: www.learnthenet.com/English/html/09netiqt.htm)

It is becoming clear that English is not just one uniform code, but many codes. There are all sorts of ways in which the form of English can vary in both spoken and written variants. We are certainly interested in the cultural significance of these variations and, in particular, their links with an issue discussed in Chapter 1: the perception of *value* in cultural communication.

Variations of form in English: accent and dialect

All of us have had the experience at one time or another of having our use of language challenged or 'corrected' by others – teachers, perhaps, or parents. Candidates for written examinations are often advised to pay attention to the 'quality of written communication' in their answers and that their use of spelling, punctuation and grammar will be taken into account when marks are awarded. (This is certainly true of the exams in A level Communication and Culture.) Also, we often hear commentators complaining about 'declining standards' in the use of English, with young people often being identified as the chief culprits. 'Talk properly!' we are told.

It is often claimed that 'poor English' inhibits communication because it is difficult to understand, imprecise or ambiguous. Sometimes associations are made between supposedly 'incorrect' forms of English and various character defects

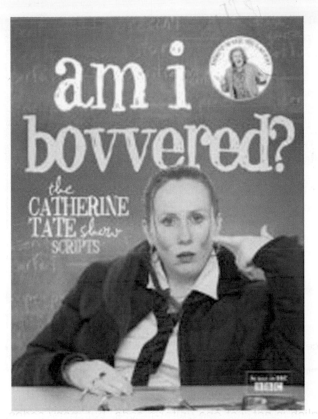

Figure 2.1 Catherine Tate's character Lauren, with her catchphrases 'Am I bovvered?' and 'Does my face look bovvered?', satirised teenagers' 'sloppy' language and the reactions of adults

such as laziness, sloppiness, aggressiveness, thoughtlessness or plain stupidity. Perhaps there is some kind of link between use of language and personality but, even so, there seems to be some faulty logic at work here. If my speech is a *symptom* of my laziness, then telling me to 'talk properly' will make no difference to the reality of my laziness any more than telling me to wipe my nose will cure my cold.

All of this suggests that there is really only one proper and correct way to use English in speech or in writing. The 'correct' forms are usually referred to as Received Pronunciation and Standard English.

Received Pronunciation

Received Pronunciation (RP) deals solely with the *sounds* of words (accent) and can be described as the prestigious speech of educated people. It is usually associated with London and the south-east and with the middle and upper classes. It is sometimes known as the Queen's English, Oxford English or BBC English. However, all of these labels are slightly misleading because we hear plenty of non-RP accents in Oxford (even in the university) and on the BBC, and RP speakers live all over the country, not just in the home counties. In some ways it is easier to define RP by examining what it isn't, that is, other accents. All regional accents whether from Glasgow, Tyneside, Cornwall or London's East End are decidedly not RP.

Films, TV and radio broadcasts from fifty or more years ago show us just how much RP has changed. Politicians, newsreaders and even children's television presenters from this era sound impossibly posh and stuck up when we listen to them today. Language use has changed so much that the RP of the 1940s and 1950s would only be used today for comedy effect – it certainly doesn't have any prestige. Today, the more neutral-sounding 'mainstream' RP is still taken as the yardstick against which to measure other accents. It is the form of spoken English taught to foreign students, at least if they are studying in a British institution. Problems begin to arise only when other accents are judged as inferior to RP rather than simply different. For most of us, the way in which we speak is an important part of our identity, so we are likely to feel personally insulted or embarrassed if our speech is criticised. It is difficult to accept that an attack on the way I speak is any different from an attack on me as a person.

ACTIVITY

Discussion points

■ In the past RP was used as a 'passport' to gain access to certain jobs and positions. Can a person's accent still open or close doors to progress in today's society?
■ Call centre operators sometimes deliberately employ only workers with certain regional accents because they think customers will find their voices to be warm, welcoming and friendly. What qualities do you associate with different regional accents?

Read the extract below from Times Online and then consider the following questions:

■ What is Estuary English?
■ What is a 'mockney upbringing'?

Where are the gels who can talk proper and pirouette?

Adam Sherwin, Media Correspondent

Casting directors are lost for words because the next generation of British actors just cannot speak proper. The rise of 'Estuary English' has left children with the intonation patterns of Lily Allen and Jonathan Ross, regardless of their background.

The decline in Received Pronunciation has not just transformed the presentation of BBC News. Film and drama producers are struggling to fill period roles that require unrepentantly middle-class vowels. BBC One is holding an open casting session tomorrow to try to find two girls to star in a film-length adaptation of the classic children's novel Ballet Shoes. Victoria Wood and Marc Warren have signed up to star in the story, by Noel Streatfeild, set in 1930s London. But the challenge of finding two ballet-dancing leads who can act, twirl and – most importantly – speak in middle-class accents has defeated the producers.

'We've been to drama schools, ordinary schools and children's agents, but we still haven't found the right girls,' said Susie Parriss, the casting director.

'It doesn't matter whether you go to public schools or comprehensives, children just speak common estuary now. That is the trend. But this story requires our leads to speak with a clear middle-class accent.' The great names of British theatre fear that young acting talent may never recover from a 'mockney' upbringing. Scripts often have to be rewritten to accommodate actors trained in regional speech patterns at drama school. Dame Eileen Atkins, who appeared in the TV adaptation of David Copperfield in 2000, has told young actors that they will have to master Received Pronunciation if they want to take on important, classical roles. Otherwise, she said, they will play parlour maids forever.

(Source: http://entertainment.timesonline.co.uk/tol/arts_and_entertainment/film/article2120715.ece)

Standard English

The relationship between Standard English (SE) and regional dialects of English is similar to the one that exists between RP and regional accents. A dialect is a variation of language based on vocabulary and grammar rather than the sound of words. SE does not include words or grammatical constructions that are usually confined to a specific region or a particular situation. Books, newspapers and official records are written in SE and it is widely used in education. If your written work has been 'corrected' by a teacher, it was probably in order to bring you into line with SE.

Peter Trudgill, a prominent British linguist, estimates that only about 12–15% of native speakers use SE and of these only about one-third use RP. It seems that both SE and RP are used by a fairly small but socially powerful minority.

As with RP, debates rage about whether SE and non-standard alternatives are just different or whether the use of SE is always preferable, especially in writing. We find non-Standard English (NSE) used in many situations and by many speakers, not just in regional dialects. NSE is used by subcultural groups based on age or ethnicity. An example of this is Black English Vernacular, sometimes considered a language in its own right. Some words and phrases from Black English Vernacular have been adopted by variants of English, often fuelled by the crossover popularity of rap and hip hop music (see The Ultimate Rap Dictionary at http://the_yz.tripod.com/dictionary/). Non-standard varieties are constantly borrowing (or stealing) words, phrases and grammatical constructions from each other as they evolve. Some grow rapidly, others die out altogether. Regional dialects can inspire strong feelings of affiliation and attempts are made to preserve these forms of speech which are seen to be under threat from the influence of more powerful or more prestigious language varieties.

Tooterin' folk in Norfolk talkin'

Norfolk dialect has no double-vowel sounds. So a tutor sounds more like a car horn – a 'tooter' – and if you had a computer tutor, you'd probably abbreviate it to a 'pooter tooter'.

As for grammar, the word order can be different and there is no 's' in the third person singular. So, 'he run home when she cook the meal' would be quite correct. During the Second World War, testing people's pronunciation of village names such as Wymondham (which the locals pronounce Windum) and Costessey (Cossy) was a way of identifying suspected Germans.

But it is the dialect's colourful vocabulary that has captured the children's interest. A 'bishy-barney-bee', the most striking example, is the local word for a ladybird (it is said that it was inspired by a Bishop Barnabas of Norwich, who wore a similarly coloured cloak).

Also popular are the 'tittermorter' (a seesaw); 'trickalating' (decorating); and 'slant and dicular' (something not squarely hung). There is also a Dutch influence in words such as 'dwile', which means flannel cloth.

'There is no rule for spelling,' Mr Brooks assures me as we move on to more guessable, everyday phrases: 'fair ter middlin', 'the best part of sum tyme' and 'cum on in out onnit' (come out of the rain).

(Source: www.telegraph.co.uk/education/main.jhtml?xml=/education/2006/07/22/edfeat22.xml&sSheet=/education/2006/08/09/ixteleft.html)

Even if we accept that SE has a certain role in education and formal situations, that is certainly not to say that it is any better than non-standard varieties. The American linguist William Labov argued that non-standard varieties were every bit as expressive and complex as SE (he studied Black English Vernacular in New York). During your course of study in Culture and Communication you will encounter many non-standard forms of English; the use of language has a very important part to play in cultural identity and in cultural practices. NSE is often used exactly because it unites us as members of a group, because it signals our identity or because of its expressive qualities. These expressive qualities feature often in our everyday conversations as well as in the lyrics of popular songs, where SE is rarely heard. Take these few lines from a famous old Elvis Presley song:

> You ain't nothin' but a hound dog
> cryin' all the time.
> Well, you ain't never caught a rabbit
> and you ain't no friend of mine.
> When they said you was high classed,
> well, that was just a lie.

There are three examples of double negatives ('ain't nothin', 'ain't never' and 'ain't no'), use of non-standard words (ain't), non-RP contractions (cryin') and incorrect subject–verb agreement (you was). In addition, there is a tautology as 'hound and 'dog' mean the same. The referents of the pronouns 'you' and 'they' are unspecified.

Let's try a corrected version:

You are nothing but a hound, crying all the time.
You have never caught a rabbit and you are not a friend of mine.
When unspecified people said that you were of high class, they were lying.

It doesn't really work, does it!

Styles and register of language

As we noted earlier, context has a very important part to play in the understanding of any act of communication. As we move between different roles, different physical environments and different cultural locations, we make more or less subtle changes in the forms of language that we use. Sometimes this means moving from one language to another. For example, you may speak Gujarati at home with your family, but change to English at school.

In the same way, the change may be between different dialects of a language rather than between two distinct languages. For example, a speaker may use Black English Vernacular with one group of friends, Birmingham dialect with another group of friends and Standard English at work. These changes between languages or between dialects are known as *code switching*.

Code switching, of course, depends on the user's knowledge of two or more languages or dialects. More subtle changes of form can take place within the same dialect (or between two very similar dialects). This is called *style shifting*. Our language style varies in the choice of words, grammatical constructions and pronunciation. For example, we may recognise that some situations, such as an interview, call for a more formal style. In accordance, interviewees are likely to adjust their pronunciation at least some way in the direction of RP and cut out slang expressions in the hope of making a good impression.

In different settings we make small but telling adjustments to our language style in order to let people know our attitude towards them. Even in friendly conversations, power plays a part as we use different styles to signal domination (unspoken message: 'I'm the important one here!') or deference (unspoken message: 'I accept that you are more important than me!').

Generally, we adjust our language to make it more like the language style of the person we are addressing if we want to convey warmth, friendliness and empathy. This is called *convergence*. On the other hand, moving language style away from the other person's way of speaking can signal status or the desire to avoid intimacy. This is called *divergence*.

Convergence and Divergence

Write a short piece of dialogue (based on your own experience) showing style shifting, convergence or divergence.

Look at the following examples (all are entirely imaginary). How do you think convergence or divergence is being signalled in each example?

Example 1

A: Hi. I'm new here, just starting today. Where should I sit? My name's Paddy by the way. Nice to meet you.

B: Good morning Patrick. My name is Mrs Johnson. I have cleared a place for you at the desk over there.

Example 2

A: Ree – lax everybody! You're a-listen' to Country Music Hour on your very own Radio 50 plus.

Example 3

A: Hi mum. Great news! I'm just phoning to say that I've booked the flight and I'll be home for New Year's Eve. Can't wait to see you!

B: Lord! You sound so English these days.

Similar in many ways to style, the term **register** is also used to describe variations in the use of language associated with a particular context such as a job, an area of technical expertise or social setting. As a student, part of the task is to learn the register of your subject so that you are able to write and speak as, say, a historian or a geographer or a biologist. In your investigations of cultural practices and products you will need to identify and explore distinctive styles and registers. Both terms have a range of application that extends beyond verbal communication, so it is just as valid to discern the styles and registers of a film or a website or of an individual's clothing and appearance.

By George, she's got it…

His daughter's sloppy speech made **Jack Shamash** book elocution lessons – and the results speak volumes

Through the open door of the sitting-room, I could see Yolanda, my eight-year-old daughter, standing very straight. She paused before speaking. "*Goblin Market*, by Christina Rossetti," she announced. There was another pause. Then she started reading the poem, which includes lines about "swart-headed mulberries" and "unpecked ripe cherries".

Yolanda was having her first elocution lesson. It seemed rather old-fashioned but, like many parents, I was upset at the sloppy way that my child talked and was anxious to do something about it. Yolanda goes to a primary school where a large number of children speak without regard for dropped aitches. The Ts and Gs at the end of words seem to be regarded as an optional extra.

A report published recently by the Qualifications and Curriculum Authority said that schools in France and Russia gave far greater emphasis to spoken language than British schools did, and that was one reason why our children were poor at expressing themselves.

As a child, I had an elocution teacher, an ancient woman called Miss Rose. She wore a strange black hat with bits of netting hanging down from it and smelled of mothballs. She was unpleasantly hectoring and would say things such as: "My time is precious." She spoke as if she was trying to be heard in the back row of the stalls and had once taught Fenella Fielding, the actress with the deep voice whose output included "Carry On" films.

Miss Rose made me recite poems such as *Hiawatha* by Longfellow. Each lesson would start with me reading a list of words: "Kettle, battle, rattle, cattle." I thought she was ghastly, but she did help me make myself understood.

I first raised the subject of elocution lessons with Yolanda a few months ago, when she was speaking particularly badly. "If you don't improve, I'm going to get the oldest and smelliest elocution teacher I can find," I told her.

Yolanda said she didn't mind having elocution lessons, as long as the teacher wasn't smelly. So I took her at her word. But finding an elocution teacher wasn't easy. I

phoned the Royal Academy of Dramatic Arts in London. Jane Brown, the senior voice specialist, said RADA staff would charge up to £65 an hour for lessons – far beyond my budget.

However, she explained, elocution was important. "You need to build up clarity, eye contact and volume, and learn to breathe at the right times, otherwise you can't be understood," she said. "The beginning and end of words are crucial. If you lose the end of the word, you don't complete the thought."

Elocution was not about snobbery, class or attempting to sound like Hyacinth Bucket, she emphasised. Regional accents were quite acceptable.

I decided to find a tutor through a tutorial agency. The first person I rang had obviously had a bad experience. "I think elocution is dreadful," she told me. "I was taught by the nuns and hated it."

The next agency was more helpful. "Why do you want to find one?" the woman asked. I said I wanted my daughter to express herself better. "And I think it might help her get into a good

school," I added. She immediately warmed to the idea and said she would ring back.

Two hours later, I was telephoned by Mr Noel Blair Diprose. He told me that he was an associate of the London Academy of Music and Dramatic Art and that as a youth he had trodden the boards with Margaret Rutherford. Lessons would be

Distinctive properties of paralanguage also serve to identify a context or genre. Looking at the following examples, you will probably recognise immediately the tone or rhythm or qualities of voice associated with them:

Once upon a time there was a princess who lived all alone in a tower.

They have declared their marriage by the joining of hands
and by the giving and receiving of *rings*.
I therefore proclaim that they are husband and wife.

Silence in court!

Good evening. This is the Six O'Clock News.

Knock, knock.
Who's there?
Cowsgo.
Cowsgo who?
No they don't. Cows go moo.

Crewe Alexandra 1 Stockport County 3
Accrington Stanley 1 Huddersfield Town 1
Oldham Athletic 2 Walsall 0

If you try to read these aloud with anything but the 'right' paralinguistic features, they sound very odd. You may have the basis of a stand-up comedy routine.

Physical appearance

Clothing, hairstyle, make-up, body adornment, jewellery, tattoos, piercings, glasses, facial hair, accessories such as handbags, briefcases, purses.

You only have to think of the huge industries associated with the above examples to recognise the cultural significance of physical appearance.

INFORMATION BOX – HALIFAX REVEALS EXTENT OF SPENDING ON FASHION ACCESSORIES

i

People in the UK spent a total of £43.7 billion on clothing and footwear in 2005, accounting for 5 per cent of the total household disposable income spending last year, according to Halifax Credit Cards.

This equates to an average of £1789.93 per household across the year, or £34.42 per week.

continued

The amount revealed by the research represents a 56 per cent increase on ten years ago, when £28 billion, or £21.98 each week for a typical household, was spent on fashion accessories.

(Source: www.thriftyscot.co.uk/Finance-News/102006/halifax-reveals-extent-of-spending-on-fashion-accessories.html)

Physical appearance, of course, includes not only those things with which we cover or adorn our bodies, but also the shape and size of our bodies. The preoccupation with body shape and size is reflected by practices such as slimming, body building and cosmetic surgery. It is the body's capacity to communicate aspects of an individual's identity which makes us so aware of our physical appearance. This is a theme to which we shall return in Chapter 3.

We are used to thinking of clothing and appearance as means of *self*-expression, but this is a fairly recent development in historical terms. Many societies had (and some still do have) highly regulated codes of dress, often linked to rank and status. In the Middle Ages, the monarchy restricted access to certain types of clothing to make sure that the power and authority of the king and queen and members of their court was clearly visible (see information box opposite).

Figure 2.2/2.3 The power of the body to communicate leads many people to control or shape their physical appearance

Figure 2.4
Queen Elizabeth I

Tudor monarchs such as Elizabeth I (above) used Sumptuary Laws and Statutes of Apparel to control what people could wear. For example, only royalty were permitted to wear ermine trims while fox and otter trims were restricted to members of the nobility. Similar laws were common throughout Europe with penalties running from fines to imprisonment or execution.

Self-expression in contemporary culture is also limited by requirements to wear uniforms or to observe dress codes. Such requirements are not restricted to schools and services such as the military, police or nursing personnel. Many corporations and organisations expect their employees to communicate a corporate rather than an individual identity and this often includes the wearing of company colours or brand logos.

Body movement (or kinesics)

Gesture, facial expression, posture, head nodding, orientation (where you put your self in relation to others).

A further subdivision of this category makes the following distinctions:

Emblems These are gestures with the specific cultural meanings attached, often used as direct substitutes for words. Often, emblems are used in situations where speech is made difficult or impossible such as very noisy environments or places where communicators are too far apart to hear each other properly.

Illustrators These gestures reinforce the words of a speaker; for example, by point-ing to something in a shop while saying 'I'll have one of those'. All cultures have a rich repertoire of illustrators spoken messages, but this is certainly an area in which widespread cultural differences can be observed. To many people, shaking the head may seem a natural way of reinforcing dissent or disagreement – but not in Bulgaria, where head shaking signals agreement. There is also wide variation in the sheer quantity of illustrators used. Consequently, people from cultures who use illustrators frequently and expressively consider those from cultures who don't to be cold and aloof, and vice versa.

Adapters These almost unconscious gestures relieve stress or boredom; for example, by drumming fingers on a desk or scratching the back of your head. Often, adapters signal nervousness or anxiety in situations, such as giving a talk or being interviewed, so we do our best to control them. It is sometimes maintained that these involuntary gestures can reveal an intention to deceive. Looking for signs that someone is lying may be interesting, and we all do it, but does it really have any reliability or validity? The problem is that we can never be sure about adapters; they may not be as unconscious as they seem. In most jurisdictions, including the UK, evidence gathered from lie detectors (polygraphs) is inadmis-sible. If the careful collection of data based on the measurement of blood pressure, heartbeat, body temperature and so on during interview is not considered safe, then conclusions based on observations of twitching, fingernail chewing or nose tapping are, at best, unconvincing.

Posture is another one of those non-verbal areas which is heavily laden with value judgements. Just as we mentioned the perceived importance of elocution (in paralinguistics, previously), correct posture has often been associated with a positive attitude. Most of us have been instructed to 'Stand up straight!' or to 'Put your shoulders back!' at some time. Teachers and students alike, we have all engaged in low-level classroom disputes about sitting, leaning, slumping, slouching and 'paying attention'.

Closeness (or proxemics)

Proxemics is the study of how we use space and distance, including seating arrangements, queuing and territoriality. You will certainly be used to the idea of 'personal space' and the 'invasion of personal space'. This is the area of NVC which deals with our 'comfort zone' in relation to others. As you would expect, culture, gender and situation are important variables here.

The importance of context is apparent if you think about a train journey which you start as the only passenger in your carriage. You certainly would not expect the next passenger to sit near you, let alone next to you, if you are typical of northern European cultures. However, as you continue your journey you may begin to feel slightly uncomfortable if almost everyone else has a stranger sitting next to them, except you.

We have a number of non-verbal devices and techniques at our disposal to 'ward off' anyone who threatens to invade our space. These include the use of objects as 'markers', such as putting down a bag or a coat to indicate your ownership of a space. A stare or a scowl can have the same effect, warning others to 'stay out of my space'. In your study of cultural practices you could look out for the cultural products used as 'markers' of territory. For example, do you or your friends have your own room? How do you use objects as 'markers' to stamp your identity on this space?

Touching (or haptics)

Physical contact such as holding, hitting, kissing, stroking, shaking hands, guiding.

The study of touching is obviously linked to proxemics; obviously, you have to be close to someone to touch them. Getting very close to someone else and making physical contact is not always a sign of empathy, it can also be highly aggressive and intimidating. Touch plays a particularly important role in our early development. Touch between infants and their parents or carers is very frequent up until the age of about two years when the amount of touching begins to decline. As adults, there is plenty of evidence to suggest that touching is good for us, yet there are many rules and taboos regulating physical contact.

In the company of others, most of us are very sensitive to any differences in expectations of touch, whether these are individual or cultural differences. Furthermore, sensitivities about touch sometimes extend beyond the body to our possessions, hence the warning: 'Don't touch that, it's mine!'

Eye movement (or occulesics)

Eye movement, length and direction of gaze, changes in pupil size.

We are hypersensitive to the information imparted by eyes. They fascinate us more than any other part of the body – most of the time, at least. The 2007 film *Beowulf* used state-of-the-art computer-generated imagery and performance capture to create impressively realistic versions of the human body, yet many reviews commented on the 'dead, soulless eyes' of the characters. Apparently, it isn't easy to recreate the depth and subtlety of human emotion expressed by the eyes.

As with adapters (see Body movement, previously), it is sometimes argued that the eyes reveal the truthfulness of what is being said. This is why children are often instructed to 'Look at me when you say that', but the idea that a lie can be detected simply by watching someone's eyes is contradicted in most cases by a little introspection. Which of us could say that we have never looked someone straight in the eye and told a fib?

Smell (olfactics)

Although humans do not have a particularly well-developed sense of smell when compared with other species, this non-verbal code still has some significance. Perfumes and deodorants can send powerful messages (though possibly not quite as powerful as some manufacturers claim) and so, in a different way, can the natural body odours we often try to suppress.

Additionally, a rapidly growing industry has developed around the use of smells (or 'fragrance delivery systems') in domestic and commercial environments. One company's website sets out the following claims:

Aromas and scents can soothe your soul, balance and harmonize your body, mind, and spirit. Aromas can stimulate your senses, make you more alert. At an exhibition or at a store a nice aroma will increase your readiness to purchase. Since the Egyptian Pharaoh era, aromas have been used for healing and stimulation.

The appropriate aroma will

- create a relaxed atmosphere
- make you more alert, freshen the air
- add to life style
- make display in museums more authentic
- add to shopping experience

Where STIERS aroma machines are used: shops, stores, offices, doctors, theatres, exhibitions, movie theatres, events, shows, clubs, restaurants, exhibitions at home and in museums.

(Source: http://www.fragrancemachine.com/)

There are also, of course, plenty of taboos around body smells. As Knapp delicately puts it:

> **anticipation of expelling flatus may lead to rapid termination of an interpersonal contact.**

(Knapp, 1972 p. 77)

Complex messages

Having carefully placed NVC into these categories we should acknowledge (without wanting to undo our good work) that it is rare enough for these non-verbal codes to operate in isolation from one another or, indeed, separately from language. As we participate in communication we create and perceive messages using signs from a range of verbal and non-verbal codes. To make this situation even more complex, these signs and codes do not always pull in the same direction.

It would be quite easy to decode and understand interpersonal communication if all the signs supported the same meaning. Sometimes this is the case; for example, if I bang my fist on a desk, stare hard, lower my head, scowl and shout 'I'm very angry with you', then a combination of codes are all mutually supportive of the same basic message. However, we often exploit the rich potential of all these codes at our disposal in order to create complex and deliberately ambiguous messages. We can say one thing but mean another. We can tease each other by deliberately offering two entirely contradictory but simultaneous signs. Nuances and subtleties of meaning are achieved much more readily if we use a variety of verbal and non-verbal codes together with associated styles and registers. The ability to do this is, perhaps, the single most important feature of cultural belonging and a set of skills referred to as *communicative competence*.

INFORMATION BOX – COMMUNICATIVE COMPETENCE

i

This idea refers to our ability to use language not just accurately but appropriately. A competent communicator will:

- Recognise and use different verbal and non-verbal styles as they are suited to different social situations.
- Recognise the subtle interplay of verbal and non-verbal elements in communication.
- Compensate for possible misinterpretations in communication with others.

continued

The idea of communicative competence was developed by the American linguist Dell Hymes. He thought that a study of language which focused simply on 'rules' and grammar was too narrow. As children, we don't just learn our language; we learn when to speak, where to speak, how to speak, how to link language with other forms of communication and how to assess our performance as communicators.

The functions of non-verbal communication

Inevitably, we have already supplied many examples of NVC in action as we have exemplified the various categories discussed above. Here, though, we shall look at some of the key functions of NVC, exploring the ways in which non-verbal behaviour frequently involves the simultaneous use of cues from several categories, often working alongside language.

Communicating feelings, emotions and attitudes

Non-verbal communication has a particularly important role to play in establishing and maintaining relationships, otherwise known as an *affective function*. Of course, we use language as well to acknowledge the presence of others and to tell them what we feel about them, but we rely more heavily on NVC in this area of personal communication. Looks, glances, changes in orientation and proximity allow others to know what sort of relationship we want to have. We use NVC to establish a level of intimacy that is mutually acceptable.

The ambiguity of NVC can offer many advantages in the affective function. Imagine the following scenario. Someone you know vaguely is making friendly signals but, for whatever reason, you want to reject these advances. You could just say directly 'Look, I don't want to be friends', but this approach risks anxiety and embarrassment for both of you. Much less risky is the gentle use of gesture, facial expression and other non-verbal cues to dissuade your would be friend without a word being spoken. Not only does this have the advantage of saving face, it puts you in a position where you can easily change your mind. It is easy to claim that non-verbal messages have been misinterpreted or unintended, but more difficult to claim convincingly that 'I didn't mean what I said!'

The phenomenon of *non-verbal leakage* – messages 'slipping out' in spite of our attempts to control them – ensures that high credibility is given to non-verbal cues in the area of feeling, emotion and attitude. This puts a lot of power in the hands of a skilled communicator, as deliberate messages can be disguised as involuntary non-verbal cues. Is the politician who removes his jacket and loosens his shirt cuffs in the course of his speech just reacting to the heat of the TV lights? Or is he deliberately trying to communicate his informality and solidarity with 'ordinary people' by this apparently natural gesture? As the late comedian Bob Monkhouse caustically remarked, 'If you can fake sincerity, you've really got it made!' Perhaps he was just reinforcing the importance of communicative competence.

Interpersonal attitudes, especially degrees of affection and empathy, can also be indicated by body closeness and orientation. Just as with the phenomena of convergence and divergence, we tend to move away from those we dislike and move closer to those we like. In the latter case, we are also likely to mimic posture and orientation – an action known as postural echo, a non-verbal version of convergence. It is a technique deliberately employed by carers and counsellors to put people at ease.

Figure 2.5/2.6
Postural echoes

Communicating power and status

Within stratified organisations such the army, positions within the hierarchy are very clearly signalled by uniforms, badges and behavioural codes such as saluting. In other organisations the non-verbal rules of the pecking order may not be so overt, but they are just as carefully observed. In his *Book of Tells* (a 'tell' is a non-verbal cue), Peter Collett shows how the seemingly innocent handshake can have all sorts of implications for establishing dominance and subordination. He lists eight variants of the handshake as follows:

- The Bonecrusher
- The Limp Handshake
- The Firm Handshake
- The Limpet Handshake
- The Clammy Handshake
- The Reinforced Handshake
- The Relocated Handshake
- The Upper Handshake

Of these, the Limp Handshake may seem the most likely to offer evidence of submissiveness, but this is not necessarily so, as Collett's more detailed explanation reveals:

> A limp handshake occurs when someone offers a hand that is totally relaxed. It doesn't exert any pressure on the other person's hand and it doesn't contribute to the mutual production of the handshake. A person who offers a limp handshake is someone who, in more senses than one, doesn't connect with the other person. Like their hand, they remain passive and detached – they're simply not focused on the person they're greeting. This often happens with people who are self-important or who have to shake hands with lots of people. . . . Women who want to cultivate an impression of languid femininity often present a rather limp hand to the person they're greeting. Strong people often do the same, but in their case it's to emphasise their strength. It's said that Mike Tyson offers a relaxed, almost tender hand when he greets people outside the boxing ring – the complete opposite to what happens inside the ring.

(Collett, 2003, pp. 168–9)

There are fairly obvious examples of non-verbal behaviour in which power is exercised by force; for example, hitting, kicking, punching and physical restraint. But power certainly doesn't have to work in these ways – control is more usually achieved by using the mildest rather than the most forceful methods. In most situations, a resort to physical methods of control is seen as a failure, but our non-verbal repertoire still offers numerous techniques for exercising domination or expressing submission.

The power dimension of NVC is acknowledged within the principles of assertive-ness training. Courses in assertiveness training seek to build confidence through the development of communication skills which include the recognition and ability to resist manipulative non-verbal controls.

Replacing and regulating language

We have already looked at how emblems, illustrators and adapters work alongside spoken language to replace, reinforce or modify speech. The role of NVC in inflecting the meaning of a sentence can be explored by 'performing' the following sentence in different ways:

Well, I really enjoyed the party last night.

Starting with just paralinguistic features such as pitch, tone, emphasis and the enactment of different verbal registers, it is easy to convey at least eight or ten distinctly different messages. If you start to throw in other non-verbal cues such as eyebrow lifting or illustrators such as the use of index and first finger of both hands to indicate inverted commas around one word or another, the number of potential meanings rapidly increases.

Non-verbal cues also make a significant contribution to conversation management. These are the rules of turn taking which allow us to have coherent discussions without constantly talking over the top of each other. Paralanguage, gaze, eye contact and head movement all play a part in the complex choreography of conversational turn taking. It's a set of rules that takes some time to grasp. As children, we are often told off for interrupting or talking at the same time as an adult – mostly because we haven't yet learned the complicated rules of how to play the conversation game.

Even heated arguments tend to observe the basic rules of turn taking, so that the participants indicate to each other using eye contact and tone of voice when they wish to hold or relinquish the conversational floor.

As you will have come to expect by now, this is yet another area in which power is never far from the surface. This would be the case when a speaker realises that someone else wants an 'in' to the conversation and decides to set a trap. First, the potential interrupter signals that they wish to speak by raising the head and holding eye contact for a fraction longer. This is acknowledged by the speaker who, with a nod begins to slow down as a natural grammatical break approaches.

However, as soon as the unfortunate interrupter jumps into the space that has been offered, the first speaker re-starts, slamming the conversational door in the face of the other person and forcing them into an embarrassing and demeaning climb-down. We have all been victims of this trap situations where we have found ourselves mouthing and floundering in disarray as we are excluded from the conversation.

Conversational power plays and tricks such as this are strongly differentiated by gender. Women, typically, have a more cooperative conversational style, providing the speaker with positive feedback through nods and expressions such as 'Mmmm' to indicate active listening. Men, typically, provide less non-verbal feedback and are more likely to violate the rules of turn taking (Gibbon, 1999, pp. 126–9).

Other functions

Our list of functions is not by any means exhaustive. There are many other uses to which we put our non-verbal codes including:

- Self-expression
- Group membership
- Persuasion and rhetoric
- Indicating role

You are likely to encounter all these in your studies. We hope that this basic introduction to the complexities of non-verbal communication helps you to understand and analyse examples as you discover them in new situations.

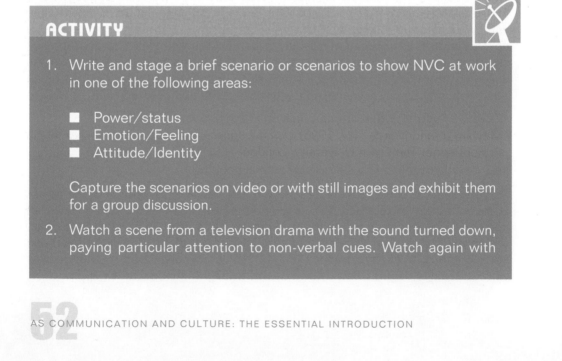

ACTIVITY

1. Write and stage a brief scenario or scenarios to show NVC at work in one of the following areas:

    - Power/status
    - Emotion/Feeling
    - Attitude/Identity

    Capture the scenarios on video or with still images and exhibit them for a group discussion.

2. Watch a scene from a television drama with the sound turned down, paying particular attention to non-verbal cues. Watch again with

sound. How much of a contribution has the performance of non-verbal codes made to the meaning of the scene and the identity of the characters?

Repeat the exercise using an interview with a politician from a news or current affairs programme.

3. Look at the following situations. In each case try to identify a verbal form, a verbal function, a non-verbal form and a non-verbal function that could be associated with the situation.

    ■ **A judge** addressing a member of the jury who is not paying attention.
    ■ An upset and lost child approaches **you** in a busy supermarket.
    ■ **You** want to get past the doormen and into a crowded nightclub.
    ■ **A new teacher** meets a Year Ten class for the first time.
    ■ **A mother** wants her teenage daughter to come home before midnight.

References and further reading

Collett, Peter (2003) *The Book of Tells*, Bantam Books, London

Crystal, D (1987) *The Cambridge Encyclopedia of Language*, Cambridge University Press, Cambridge

Gibbon, Margaret (1999) *Feminist Perspectives on Language*, Longman, London

Hall, Bradford J. (2005) *Among Cultures: The Challenge of Communication*, 2nd edn, Thomson Wadsworth Belmont, Caifornia

Hartley, Peter, 2nd ed (1999) *Interpersonal Communication*, 2nd edn, Routledge London

Knapp, Mark L. (1972) *Nonverbal Communication in Human Interaction*, Holt, Rhinehart and Winston, New York

Maybin, Janet (1996) 'Everyday Talk' in Maybin, J. and Mercer, N.

Maybin, J. and Mercer, N. (1996) *Using English: From Conversation to Canon* Routledge/The Open University, London

3 IDENTITY AND THE SELF

We have already stressed that a course in Communication and Culture places you, the individual, at the very centre of our concerns. In this chapter we shall examine the codes that make us who we are and which we use to express our identity.

The first two chapters established the interdependence of communication and culture to the extent that each are only fully explicable and understandable in relation to the other. But what about personal identity? What is the relationship between identity and culture and how is this relationship communicated?

Consider these two points of view.

> I am who I am because of the time and place I was born and the culture I was raised in. My family gave me a set of values and so has my town, my religion, my community and my country. Add these all up and that's who I am – me.

> I have got an identity – at least my friends seem to thinks so, but I'm not really sure who I am. I know that I'm more like some people than others, but this changes as I try out new identities. I don't really want to take on an identity if it means that I can't be different when I want to be.

Which of these two approaches do you find yourself in most agreement with? The first view sees identity as a *product* of culture – we are fashioned by social and cultural forces together with a sort of genetic blueprint which moulds us into the individuals we are. The second view has a different take on the relationship between culture and the individual. Here, culture provides a set of resources which we are free to use in the construction of our own identity. Rather than being fixed into place by powerful forces, identity is more like a butterfly.

Neither one of these approaches is right and neither one is wrong, but they do represent the two sides of a debate about the nature of identity which runs through this chapter. You may disagree with the first argument on the grounds that it seems to suggest that identity is simply predetermined or 'programmed' by forces beyond our control, leaving little space for individual difference. On the other hand, you may find the second argument unappealing because it seems to reduce identity to little more than a collection of symbols drawn from the resource bank of culture on a given day. 'What about the "real me"', you could ask, 'Surely I'm more than the contents of my wardrobe and the tracks on my MP3 player?'

As with so many debates in Communication and Culture, it is unlikely that we shall be coming to a definitive resolution any time soon. As you will discover, there are lots of questions, lots of debates, arguments, points of view and theories – but few conclusive answers. However, in our exploration of identity, you should be able to assess these two contrasting positions in relation to evidence and ideas. Also, you may find alternatives to the view that identity is either fixed and stable or fluid and capricious.

Our next task is to introduce you to some basic concepts and terms used in the study of identity, starting with self.

Self-concept

Let's look at the ways in which we, as individuals, respond to our individuality. The 'self-concept' is the idea we have of ourselves as individuals. Self-concept consists of three elements, each of which makes an important contribution: self-image, the opinion or picture we have of ourselves; ideal self, the person we would like to be; and self-esteem.

Self-image

ACTIVITY

Either (a) answer the question 'Who am I?' 20 times, in each case responding in the form 'I am . . .'.

Or (b) answer the following list of self-probing questions.

- Who are you?
- What do you do?
- What do you do well?
- What do you do badly?
- What is your strongest feeling?
- What is your strongest belief?
- What is your strongest desire?
- What is your oldest memory?
- What is your most shameful lie?
- What has been your greatest triumph?
- What has been your most wretched disaster?

continued

- Who do you love?
- Who do you hate?
- Who do you like?
- Who do you dislike?
- Are you too tall or too short?
- Are you too thin or too fat?
- Are you too clever or too stupid?
- Who would you like to be?
- Which question would you like to be asked?

If you responded to (a), the interesting thing to do is to try to spot trends in the results. If you chose (b), it is valuable to go back and calculate how many of the answers you gave are genuinely honest and thus useful. How many of your answers are really a response to the need to have an answer and/or the need to have a potential audience?

Kuhn and McPartland (1954) conducted this experiment, asking option (a) above, on both 7-year-olds and undergraduates and they reached some interesting conclusions. First, they were able to see responses to the 'Who am I?' question falling into two categories which they related to:

- **Social roles**: the parts we play, either 'ascribed' (or given) rather like daughter or son or 'achieved' roles (such as student or part-time worker)
- **Personality traits**: statements about what we think we are like, such as 'I am very easy-going' or 'I am very hard-working'.

Kuhn and McPartland also found that the main difference between the 7-year-olds and undergraduates was in the proportions of 'social roles' and 'personality traits'. On average 7-year-olds recorded five social role statements while the undergraduates recorded ten. This suggests that as we get older we progressively describe ourselves in terms of the jobs we do or status we have. This has a convincing ring to it, for on meeting people for the first time the thing adults most often offer, after their names, is their occupation.

The other aspects of self-image relate to the various versions of the self which are being imaged. We can distinguish between the intellectual self, the emotional self and the body self (or body image), though we could also add social and physical or physiological selves. Body image is a particularly important factor in growing up in a society where stereotyped body images are common. This is the point at which self-image becomes influenced by the other components of self-concept, in particular, the ideal self.

Ideal self

ACTIVITY

Note: this activity is not intended to be a traumatic experience where you put yourself down. Loosen up – education should be fun!

Ideal self is the kind of person you would like to be at best. Examine the three designations:

- Intellectual self
- Emotional self
- Bodily self.

Sum up the ideal male or female according to society or the media. How far is your ideal self similar or different to these?

Ideal self is an easier concept in theory than it often is in practice. Trying to probe the ideal self in any kind of public context results in **gatekeeping**; we filter out information that could cause negative perceptions. In expressing our ideals, we will often resort to projecting these on to other, often public people. To conceive of your ideal self in terms of another person is usually to get role models and ideal selves confused.

ACTIVITY

Who are your role models and heroes/heroines? What qualities do you admire in them? If you would like to be more like these people, what more than their success (money, fame, adulation, and so on) do you want?

Rogers (1961) would see in role-modelling evidence that we have a number of layers or levels of self-consciousness. The modelling of ourselves in terms of other, often public and famous people, is part of a process that creates, presents and maintains our own 'public self'. This 'public self' is a significantly more superficial version of the self than the one we 'show' to close friends and family, let alone the 'core' self that remains with us at all times. His concentric circle model shows the interconnectedness of these 'selves'.

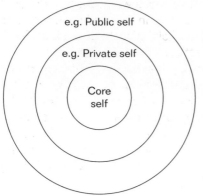

Figure 3.1 Rogers' concentric circles model

Self-esteem

Rogers suggests that the gap between self-image and ideal self is likely to be a measure of an individual's self-worth or 'self-esteem', as the third component of self-concept is usually known. Coopersmith (1967) defines self-esteem as 'a personal judgement of worthiness'. In other words self-esteem is a currency of self-regard: it measures and records how good you feel about yourself. High self-esteem is obviously aided by such socially valuable attributes as physical athleticism and/or attractiveness, but it is most significantly helped by the respect of others.

Of the four key factors identified by Dimbleby and Burton (2006) in the creation of a sense of self, three are directly concerned with the relationships we have with others:

- Reactions of others
- Comparisons with others
- Identifications with others
- (The fourth is the roles we play).

ACTIVITY

'Identifications'

- Who are the significant others for you?
- Whose reactions matter to you?
- Whom do you compare yourself to?
- Who are you compared to?
- With whom do you identify?

We have already to some extent dealt with identifications when we talked about role models. Much research has been done, particularly in the fields of education, management and sports psychology, into the beneficial effects of positive feedback. This is sometimes called the 'Pygmalion effect'. (This is a reference to the play by George Bernard Shaw where Professor Higgins makes a bet that he can turn a Cockney flower girl into the RP-speaking toast of London society. In other words, he believed he could change someone's identity.) Researchers might, for example, privilege schoolchildren according to illogical criteria such as eye or hair colour. Most often these children would end up heading the class academically. This suggests that our expectations are a powerful tool for changing attitude, behaviour and perception. This is usually referred to as the **self-fulfilling prophecy**, a vicious or, sometimes, beneficial cycle.

Here the established expectations cue behaviour, which further supports the expectations. Put another way, you expect laziness from a child who then conforms and confirms your initial expectations. Of course, it can work in a positive way, as a motivational tool where high expectations encourage positive behaviour and achievement follows.

In both cases the issue is essentially self-esteem, which at its positive and negative extremes can have potentially miraculous and/or crippling results. Low self-esteem results in low motivation, a lack of self-confidence and a lessening in the effective use of verbal and non-verbal communication. High self-esteem improves all of these, facilitating social interaction, persuasion, and increasing the quality and volume of communication.

ACTIVITY

Self-esteem is a flexible attribute, often extremely susceptible to fluctuation. What raises your self esteem and makes you feel good about yourself? What lowers your self-esteem and makes you feel bad about yourself?

It is likely that your lists were dominated by the influence of other people, those whose responses make a difference to you. These interested others act as a kind of validation of our behaviour, reflecting (if we're lucky) the kinds of versions of ourselves that we think we are projecting. This is what Cooley (1992) called **'looking-glass theory'**, the version of the self we find in others' responses. On a superficial level this is evident. When we get dressed up for a night out, we partly see ourselves in other people's reactions to us. The theory is similar to 'the self-fulfilling prophecy' in that expectation is created by response. We receive judgements and evaluations of our behaviour from others and then modify our behaviour accordingly. Cooley was interested in the ways we modify behaviour according to the differences between 'reflections'.

These variations depend very much upon our stability and consistency as *personalities*, our capacity to perceive and interpret feedback accurately and our ability to respond appropriately to others. The depth of our engagement with a person or situation will usually influence the significance of the mirror effect – the greater the regard we have for another person, the more we are interested in their perceptions of us.

ASIDE

It's perhaps worth stopping at this point and doing something a little more active than reading or listening. The assumption appears to be that self-knowledge and self-actualisation are all round good things and the endpoint of our endeavour, the purpose of our lives. This in fact appears to be the knack in both personal and professional spheres. Trainee teachers, for example, are told that they need to 'be themselves' in the classroom as if only one part of this proposition is difficult and alien. Similarly those 'dating gurus' (who promise they'll get you 'hitched') will often claim that knowing yourself is a prerequisite to anyone else wanting to know you. With the self so easily under discussion everywhere, it's perhaps time we discovered how difficult the question of identity can be.

ACTIVITY

As this book may not yet have warmed you up enough to persuade you to loosen your clothing and bare your soul, we'll avoid the confessional at this stage. Instead, let's consider how we are seen by others and consider the extent to which it might be possible to reconstruct you from their accounts .

Start with a simple word/phrase game.

Think about how the following would describe you in terms of what they might:

a) see (how you look)
b) feel/think (what you're like)

Choose three or four from the following list:

1 parents
2 brother and or sister
3 girlfriend/boyfriend/partner/significant other
4 best friend (same gender)
5 best friend (other gender)
6 teachers
7 neighbours
8 those who like you least

It's important at this stage that this is a projection exercise since we're interested in who we think we are and unless you happen to be famous or infamous enough to be the subject of a TV documentary, you're not usually going to get to listen to the testimonials of your friends and families (though there's a lovely format for your coursework presentation). Of course this exercise will almost inevitably get you talking about these issues and comparing notes.

While it is tempting to think that the truth about ourselves can be found in the intersections of the above perspectives, in a kind of supercharged triangulation (cross-referencing), this is not the case. Clearly the nature of the question dictates to some extent the nature of the answer and method leads to madness. Who we are depends on not only who we ask and the context in which the question is asked but also on whether the question is asked and which question is asked. This is partly because of the conundrum which recognises that while the 'self' is unquestionably ever present in our lives, we are only aware of it when considering what it is, in the acts of introspection and self-presentation.

One regular such occasion comes when we are preparing personal statements for job applications or university entrance. Here we are airing ourselves for a purpose, representing but also creating and embroidering. More interesting are the customised websites such as *MySpace* and *FaceBook*, stages on which we can rehearse the 'faces we must make to meet the faces we must meet' (as T.S. Eliot put it). In virtual environments such as *Second Life* we can go a good deal further.

Figure 3.2a/b Different versions of 'Me'

ACTIVITY

Let's leave *MySpace* and *Second Life* for later and try to put our thinking about ourselves to use in producing some kind of contextualised summary of who we are. Choose one of the following which are quite different ways of saying who we are (or in the final case 'were'). In each case allow yourself no more than 250 words

1   An 'About me' entry for a dating website. Choose either with or without picture (if with picture consider what kind of image you would send. Would it, for example, be a picture of you?). Think about the extra freedom/responsibility that the absence of an image allows.

2   A police statement as if you've seen yourself behaving suspiciously 'down the precinct'/'outside a primary school'/'on the way to college'. What are your standout (salient) features?

If we cannot take account of this diversity and difficulty, we are in danger of reducing our understanding of who we are to a simple (but vital) process of gatekeeping, where the only real struggle is with the 'outing' of information.

One of the problems we have when we are trying to understand our identity as it appears to be presented in the public domain is to do with this very context. That public context is a context dominated by ideas about narrative and coherence. Raymond Williams, the cultural theorist discussed in Chapter 1, referred to 'dramatised' society in the 1980s. He meant that we tend to see ourselves and others as if we were all characters in a story. In this way we learn the language and other codes through which we are expected to understand and talk about ourselves. This is a language that is very much subject to change since it takes its character from those fictional, non-fictional and semi-fictional personages who dominate the public consciousness at this time; be it Hannibal Lecter, David Beckham or Jade Goody.

At one level this means that, for example, for a long time in this country over-officious bureaucrats have been described as 'little Hitlers' but at a much more subtle level it provides a more invidious scheme for any discussion about what people are like. This is partly because all communication is interested, it has intention, purpose and angle: it means something to someone. We are shown the world by others in order that the way we see it might be affected in some way (changed or confirmed). Central to this process is the negotiation of identities on both sides of the screen (and for screen read microphone, page and any other form of public communication).

The next activity directs your attention to the ways in which identities are created for fictional characters, but you could also extend the exercise to think about the characters, the personae, created for celebrities.

ACTIVITY

Introducing Concepts of the Self

Your task is to create a character for a film (or a novel or a play). Make a few notes under each heading.

- Physical appearance (body)
- Physical appearance (clothing and adornment)
- Social categories (age, gender, occupation, ethnicity and so on)
- Aspirations
- Three things liked about self (by the character)
- Three things disliked about self (by the character)
- Social skills and emotional attributes
- Key relationships with others
- What do other people say about this character

    a) to their face?
    b) behind their back?

- A phrase or saying that sums up this character's attitude to life

Having devised your character, describe him or her to others in your group. How would they analyse your character in terms of self-image; self-concept, ideal self and self-esteem?

The Johari Window

Our sense of self, then, is powerfully influenced by our involvement in communication with others. We have looked at various models which can be used to describe and analyse this relationship. We think that one of the most useful of these is the Johari Window (or, at least, our adapted version of it). The original was developed in the United States by Joseph Luft and Harry Ingham (hence Jo-Hari) as a graphic model of interpersonal awareness and relationships.

The four 'panes' of the window relate to different aspects of the self. It works best if you think of your own Johari Window in relation to another individual or group. Your *Open Self* consists of information about your behaviour, life story, attitude, feelings, emotion, knowledge and experience that you willingly make available to others. However, this may well depend on who those others are. You may 'open up' to some people but not to others.

The *Blind Self* consists of those aspects of yourself which are known to others, but not to you. These could, of course, be positive or negative qualities. This could

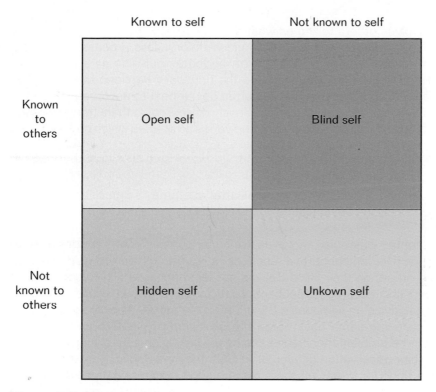

The Johari Window

	Known to self	Not known to self
Known to others	Open self	Blind self
Not known to others	Hidden self	Unkown self

Figure 3.3 The Johari Window

also include things which you imagine to be true of yourself but which others would refute.

The *Hidden Self* contains the aspects that you know of yourself but keep hidden. Again, it depends who is looking at your Johari Window. You probably reveal more of yourself to those you know and like, particularly those people with whom you have had long-standing relationships.

The *Unknown Self* supposes that you have hidden depths; the area of yourself known neither to others or yourself. This unconscious area includes the talents you didn't know you had, perhaps, or strengths and weaknesses that are only revealed by a new experience. Once you become aware of any of these attributes through self-discovery, therapy or simply by accident, then they move out of the unknown area.

From our point of view, the really interesting thing about the Johari Window is not the snapshot it provides of a static self, but the insight it offers into the relationship between communication and identity. All of our relationships, whether with other individuals or with groups, have the capacity to change the shape of the window. The two communicative processes responsible for these changes are:

- feedback
- self-disclosure.

Feedback involves others telling us what they perceive in our Blind Self, just as we discussed in relation to the looking-glass theory. This process, of course, doesn't just involve you as a recipient of feedback, but also as a provider of feedback to others. Negotiations around the boundary between the Open and Blind Self are delicate. For example, we often do our best to encourage others to provide positive feedback whilst simultaneously discouraging them from supplying any unpalatable information. Here are some verbal strategies which could be used to do this:

> 'I must look awful in this old top.'
> 'Do you think I should give up football after yesterday's game?'
> 'Tell me frankly, be as honest as you like, how do you think I did in the play?'

These comments – otherwise known as fishing for compliments – are designed to invite only positive and supportive reactions. It is often difficult to give unbiased feedback to others on their Blind Selves, not least because all of us are aware that the giving and receiving of feedback is a reciprocal affair; we usually only offer comment and advice on someone's Blind Self in the certain knowledge that they are likely to do the same back. Even the provision of positive and uncritical feedback can be problematic. If someone heaps praise on you, giving you all the benefits of their observation of your Blind Self, they are implicitly inviting you to do the same thing for them. Yet there may be good reasons why you don't want to reciprocate; the exchange of information such as this is usually associated with close friendship and it may be that this is a level of intimacy you want to avoid.

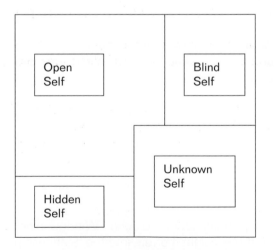

Figure 3.4 Johari Window: as a relationship is developed, the Open Self expands at the expense of the Hidden Self through self-disclosure and at the expense of the Blind Self through feedback

A similar situation exists on the boundary between the Open and Hidden Self. In the normal course of events, as you get to know someone, you begin to entrust them with information from your Hidden Self. If they reciprocate, you will probably feel confident enough to tell them more things about yourself. After a while, perhaps you may reach a level of mutual trust where secrets and confidences known only to very few others are exchanged. There are two potential causes of embarrassment here. Most of us can recall occasions when we have 'said too much' and have got carried away with supplying details of our innermost feelings. On the other hand, it can be difficult to deal with an 'over-discloser': someone who routinely tells you more than you really want to know about themselves – and more. This situation can be quite intimidating; as with the feedback example you could feel manipulated into a position where you are losing control of the level of intimacy you feel comfortable with in a particular relationship.

This is where culture enters the equation. Dialogue around the two boundaries, between Open Self and Blind Self on one hand and Open Self and Hidden Self on the other is clearly delicate and sensitive. We know that getting it wrong exposes the self image to danger. Therefore, we rely on codes of behaviour, sets of rules shared and understood within our cultural or subcultural group to negotiate these dangerous waters. One rule, for example, might state that if someone offers you a small amount of information from their Hidden Self, then you should recip-rocate with your own self-disclosure, but this should be proportionate to theirs.

The Johari Window is useful in helping us to focus on the behavioural codes in relation to boundaries. It can applied to your own roles and skills as a communi-cator in any number of situations, perhaps by considering the following questions:

■ Do I over-disclose or under-disclose?
■ Do I encourage honest feedback from others to open up my Blind Self?
■ Do I give suitable feedback to others without being intimidating or manipu-lative?
■ Am I in control of the level of intimacy I want in my relationships?
■ Am I fully aware of the behavioural codes concerning self-disclosure and feedback?

These are very personal questions, designed for reflection rather than open discus-sion. In thinking about these issues, the Johari Window should be an empowering concept for self developments well as useful analytical tool in your studies of communication and cultural practices.

Protecting the self: cognitive dissonance and self-maintenance strategies

Self-disclosure is not the only protective mechanism known to the self-concept and its attendant self-image. We may be theoretically vulnerable to the responses of others, which is why we have strategies through which to counter their effects.

This is essentially a *dissonance theory*. The self is faced with two sets of oppositional data – positive information from the self-concept and negative information
being fed back from the world of experience. These two sets of information may
be cognitively dissonant (they do not 'rhyme' intellectually; they are difficult to
reconcile). Dissonance theory suggests that the likely response to such a conflict
of information is for us artificially to weaken one side of the argument. The classic
example offered by Richard Gross (1996) is with smokers who believe, know and
understand that smoking increases the risk of serious disease. Their response to
this cognitive dissonance is often a sort of overreaction:

- They belittle the evidence.
- They associate with other smokers.
- They smoke low-tar cigarettes.
- They convince themselves that smoking is a highly pleasurable activity.
- They stress the dangers of smoking and make it a personality feature.

This is exactly what Gergen and Gergen (1981) were dealing with when they
identified the various ways in which we protect ourselves from negative feedback.
These so-called 'self-maintenance strategies' are really a series of dissonant
responses for keeping our idea of the self intact. What we do is one or more of
the following:

- Mix with like-minded people. (How many of your closest friends like the same
  kind of music as you?)
- Mix with people of lower status or ability. (We go around with our 'inferiors'
  in order that we look and feel good.)
- Change our behaviour to conform to norms. (One of the ways that the self
  protects itself is by changing its 'clothes' and adopting the 'uniform' of
  accepted ways of behaving in which it will be less likely to attract attention
  and challenge.)
- Form a low opinion of detractors. (Feedback is effective in proportion to the
  status of its source; if the source is stupid/unreliable/dishonest, then the
  feedback will be too.)
- Disbelieve what others say. (This is why we never believe our parents when
  they tell us our new boy/girlfriend will bring us nothing but trouble.)
- Misunderstand negative feedback. (If we don't fully understand criticism, it
  can't fully 'hurt' us.)
- Consciously evoke response. (We behave or dress in a way that will artificially
  provoke the feedback we want – such as dressing smartly for an interview.)
- Selectively evaluate the self. (A simple device which stresses some aspects
  of who we are instead of other less positive aspects.)
- Self-handicapping. (This is a favourite strategy with students of all ages; by
  not attending or trying or revising, we leave little room for real failure (and no
  room for success).)

ACTIVITY

Self-maintenance strategies are employed by us all to a lesser or greater degree: they are designed to keep us comfortable and sane. Spend some time observing your friends and colleagues, and try to collect evidence of Gergen and Gergen's strategies. Do different subcultural groups use different self-maintenance strategies?

Gergen and Gergen offer a useful list of mechanisms which are a mixture of the internally defensive and externally offensive (the best form of defence being attack). Identity is at the very least in this sense the result of ongoing conversations we have with ourselves and others about who we are.

Take today, the literal day you are reading this. What you're wearing (let's assume you are wearing something) has clearly been chosen, one assumes by you, but the care and deliberation with which it has been chosen depends on what you intend for today beyond reading this. It would be very difficult to imagine anyone who would dress in a special way to read this book but the codes and conventions of dress are certainly important to conceptions of the self.

ACTIVITY

Consider the dress codes for the following contexts and your responses to them. Describing the codes is the first step, in which such issues as colour, texture (materials) and styling might be useful to consider. In addition, identify the factors that modify these codes (gender often has an impact). Finally, discuss the meanings contained in these assumptions.

1 Secondary school
2 School (PE)
3 College
4 Working in a fast-food outlet
5 Working in a bank
6 Going to a shopping centre
7 Going to a city centre nightclub
8 Going to a party at a friend's house

Dress provides an interesting example because it is always to some extent a representation (or projection) of who we are or perhaps who we would like to be or who we think we are allowed to be. Again the qualification in the last sentence returns us to our perpetual theme: it is extremely difficult to say anything unequivocal about identity since all we can do is to provide readings of it. Also, rather unnervingly, the reason for much of this difficulty is not because we're all so individualistic but rather because we're all coping with similar meaning systems and sets of expectations, which means that isolating the individual and personal elements is difficult.

INFORMATION BOX i

The theorist Muscovici claims that our idea of the individual is very much a Western creation, deriving from the Western political attitude to individualism.

Consider the appearance of your Communication and Culture group as a sort of temporary outcome of sixteen or so years of growing up in a culture apparently committed to personal expression and the right for individuals to be themselves.

ACTIVITY

This activity investigates the degree to which individual expression is a factor in the way we present ourselves. Take a formal picture of your teaching group (or failing that a group of your friends). Try to identify the significant points of difference and similarity and then divide these into two sets. Head one list STYLE/CHOICE and include those differences which are a matter of personal choice/personal taste (e.g. a particular kind of hairstyle). Head the other list BIOLOGY and list the factors that we have no control over (such as height and gender).

Putting the biology list to one side for a moment, consider the extent to which 'styles' are largely a) individual or b) shared by groups (one group for example might be 'females', another might be those who like a certain kind of music). Do religious beliefs have any part to play in the appearances you have observed?

If your college/school has a dress code or your school insists on a uniform, you have two choices. Either organise a non-uniform day and say it's part of your A-level course or merely see these obvious impositions as explicit examples of what is otherwise implicitly dictating how we see ourselves as people in this culture. In many ways we are looking for the uniforms of our apparently unsupervised lives. The musician Frank Zappa once chided his fans who were mocking the front of stage security guards at his concert with the words 'Everybody in this room is wearing a uniform and don't kid yourself!' Or as the principal of a local sixth form college says every year to parents: 'We don't have a uniform here but they still all wear jeans' (pause for laughter).

The relationship between what is biologically given and what is culturally added is central to all our work (and is referred to elsewhere as the nature/nurture debate). Here it is enough to note that there is more going on than can be easily be explained by the 'facts' of how we are biologically determined. Clothing, for example, that is still largely gendered represents a lot more than the accommodation of biological differences. In pragmatic terms all our sex differences demand physically is a little extra support either above or below the waist. What male and female costume describes is something far more complicated involving attitudes and expectations, gender rather than sex. As you can see it is extremely successful if success is to be judged by how many of us buy into it or how few opt out. It seems a feature of our culture that we learn gender roles and how to play them and are not encouraged (or given room) to question them. It seems obvious that this learning is partly achieved through the role-modelling that goes on across our cultural experience – in the family, in school, in the media. This process of socialisation (getting us ready to be effective members of society) is what has brought you to your current position as students on the verge of adult responsibility (unless you can manage some more 'preparation' at university).

The British sociologist Basil Bernstein said that socialisation is 'a process for making people safe'. It does this partly by alerting us to the dangers. These dangers alter as we develop. In our earliest years the danger seem most obviously physical, and socialisation includes such things as teaching 'road skills' and the recognition of what to do about strangers. Later the dangers become more subtle but not less problematic and they justify or at least sanction a conservative tendency to stick to established social norms. That's the reason why all parents try to prevent you from having a full-facial spider's web tattoo (with the spider sitting within a centimetre of your left eye), because they see this act as dangerous to your chances of being accepted as a fully paid up member of society with all the benefits that this implies. Similarly in the battlefield of adolescence it is not surprising that we sometimes prefer to keep our heads down and to fit in, preferring conformity to alienation.

Gender roles are quite straightforwardly and unproblematically taught in most families and reinforced on every billboard and shopfront and in every mainstream Hollywood film. Little boys are told, 'Don't play with that doll, you're not a girl' and little girls still apparently ask for toy ironing boards for Christmas presents. Meanwhile girls are outperforming boys at most levels of education, we have laws on equal pay and some claim that this is the era of post-feminism because all of the significant battles over equality have been won. Clearly, like identity, gender is not a given, rather it is an issue on which positions are taken. However, it seems uncontroversial to suggest that, on Bernstein's terms, a lot more effort is taken with making girls 'safe' than boys.

Figure 3.5 Girls and boys – look at the way both girl toys are dressed in pink and the boy toys in blue, green and red

It may be that the paraphernalia associated with being female carries greater meaning and expectation from the naming through the rearing and raising to the costumed performance. It is interesting that the wholesale importing of American-style proms in recent years emphasises this very well since it offers an extreme version of the more low-key differences you will have noticed in gender appearances in the last activity. Here we see a self-conscious imitation of the dress and fashion styles associated with celebrity, especially the celebrity rituals of the gala award evening or the film premiere. Like other rituals linked to rites of passage (transitions from one life stage to another), the prom has become an arena for highly prescribed dress codes, where any individual choice operates within very clear constraints. Like so many cultural codes, these constraints do not necessarily operate through written 'rules', but they impose just as strong a weight of expectation.

This is not theoretical stuff, these are the issues that, largely subliminally, provide the context for all of our self-presentations. We are all relatively 'feminine' and 'masculine' even though it's clear that these two powerful signifiers are far from being fixed in their meanings. As with so many of culture's binary oppositions, it is hard to define either masculine or feminine except in relation to the other, so that feminine is the absence of masculinity and vice versa. At the level of social theory, 'feminisation' is seen as a powerfully transforming presence within all those areas into which women have moved professionally over the last century – from education through psychiatry to religion. Closer to home, though, a rather more problematic discussion has emerged through the channels of popular culture.

Figure 3.6 David Walliams and Matt Lucas of *Little Britain*

to think theatrically in terms of 'double acts' and then of your own 'work' with your closest friend.

If we consider high-profile comedy pairings (for example Morecombe and Wise, the Two Ronnies, Matt Lucas and David Walliams, Julian Barrett and Noel Fielding, French and Saunders), we are immediately aware of the front that is being established. We are being 'sold' physical differences as an index (a connection is being made) of character differences. These are used consciously to create a context for comedy, a staging for humour. The teamwork is often slick and professional but the principles are the same as for our own two-person performances. We play off other people, and that play begins with appearance and goes from there.

ACTIVITY

Choose three friends whom you might see individually. Briefly describe the 'teamplay' in each of the three pairs you form when you're with them individually. How does it differ and what difference, if any, does it make to you as a presented self?

Role

Given that Goffman uses a theatrical metaphor, it seems surprising that it should have taken us so long to come to role. Role refers to the parts we play and is, in essence, the focus of Goffman's model. Though Goffman admits that 'All the world is not, of course, a stage', he also points out 'the crucial ways in which it is not easy to specify'. When we considered the business of defining the self, we identified 'social role' as a significant theme of the responses. The research, by Kuhn and McPartland (1954), also indicated that 'definition by role' becomes more prominent as we mature (undergraduates referred to the idea of role twice as often as 7-year-olds did).

Goffman sees the parts we play as an organising principle of our self-presentation. He would see most of us moving from role to role across the day. We may wake up as a wife or husband, walk downstairs into the role of father or mother, before playing the commuter in the early morning rush hour. We may arrive at work to the unexpected role of friend or confidant before we assume the role of employee or employer. The workplace is alive with role differentiation, and potentially role conflict, where the role of 'mother of a sick child' conflicts with the role of 'full-time worker'. Work is often obsessed with rank and status. This makes offices and staffrooms settings for conflicting and overlapping roles. The evening may produce a new set of roles; you may be the guest at a party, a boyfriend or girl-friend, or a part-time worker in a pub.

with a 30-year-old in 'child' ego state. They have their own patterns of behaviour and particular uses of speech and body language. In the course of normal communication each will become dominant in its own contexts. The idea is that when we are communicating we choose from which ego state to speak and our receiver does the same. When we get recognition for our communication, in the form perhaps of a smile or a nod, we receive what Berne called a 'stroke'. A stroke is a form of recognition, an acknowledgement by somebody else that we exist and for Berne it is the most important reason we communicate. We transact to receive strokes. With small children strokes are literally physical, whereas with adults strokes can also take a verbal form. Berne claimed that without strokes 'the spinal cord will shrivel up'. Clearly, negative recognition produces negative strokes and everything deteriorates.

According to Berne, there are three ego states:

- **The Parent**: Claude Steiner, an associate of Berne's and a leading writer on TA, describes the parent ego state as 'like a tape-recorder . . . it is a collection of pre-recorded, prejudged and prejudiced codes for living'. When we are in our parent state we become our parents or the people who raised us. Berne distinguishes between the 'Critical Parent' and the 'Nurturing Parent'. In terms of motivation, the Critical Parent prefers the stick and the Nurturing Parent prefers the carrot. For Steiner, 'The parent uses old tapes to solve problems and is therefore at least 25 years behind'. We probably have all known teachers who are stuck fast in their 'Critical Parent' state.
- **The Adult**: the adult uses reason and logic to solve problems. This is the ego state in which we think and feel in relation to experience. In Steiner's words, 'The adult is a human computer'. The adult has its emotions under control.
- **The Child**: This state contains all the impulses that come naturally to an infant. But just as the Parent has different aspects, so does the Child.
- **The Natural Child** is spontaneous, curious, loving and uninhibited, the part of you that feels free and loves pleasure. In the natural child you communicate freely and openly. It is just like the toddler that responds with love and affection when its needs are met, and angry rebellion when they aren't. Many adults repress their natural child and exaggerate the parent.
- **The Adapted Child** is the state developed when you learned to change (adapt) your feelings and behaviour in response to the world around you. Feelings of guilt, fear, anxiety, envy and pride are all characteristic of the Adapted Child. These feelings may help us to learn the skills we need to get on socially – saying 'please', 'thank you' and 'I'm sorry', but the Adapted Child can become the most troublesome part of our personality. In the Adapted Child state people often react to external demands by:

  - complying
  - sulking
  - avoiding situations.

It is the Adapted Child that may:

- try to please everyone
- turn its back on people with problems
- put off work until a deadline passes.

- **The Little Professor** is creative, thinking and manipulative. The Little Professor can:

  - develop new ideas
  - intuitively sense solutions to problems
  - imagine new ideas.

Recognising ego states

With a little practice and basic understanding of the Parent Adult Child states (PAC) outlined above, it is not too difficult to recognise these ego states. Once you begin to identify your own ego states, it is easy to recognise the PAC states of others.

The following table may help you to begin this process.

	Controlling parent	Nuturing parent	Adult	Natural child	Adapted child	Little professor
Words	Bad, should, ought, don't	Good, nice, well done	How, why, who, yes, no	Fun, want, mine	Can't, wish, please, thank you	I've got an idea
Gestures Postures	Pointing finger, pounding table, shaking head	Open arms	Straight posture, level eye contact	Energetic, loose-limbed	Slumped, dejected, nail-biting	Batting eyelashes
Tone of voice	Sneering, condescending	Loving, encouraging, concerned	Calm, clear, even, confident	Loud, free	Whining, sulking, defiant	Teasing
Facial expression	Scowl, hostile, disapproving	Smiling	Controlled, alert eyes	Grinning, twinkling eyes	Fearful, pouting	Wide-eyed, 'innocent'

website. In particular, he removed all photos of himself involving 'drinking alcohol.' Because of that he is not concerned about strangers, managers or mentors seeing his information online.' 🙷

(DiMicco and Millen 2007)

Another worker in the 'reliving college days category' revealed a distinctly different approach:

🙶 **When he joined the company, he did not change anything about his profile or the pictures of himself. His current profile links to many photos of him drinking alcohol (including directly out of a beer keg) and attending numerous college parties. He feels that *Facebook* is 'for fun' and relates only to 'personal life' and hopes that if his manager ever did see his page would understand that it has 'nothing to do with his professional life'.** 🙷

(ibid)

Enthusiasts for the liberating potential of social network sites stress the endless opportunity for the creation and manipulation of your own identity, and it is certainly the case that there is no requirement for authenticity. The views expressed above suggest that online identity may, in the case of social networking, have unforeseen consequences, largely because it is difficult to influence the perceptions of others in the same ways that we can for offline identity. A more positive approach to online identity formation would stress the opportunities provided by social network sites for creative self-expression, for making new friends and for building self-esteem by encouraging supportive feedback from others. It may be the case that social networkers are rapidly acquiring an awareness of the pitfalls as well as the potential of an online identity and that they already take steps to protect their current and future interests as they project versions of themselves into cyberspace. However, the intention of this example is not to criticise or endorse online identities in social networking sites, but to suggest that this is a fascinating and fast-evolving area for your further discussion and investigation.

ACTIVITY

Social Networks: Issues for Group Discussion

- Which social networks sites are preferred, and why?
- What sort of information would you include/exclude from your online identity?
- What sort of online identity earns the highest status?
- How do you control access to your identity?
- What are the safety issues in social networking/online communities?
- What are the advantages of online interactions over offline?
- Read the article *Your digital dirt can come back to haunt you*. What are the ethics of online 'snoopers' such as:

  - employers
  - prospective employers
  - colleges and schools
  - parents
  - teachers
  - ex-partners?

Your digital dirt can come back to haunt you

27 Oct 2006 | Filed under: Job Searching. Recruitment. Technology & IT.

As we're often being reminded, the Internet has irrevocably changed the way that we look for and apply for jobs. But the web works both ways. So you may want to think twice about what you say in your blog or avoid posting photos from your last toga party online just in case a potential employer takes a look and changes their mind about you.

And this is no idle warning. According to a new survey by CareerBuilder.com, a quarter of hiring managers in the US have used Google or other internet search engines to find out more about potential employees.

continued

A web-savvy one in 10 have even gone beyond simple 'Googling' and used social networking sites as part of their candidate screening process.

The survey of more than 1,000 hiring managers nationwide revealed the astonishing fact that half of those who have Googled candidates have rejected one or more based on what they found.

More startling still, almost two-thirds of hiring managers who used social networking sites to research candidates have also been put off hiring people as a result.

So what is it that they are discovering online that is having such a profoundly negative effect on recruiters?

Almost a third find that a candidate has lied about their qualifications. A quarter find that they have poor communication skills (so make sure that you proofread those blog entries) and a quarter have found that a candidate was linked to criminal behaviour. One in five candidates also posted information about drinking or using drugs.

Be careful, too, about what you say about previous employers or colleagues. One in five hiring managers told CareerBuilder's survey that they took exception to candidates bad-mouthing their previous company or fellow employees while 15 per cent of candidates shot themselves in the foot by sharing confidential information from previous employers.

Those ever-so-funny-at-the-time snapshots could also ruin a career before it has even begun. One in 10 recruiters has come across candidates who have posted provocative or inappropriate photographs of themselves, while almost as many (eight per cent) have been put off a candidate because they deemed that their screen name was unprofessional.

'While sharing information online can have a potentially negative impact on your job search or career plans, it can also be leveraged as a tool to differentiate yourself to employers,' said Rosemary Haefner, Vice President of Human Resources at CareerBuilder.com.

'Highlighting professional and personal accomplishments and showcasing your creativity can help a candidate make a positive lasting impression on employers and validate why he/she is the right person for the job.'

In other words, the web-savvy job seeker can just as easily use the medium to boost their chances of landing that dream job as they can destroy them.

Two-thirds of the hiring managers surveyed said that they had found background information on candidates that supported their professional qualifications for the job and four out of 10 had gained the impression that a candidate was well-rounded and showed a wide range of interests.

Around a third also found material online that suggested a candidate had great communication skills, conveyed a professional image and would be a good fit within the company culture.

Rosemary Haefner recommends a simple mantra that we all ought to bear in mind to safeguard their online reputations: Be careful, be discreet and be prepared.

Don't post anything on your site or your 'Friends' sites you wouldn't want a prospective employer to see – and that includes derogatory comments, revealing photos or lewd jokes.

On social networks, consider setting your profile to 'private', so that it is viewable only by people of your choosing.

And finally, check your profile regularly to see what comments have been posted. Use a search engine to look for online records of yourself to see what is out there about you. If you find information you feel could be detrimental to your candidacy or career, see about getting it removed – and make sure you have an answer ready to counter or explain 'digital dirt'.

Earlier this week, the Head of Content at UK digital consultancy Cimex warned that blogging, in particular, represents a 'weapon of mass destruction' that could jeopardise the future of thousands of young career hopefuls.

'There is very little guarantee that a blogger can properly delete his (or her) adolescent ramblings later on in life,' warned Dan Williamson in a letter to the *Financial Times* newspaper.

continued

Turning to MMORPGs, whether games such as *World of Warcraft* or interactive environments like *Second Life*, the opportunities for experimenting with identity seem endless. Typically, participants create a character, give it a name and assign an avatar (a digital model that represents you in virtual reality). This process enables you to create an idealisation or projection of your offline self, without even the restrictions of social networks like Facebook. You are completely freed from the constraints that normally operate on the construction of identity: age, gender, body size and shape, ethnicity, nationality and even species all become irrelevant. Your online identity is entirely a product of your desires and your creative imagination. However, research has suggested that conventional parameters of identity do have an influence on the identity choices made by players in MMORPGs. For example, female players are more likely to see their characters as idealised versions of themselves whilst age has a greater effect on male players. Female players are more likely to interact as they would in real life whilst males are more experimental. The non-verbal codes which we discussed in Chapter 2 are also reproduced in virtual environments. Although they may be able to fly and teleport (as in *Second Life*) or perform superhuman feats, it seems that people tend to stick to the same social rules whether in the real world or a virtual world; for example, by observing codes of proximity, direction of gaze and touching. On the other hand, just as clothing influences our self-perception and identity in the real world, so the size and shape of an avatar affects behaviour in virtual environments. An attractive avatar makes its owner feel more confident and behave more purposefully (Yee et al., 2007; Yee and Bailenson, 2007).

It seems certain that in future we will be spending more of our time in virtual environments, not just playing but also meeting people, shopping, working and learning. As this is the case, we need to think carefully about the implications for our sense of identity and codes of self-expression.

Figure 3.8 Virtual worlds – the Habbo Hotel

Figure 3.9 *Second Life*

References and further reading

Argyle, M. (1983) *The Psychology of Interpersonal Behaviour*, 4th edn, Harmondsworth: Penguin

Bennett, P., Slater, J. and Wall, P. (2006) *A2 Media Studies: The Essential Introduction*, London: Routledge

Cooley, C.H. (1992) *Human Nature and the Social Order*, New York: Transaction Publishers

Coopersmith, S. (1967) *The Antecedents of Self-Esteem*, San Francisco: Freeman

Dimbleby, R. and Burton, G. (2006) *More Than Words: An Introduction to Communication*, 4th edn, London: Routledge

DiMicco, J.M. and Millen, D.R. (2007) 'Identity management: multiple presentations of self in Facebook'. Online at: http://delivery.acm.org/10.1145/1320000/1316682/p383-dimicco.pdf?key1=1316682&key2=1520195911&coll=ACM&dl=ACM&CFID=15151515&CFTOKEN=6184618 (accessed 12 November 2007)

Gergen, K.J. and Gergen, M.M. (1981) *Social Psychology*, New York: Harcourt Brace Jovanovich

Goffman, E. (1990) *The Presentation of Self in Everyday Life*, Harmondsworth: Penguin

Gross, R. (1996) *Psychology: The Science of Mind and Behaviour*, London: Hodder and Stoughton

Kuhn, H.H. and McPartland, T.S. (1954) 'An empirical investigation of self-attitudes', *American Sociological Review*, 47

Rogers, C. (1961) *On Becoming a Person*, Boston, MA: Houghton Mifflin

Rosen, C. (2007) 'Virtual friendship and the new narcissism', *The New Atlantis*, 17, 15–31. Online at: www.thenewatlantis.com/archive/17/rosen.htm

Yee, N. and Bailenson, J.N. (2007) 'The Proteus Effect: self transformations in virtual reality', *Human Communication Research*, 33, 271–90. Online at: http://vhil.stanford.edu/pubs/2007/yee-proteus-effect.pdf

TOOLKITS – THE PROCESS AND SEMIOTIC APPROACHES

4

You have already discovered that Communication and Culture as a subject is principally concerned with how we make meanings as individuals and collectively. It will be clear that 'meaning making' is by no means a simple and straightforward activity, however much it may seem so to communicators. In this chapter we shall be examining some different approaches to the complexities of meaning making, but we must begin with an understanding of just what it is that we are trying to understand and analyse. Our starting point is the text.

What is a text?

As active communicators we create and respond to texts within the cultural environment. Before going much further we need to pause in order to consider the terms 'text' and 'textual' in some detail, as we shall be using them frequently. In our terms, a text is a message or a 'piece of communication'; it is something that we make meanings out of. It is worth pointing out that the derivation of the word is from the Latin *textus*: 'something woven' and it may be useful to think of the 'weaving together' of meanings in a text.

The best way to explain the concept of a text is to use some examples. We are used to the idea of written words being treated as texts as they are organised into articles, essays, short stories, poems or shopping lists. These are, fairly obviously, meaningful items which we read in order to make sense of them. Furthermore, the idea that a poem or a play can be read (that is, interpreted) in different ways is no stranger to us; we have all studied the texts of literature and been encouraged to look for different meanings including our own personal responses. All we seek to do in Communication and Culture is to extend this notion beyond just the written or printed word to all areas of meaning making. Many of our texts include graphic or pictorial images which are open to interpretation in just the same way, so we would talk of reading a film or a photograph or the packaging of a tin of baked beans in just the same way.

Our extension of the ideas of 'reading' and the text doesn't stop with visual images. We also want to deal with the texts created using non-verbal codes; for example, the glance, the tilt of the head or the slightest movement away. Furthermore, we can regard all cultural products as texts: the car, the mobile phone, the airliner, the semi-detached suburban house, the Humber Bridge or the Houses of Parliament. Places, too, meet our definition of the text. This can include not only obviously constructed environments such as your local high street or shopping mall, but also more apparently 'natural' spaces which clearly have meanings to be interpreted: the Forest of Dean, for example, or Lake Windermere.

We can also identify cultural practices as texts; you could read your sister's wedding reception as a text, just as you could read a religious festival or day trip to the seaside. As you can see from this expansive set of examples, we are not going to run out of texts to study any time soon. You may ask why we should use the terms 'reading' and 'text' in this rather specialist way, a way which is rather different to everyday use of these words. The simple answer is that these terms carry the implication that meanings are almost never neutral; they are heavily influenced by culture. This is exactly the implication that we want to reinforce in Communication and Culture.

We are working towards a definition of text as 'anything that has the potential to be read or interpreted; anything that communicates meaning or meanings'. This pretty much covers it though it is worth considering that there are a number of ways in which this potential can be identified. One way is the conscious construction of messages by the sender (or 'weaver'). In this sense, the shape of the message, the signs it contains, the codes that are used are all carefully constructed by the creator of the message to achieve a desired result. Alternatively, we could identify meaning in texts from the point of view of the receiver. Here we would be interested in the interpretations of texts, irrespective of the intentions of the sender. Third, we could stress the cultural environment in which communication takes place; on this occasion putting emphasis not so much on the sender's intentions or the receiver's perceptions, but on the context in which the act of communication takes place.

We have already discussed the apparently unique properties of language (in Chapter 2) but, in more general terms, it is probably the capacity to communicate with ourselves and others at such a level of sophistication that distinguishes the human animal from other animals. This capacity to communicate is closely linked to another human characteristic: systematic and organised thought. We can act, we can reflect upon our actions and we can draw conclusions about the actions of others. As Colin Cherry observed, 'Self awareness and the sense of social responsibility have arisen as a result of organised thoughts' (1978), but such organisation of thought would be of little use without the capacity to communicate.

The concept of the code was introduced in Chapter 2 and this will certainly be a very useful component of your toolkit as you move on to the analysis of texts. Although we all use codes in our communication from our very earliest days, we are not always aware of this. In fact, our awareness of codes often only arises when we encounter unfamiliar codes, often in the form of frustration. 'If that's what they meant, why didn't they say so?' is a frequent reaction to the use of specialist terminology or jargon. It's a common complaint of students and people in the working world that others wrap up what they are saying in fancy words or jargon that seem to be designed as much to make a good impression as to make sense. Sometimes, these are justified complaints as people do, indeed, attempt to manage the impressions of others by making themselves look clever or by using a form of communication designed to include some and exclude others. On the other hand, what may seem to outsiders as 'meaningless jargon' may be an essential and precise form of communication in some circumstances. Perhaps this why we need to develop what Neil Postman, the American theorist of media and communication, called a 'crap detector' to distinguish between these two types of code.

In some ways, the toolkits which this chapter is trying to assemble for you to use are themselves codes. Just like other academic subjects, Communication and Culture has its own set of specialist terms, its own modes of interpretation and a characteristic form of expression. In order to show how this principle works, we shall use an analogy with the British system of road signs (an analogy is comparison between things which have a similar set of relations but are otherwise different).

Figure 4.1
Humpback bridge
road sign

A bizarre alternative would be a sign with a written message that said:

> **'If you continue driving or riding on the road that you are now driving or riding on you will soon encounter a humpbacked bridge. Take care to reduce speed to ensure that you do not damage your vehicle or endanger others. Use your eyes and ears because vehicle approaching from the other side of the bridge may be obscured by the hump of the bridge and may not be as careful as you are.'**

This would not be a useful or effective way of communicating information because road users all recognise the simple road sign and consciously or subconsciously remind themselves of the necessary advice. Most of us already have the key to this code, we know how to unlock the information implied by the road sign. As with all codes, it is essential that users of the code share a set of meanings that are generated by the particular signs used within the code. In this case, the community which needs to interpret the sign are British road users and it is imperative that all of them are able to read and decode this and other road signs in pretty much the same way. If they didn't, there would be mayhem on the roads. This is why an understanding of the Highway Code is considered such an important part of the driving test; there are serious safety considerations if road signs are ignored or misinterpreted.

However, this is not to suggest that alternative interpretations of the above sign are impossible. The representation of the bridge itself could, perhaps, be guessed at by someone with no familiarity with this code, though it could easily be misread as, say, 'tunnel ahead'. The triangle that frames the pictorial symbol, though, is a different sort of sign altogether. It is very unlikely that anyone totally unfamiliar with this code would have guessed that a red triangle means 'warning'. The triangle is therefore in a different category from circular road signs, where red circles tell you what you must not do and blue circles tell you what you must do. These conventions for the interpretation of shapes and colours must simply be learned. It would be too dangerous to rely on the ability of road users to guess correctly at the meaning of signs.

SCHOOL OF THOUGHT: a set of beliefs or ideas held by a group of academics. A shared way of thinking about a particular issue.

With some of the basics such as text and code now, we hope, in place it is time to move on to consider two significantly different approaches to the analysis of communication and culture. These two approaches, or schools of thought, can be distinguished by their own distinctive codes: the terms, techniques and analytical devices they use. This is why we have assigned to them both a 'toolkit', so that by the end of this chapter you will be able to use either the process toolkit or the semiotic toolkit in your practical exercises of analysing communication and culture. The first school of thought, the process school, characterises communication as the transmission and reception of messages. The second school of thought, the semiotic school, conceives of communication as the generation and sharing of meanings.

The process school

In the opening chapter of this book, we introduced a very straightforward approach to communication which reduces all communication to three simple components as follows:

Sender → Message → Receiver

We noted that this idea is sometimes called the 'railway model' because it sees the message rather like a physical thing which has to be carried along a line from A to B, from Sender to Receiver. There was a time when the word 'communication' was principally associated with transportation, the days of mail coaches, steam ships, the pony express, carrier pigeons and canal boats. If you wanted to get a message further than you could shout, it had to be written down and carried from you to your intended destination. OK, there were a few exceptions, such as signalling with mirrors and flags but, on the whole, messages had to be picked up and carried.

This all changed with telegraphy and the amazingly rapid development of electronic and mass communication (see the timeline in Figure 1.7, pages 11–12). However, the idea that communication is just like a postal system has persisted long into the era of electronic communication and many theorists have sought to explain and understand communication processes by expanding and developing the basic idea of a line between sender and receiver along which the message is either successfully transported if it gets through, or unsuccessfully transported if it fails to get through. Welcome to the process school of communication.

Process approaches have been particularly widely used in technical and organisational contexts. This is because they tend to focus on success or failure in communication. Most businesses depend upon effective communication so they are keen to identify reasons for communication failure and ways of making their communication more effective. Similarly, communication technicians working with, for example, radio, television, telecommunications or satellite communications are always keen to find ways in which they can maximise the efficiency of their systems.

One such approach to the study of communication originated in the study of telecommunications. Claude E. Shannon was employed by the Bell Telephone Corporation in the 1940s. In order to solve problems occurring in the telephone system, he devised a mathematical model of communication. His objective was to find ways to reduce or eliminate the disruptions to the system. He called these disruptions 'noise', and believed that if you could put a mathematical value on noise, then you could work out how much the signal would need to be boosted in order to overcome the problem. You should note that the word 'noise' is used here in a technical sense to mean any form of interference, so an electrical storm which spoils your television picture would be an example of noise. As the model had its origins in telecommunications, it is concerned with the transmission of a signal and the effectiveness of that transmission. This idea is at the very core of the process approach: the school of thought that sees the study of communication as being about the transmission and reception of signals and the ability to overcome 'noise'.

Shannon's great insight was to separate the physical form of the message from its meaning. The former could be measured and dealt with as a mathematical problem; Shannon referred to it as the information content. You have probably heard of the term 'bit', meaning binary digit. Shannon invented this term and is widely regarded as one of the single most influential contributors to the 'digital revolution'. He was particularly interested in the technical properties of information, but less interested in the *meaning* of messages. This is why his ideas are always going to have limitations for us as students of Communication and Culture because we are very interested in meanings.

| Source | ⇨ | Transmitter | ⇨ | Channel | ⇨ | Receiver | ⇨ | Destination |

Figure 4.2 Simple process model of communication

The source is the sender of the message, usually a person who formulates in their mind an idea or information which they wish to transmit. The transmitter is the device used to transform the message into a physical form; for example, vocal apparatus. The channel is the physical means of transmission; for example, sound waves. The receiver is the device or apparatus which transforms the message into a form which can be understood by the receiver. For example, in order to receive a message which has been transmitted via the sound channel, you will need a reception device commonly known as a pair of ears.

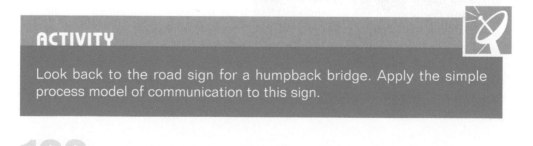

ACTIVITY

Look back to the road sign for a humpback bridge. Apply the simple process model of communication to this sign.

AS COMMUNICATION AND CULTURE: THE ESSENTIAL INTRODUCTION

As we have explained, these are fairly simple models. Before investigating some more sophisticated versions of the process approach, we can summarise some basic principles of the approach as follows:

The process approach: summary of basic principles

■ Communication seen as a process in which senders transmit messages to receivers.
■ Focus is on:

    ■ the physical form of the message, the 'information content'
    ■ the physical means of transmission, the channel.

■ Senders encode messages, receivers decode messages.
■ Success of communication can be measured by comparing the message at source with the message at destination.
■ Success in communication means eliminating, or at least reducing, 'noise' – those factors which interfere with the message to prevent it getting through.
■ Meanings, contexts and culture are of relatively little concern.

The process explanation does tend to put power in the hands (or perhaps head) of the sender, the originator of the message. The role of the receiver is more passive: waiting for the message to arrive, opening it and decoding it either successfully or not. If we now apply our process approach to a text, the following observations can be made.

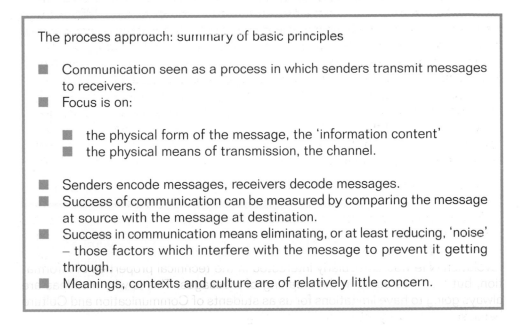

Figure 4.3 An advert for *Skins* on Channel 4 and E4

This text is the encoded version of a desire by Channel 4 to publicise their series *Skins* to a specifically targeted audience of potential viewers who would then decode this message and either comply with their efforts by watching the programme or reject the message by not watching. Significant issues here are: first, the text is a version of some predetermined intention; second, the message is essentially singular and unambiguous; third, the outcome of the communication can be quantified.

> **ENCODE/DECODE:** in process approaches these twin verbs describe the process through which a thought is converted from its abstract state and is given a physical form by the sender (encoding) and then transformed back from its physical form into an abstract state by the receiver (decoding).

The key elements such as intention, sender and audience (receivers) are often obvious, but it is sometimes necessary to tease them out. Process models of communication, such as Lasswell's Formula below, can serve as useful prompts for this exploration. In 1948 Harold Lasswell offered a five-point plan for identifying the significant features of communication. The Formula poses five questions:

Who?
Says what?
To whom?
In which channel?
With what effect?

This formula is immediately useful since it clarifies areas of investigation which we recognise as the sender, the message, the receiver, the channel (and medium) and the outcome.

INFORMATION BOX – CHANNEL/MEDIUM *i*

It is important to distinguish between these sometimes confused concepts. Whilst a medium is a means of communication, a way of communicating (a technological medium such as television or film, or a human medium such as speech or gestures), a channel is a physical connection between communicators, a route (such as sound waves or the electronic type that is carrying this message to you).

If we apply the Lasswell Formula to, for example, the *Skins* promo we might get:

- **Who?** Channel 4/the featured character and actor/*Skins* (the programme).
- **Says what?** This is a special version of that popular/familiar/controversial programme *Skins*.
- **To whom?** Those who've seen and some who haven't.
- **In which channel?** Print (technically, a visual channel).
- **With what effect?** It is seen, 'touched' and, it is hoped, watched.

The Lasswell Formula has served its purpose in efficiently identifying the text, its context and its intention. As an instrument for further analysis, however, it is limited – beyond a discussion about who the sender is. What's more, different texts produce different sets of results, with varying degrees of usefulness – even within the same genre. Lasswell may help us to identify some important components of an act of communication, but it doesn't get us very far in identifying the meaning or meanings of a message. Lasswell insists that we find a specific context for communication texts and then implies that the narrow context he has identified is the only one that counts. We will see later that the semiotic approach also privileges context, but in a very different way, to describe those wider cultural, social, political and historical conditions within which texts might be located and made meaningful. Lasswell is pretty good at the 'what' of human communication (and the 'why') but is far less interested than he perhaps should be in the 'how'. This can be a very frustrating position to be in as the next activity will hopefully demonstrate.

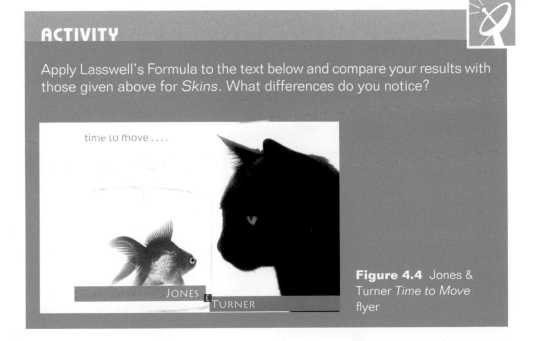

ACTIVITY

Apply Lasswell's Formula to the text below and compare your results with those given above for *Skins*. What differences do you notice?

time to move....

JONES & TURNER

Figure 4.4 Jones & Turner *Time to Move* flyer

The problem here is partly caused by a more sophisticated text, or at least a more open text (or a text that is differently closed). Whilst the preferred reading (that is, the decoding of the text intended by the sender) of the *Skins* text runs along the lines of 'this is young, raw, edgy, controversial', 'out of it'; the 'Time to move . . .' text is much more diverse. It is clearly offering much greater scope for negotiated readings which may be modified to suit the reader's interests but which go way beyond the scope of the Lasswell model. Such texts give Lasswell and the process school their Dalek moment: they simply 'do not compute' and theoretically can only be dealt with if information about the sender's intention can be ascertained.

INFORMATION BOX – DALEK MOMENT *i*

This refers to the point in any 'Doctor versus Daleks' instalment of the long-running sci-fi series *Doctor Who*, where the Doctor's timelord unpredictability outwits the superlogic of the Daleks. This results always in the flailing of Dalek 'arms' (gun and claw), the metallic whining of 'Does not compute/illogical and so on' and ultimately the explosion of the Dalek brain!

ASIDE

It may be that advertising in particular often favours these extremely open, elliptical and puzzling texts simply because the combined effect of these multiple negotiated readings and the absence of a preferred reading ironically makes oppositional readings (that is, decodings which are opposed to the sender's intention) less likely. All readings, then, in their ways are preferred readings.

Intention

So when we are examining texts in which the sender, message and receiver are clearly identifiable, it is a relatively easy job to sketch out a process analysis. However, it can be a very different matter if the text is a little elliptic or enigmatic, even after the intention is clear. The A6 flyer that follows was discovered in a Cambridge library and caught the eye with its Japanese cartoon-style aesthetic. It features, almost uniquely in advertising, the word 'ordinary' and a striking image.

Figure 4.5
Cambridge Youth
Project *Ordinary* flyer

ACTIVITY

Examine the flyer depicted in Figure 4.5.

■ What might the purpose of it be?
■ Who might send this text? Give two or three possible options.
■ Who do you think the intended audience might be (in terms of age profile, personality, and so on)?

As far as the process approach to communication is concerned, the answers to the above questions are found on the flyer's reverse side:

■ **Purpose**: 'why not write . . . for *Gunge* newspaper?'
■ **Intended audience**: 'between the ages of 14 and 25'.
■ **Sender**: The North Cambridge Youth Project.

However, what they add up to is a list of intentions, a notion of what the designers or compilers or sponsors hoped they were communicating to their target audience. They do not necessarily do justice to the quality of the design or to that of the companion piece (below) in which the man is replaced by a woman and 'ordinary?' is replaced with 'quiet?' These may be male and female versions or perhaps versions for males and females. They share reverse-side texts and have clear generic links: the floating background texts, the style of illustrations and the arrangement of elements. Despite the clearly stated intentions, the reverse side clarifications do little to identify a preferred reading of either of these striking designs.

Figure 4.6 Cambridge Youth Project *Quiet* flyer

AS COMMUNICATION AND CULTURE: THE ESSENTIAL INTRODUCTION

Knowing your audience: barriers and bridges

It's quite easy to get sentimental about the appeal of quirky texts which sometimes give us more than we expect from otherwise humdrum and largely conventional day-to-day communication. On a larger scale, in the world of mass media advertising only the bravest or best established brands risk real 'riddles' in their marketing, since the prospect of an uncomprehending audience is too awful to contemplate. Most mass market communication is strikingly formulaic and explicit, repetitive and redundant. This too has risks because if the 'says what' is too 'stupid', audiences get offended.

If we meet someone every day and they always say the same thing to us, that communication can be characterised as redundant. Most films contain a degree of redundancy, especially if they are genre films such as horror, romantic comedy or gangster. This doesn't make them any less enjoyable, it just means that certain elements such as the plot, the characters and the setting can be quite predictable. Astute communicators will try to wrap up the entropic elements of a communication with redundant elements to make it more easily understood. It could be said that the objective of an effective communicator is to make the entropic redundant, that is, to make the unpredictable, the difficult to understand, easy to understand.

INFORMATION BOX – REDUNDANCY/ENTROPY   *i*

A communication that is low on new information and which is highly predictable is said to be redundant. A communication that is high on new information and that is highly unpredictable is said to be entropic.

Imagine two Valentine's Day cards. The first contains this message;

> *Roses are red, violets are blue*
> *I'm sending this card because I love you.*

The second message reads:

> *Roses are red, violets are blue*
> *I'm sending this card because I fear an alien invasion of earth.*

The first message is predictable; each word has low information content. The second message deliberately flouts the predictability of its context and is therefore entropic.

In a development from the Lasswell Formula discussed earlier, Shannon and Weaver devised a model which emphasised the significance of noise.

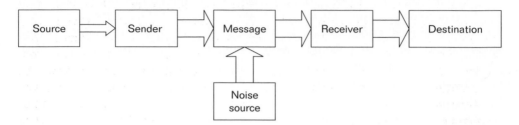

Figure 4.7 Shannon and Weaver's Mathematical Theory of Communication

As we have said, 'noise' is the technical term for any factor with the capacity to interfere with the message as it is transmitted. The higher the redundancy of the message, the more chance it has of getting through in spite of any interference. If you are listening to a radio advertisement for double glazing which you've heard a hundred times before, it doesn't really matter if the signal strength is low and you can't hear all the words. However, if someone is giving you directions by phone, it really is important that you catch every word. One way of increasing redundancy is to use repetition. Another way is to stick very closely to the format expected in a particular type of communication. This is why so many messages, particularly those communicated by mass media, are highly formulaic.

One crude (and some would argue 'simple-minded') and predictable theme of much public communication, from magazine covers to cereal ads, is the use of selective representations of women (and girls, though the line between these is deliberately blurred). In this way to select any one of the hundreds of magazines published every week which feature smiling pretty 'girls' on them (from puzzles to porn) is to pick up something whose cover is presenting no surprise or design innovation: it is structurally, though not ideologically, neutral. These images, on all shelves, are not necessarily exploitative, though they are rather bland and (obviously) cosmetic. In fact they have no particular energy at all, they are a somewhat tired cliché: a default for the uninspired designer who has probably been instructed to conform to a formula.

For the process approach, design is about the clarification of intention. It's not that other readings are impossible, it's just that they're not *valid* readings, they're 'misreadings', 'aberrant decodings'.

ABERRANT DECODING: 'reading' a text in any way other than as it is intended, usually because the receiver does not share a knowledge and understanding of the code or codes used by the sender.

AS COMMUNICATION AND CULTURE: THE ESSENTIAL INTRODUCTION

Thus when Shannon and Weaver recognise the potential difference between 'intended message' and 'received message' they are not so much acknowledging the polysemic character of communication (that is, the potential of a message to carry many possible interpretations) but rather identifying potential problems that must be solved. They are concerned only to establish those inefficiencies which might limit the transmission of intended meaning to the receiver, and through this to suggest ways in which these inefficiencies might be countered. They are concerned with accurate decoding and how it might be achieved. The Shannon and Weaver model is often referred to as the Mathematical Theory of Communication. They were trying to devise a system to eliminate the deterioration of communication using telephones. They discovered that if a mathematical value could be placed on the noise source, then the telephone engineers would know by how much the signal would have to be increased to overcome the noise source.

If we transfer this noise source argument to the consideration of our tolerance of mildly tiring male adolescent representations of 'girl/women' in a vast range of product marketing we may see that the process approach is often a little more interactive than it sometimes appears. In trying to clear channels of noise, commercial senders transmit highly redundant but also highly targeted communication. Redundancy refers to the level of predictability that can be built into a message or a text. Genre, for example, assists redundancy in that it offers a series of expectations which are to a large degree predictable. When we choose to see a horror film, we do so in the secure knowledge that significant parts of the text will be already familiar to us from our experience of other horror films. This familiarity makes us feel secure and confident.

However, genre implies a segmentation of the audience such that successful communication with one group means little communication with another. In the context of gender representation this often means flooding public space with images which are perhaps intended for a relatively small (but commercially significant) audience in a way that certainly does not make whole areas of the mass market feel 'secure and confident'.

ACTIVITY

Consider the potential barriers to communication in Figures 4.8a and 4.8b. Where would you locate these barriers; a) in the text itself, b) in the mind of the sender or c) in the receiver's mind?

Figure 4.8a *PC Format* postcard

Figure 4.8b Cover of *PC Format*, July 1998

Anything that impedes the communication process or causes it to deteriorate. There are four types of identifiable barrier to communication:

1   **Mechanical**: physical impediments. These affect the channel of communication, for example the noise of a low-flying aircraft preventing you from hearing the radio.

2   **Psychological**: internal pressures on sender/receiver. For example, you may receive a message perfectly clearly, but because of your overwhelmingly positive or negative attitudes towards the sender, you fail to decode the message as it was intended. Stereotyping often causes psychological barriers.

3   **Semantic**: lack of or partial understanding. Semantic barriers operate on the encoding/decoding stage of the process, so if the sender has used a code with which you as a receiver are unfamiliar, the message won't get through. As we have seen, sharing a culture involves sharing codes, so semantic barriers are more likely between senders and receivers from different cultures.

4   **Organisational**: structural dysfunctions in groups. This is when lines of communication within an organisation become clogged or blocked; for example, due to unproductive meetings or poor management. Gatekeepers in organisations sometimes intercept important messages.

GATEKEEPER: someone who controls the selection of information to be offered to a given channel. Thus, for example, newspaper editors are significant gatekeepers, but we are all gatekeepers in an interpersonal sense, deciding as we do what we communicate and what we omit or hold back.

In order to communicate with a general public audience, most broadcast communication has a large degree of redundancy, in that it conforms to predetermined conventions. New situation comedy on television, for example, will be keen to reference its original comic situation, its cast of soon-to-be-familiar characters, and its cumulative punchlines in the context of the genre as a whole. Redundancy, rather than anchorage, is the key to identifying intended meanings and preferred readings in this case. Redundancy is, in effect, an implication of generic or even formal conventions, a sort of insurance policy taken out by the sender to guard against potential audience misunderstanding or bewilderment.

> **ANCHORAGE:** directing receivers towards one particular meaning from a range of possible meanings. A caption can anchor the meaning of a photograph.

In contrast, unpredictability in the content or form of a message is described as entropy. Entropic content concentrates information in a demanding way, whilst entropic form usually breaks existing conventions. Entropy opposes redundancy and calls for a plurality of response rather than a conventional singularity of response. In time, of course, as broken conventions become the new conventions, the entropic becomes redundant and the process begins again. An example of this process would be Channel Four's *The Big Breakfast*, which set out systematically to break all the conventions of breakfast television and ended up being successful and greatly imitated.

The power of the sender in process approaches

ACTIVITY

Identify the sender(s) in the following communications:

- The *Sun* newspaper
- The film *Die Hard 4.0*
- The campaign of TV advertisements for Budweiser beer
- The new album from The View
- The book *Harry Potter and the Deathly Hallows*
- The television series *The Simpsons*

Identifying senders is significant in the sense that it has an impact on the way we respond to messages. This is why when advertisers choose to write advertising copy in the style of newspaper or magazine journalism, the words 'ADVERTISEMENT' or 'ADVERTISING FEATURE' declare this to be the case.

Mass media communications are usually produced by complex teams but the industry is forever asking us to individualise and personalise its communications. We are often invited to perceive of senders as individuals and big corporations like to assign themselves friendly, individualised identities. Promoting films by means of their directors and stars is an example of this. It is easier to relate to Quentin Tarantino as sender than to the large numbers of people who were responsible for making *Death Proof*.

Senders, in terms of their status and authority, are one factor that contributes to the building of audiences. Status here has a phatic function: it attracts attention. There are clearly types of text that are sold on the basis of the sender's identity. Advance orders of the latest release from popular bands, popular novelists or a film featuring a particular star are proof that the status of the sender is a vital ingredient in mass media marketing.

> **PHATIC COMMUNICATION:** aspects of language which serve to reinforce social relationships rather than to communicate information (e.g. 'Have a nice day').

Audiences are also built around certain kinds of message. We have previously discussed genre as an example of this, but the ways in which messages are composed work at more subtle levels as well. The process approach is always concerned to explore how communication can be made more efficient. For example, we have considered the relationship between two aspects of a message: its form and its content. This explicitly acknowledges that there are a number of ways of communicating a given content, at the level of both medium and channel. What process theory is keen to suggest is that some forms are in specific cases better suited than others, and therefore that the job of the communicator is to find the best formal match for a particular content to a particular audience.

When evaluating the effectiveness of any piece of communication, we are partly engaging in this debate, placing the particular text in a range of appropriateness for a particular context. It is clear that most communication texts are targeted at a specific (although not always specified) audience and equally clear that this is a contributing factor to the way in which texts and messages are composed. Equally clearly, this cannot be the last word on a process that is human and creative. Process models are used to evaluate communication in terms of its intentions and the degree to which those intentions are fulfilled. This may function as a useful starting point but it can all too easily limit both our response to texts and our understanding of their impact and effectiveness. What is intended is often clear or is easy to guess but what is achieved in and by a text is very often both more and less than its intention. There is a character in Ian McEwan's novel *A Child in Time* (1987) whose first novel becomes a surprise success just because it ends up on the wrong desk at a publisher's and is released as a novel for teenagers and not, as intended, for adults. This is the problem with assuming that what was achieved in communication is what was intended to be communicated. Communication is invariably achieved, but there's often a big difference between the desired objective (intention) and the achieved result (outcome). This difference is seen by process theorists as a measure of the success or failure of the communication.

ACTIVITY

Consider the intended meaning of the healthy gums advertisement below. What factors might impede the efficient communication of this message? Who is the sender in this case and in what ways do they establish their status within the text? Who are the intended receivers and how are they being targeted?

Figure 4.9
Don't Ignore Blood

The effect here is quite shocking and unpleasant, which is always a risk in a context that is largely upbeat and bland. The audience is being addressed directly by both image and text and is forced, in some way, to respond. The degree to which this engagement is the norm in media communication gives the lie to arguments about audience passivity. In many adverts, for example, the audience is asked to find the desired meanings for themselves.

The increasing popularity of phone-in competitions and popular referenda on all manner of subjects is further proof of the activation of the mass audience. Because feedback is being built in here, there is a good chance that the effectiveness of communication will improve. Within the terms of reference of the process school, feedback gives encoders information on how their messages are being received and therefore notionally the opportunity to improve them. Feedback, then, is seen by the process school as a means by which the sender can monitor the success of the communication.

Feedback to print-based texts can be expressed in two main ways: the direct way, which takes the form of filling in reply slips, donating money or buying a book (for example); and the indirect way, which sees the text as a starting point for various kinds of interpersonal and media communication. This is partly the reason why shock and scandal are so effective because they stimulate indirect publicity. The advertising for the clothes firm Benetton has often courted such publicity, offering controversial campaigns which prompt massive amounts of indirect (and some direct) feedback. Moreover, developments in technology, and particularly the emergence of the internet, have offered much greater opportunities for texts to be interactive because of the very fact that even with mass media texts the feedback can be almost instantaneous.

In 2001 the industry was just about getting smart to the enormous potential offered by technology, with *The Blair Witch Project* a case in point, where a campaign begun by an internet film reviewer almost unwittingly hyped this low-budget film to notoriety and international success. Here was a film which explicitly involved its audience in its promotion, its merchandising and its communication. Since then things have just exploded with internet contexts such as *YouTube* getting credit not only for launching up and coming bands but also for helping to raise awareness of a democratic uprising in Burma. Whatever the agenda of the allied powers or the Iraqi government, pictures of Sadaam Hussein's execution went around the world within the hour.

Consider the image below with the recognition and knowledge that Benetton sells colourful knitwear and then attempt the activity below it. It may be worth also contrasting cosmetics chief Charles Revlon's famous maxim ('In our factories we make lipstick; in our adverts we sell hope') with whatever you imagine is being sold here, whether ideologically, intellectually or spiritually.

Figure 4.10 Benetton *Hearts* advert, March 1996

ACTIVITY

What can a process approach to communication tell you about this striking text? In what ways does it leave you dissatisfied? (The approach not the text!)

INFORMATION BOX – REFLEXIVITY

One feature of a whole series of Benetton campaigns is their ability to court controversy by creating a cultural context which is self-referential. Crudely this means creating a way of working (a mode of address) which is unlike any other and then making the oddness, the otherness, the edginess the whole point of the campaign. Reflexivity describes what it is to be self-conscious, to be self-aware, and to reflect on who you are, what you're doing and how you present yourself in the world. It is a feature of much of contemporary communication that it is similarly conscious and aware. It is self-reflexive. In this way, for example, we are used to seeing films about the making of films, advertisements that play with the conventions of advertisements, and comedies that refer to the 'rules' of comedy.

In a process sense the three hearts 'merely' deliver the message that Benetton is there (it exists) and worth a look at with all the obvious dangers in the form of psychological, semantic and possibly mechanical barriers. This is an efficient if underdeveloped response to this text largely because it is not really interested in the details. If the hearts were pink and fluffy, the process response would be effectively the same. There is no real acknowledgement of the ways in which this text might stimulate a large-scale debate. The semiotic approach (to which we shall shortly be turning) to textual analysis will partly answer this need by providing a focus on the composition of the text from elements drawn from our cultural experience (signs) but before we leave process let's consider a model/formula that bridges the gap somewhat.

Roman Jakobson's model is really a sophisticated account of the functions of communication and the modes through which these functions operate. Jakobson (1962) identifies six essential elements in any act of communication. He arranges them in a primarily linear fashion:

	CONTEXT	
	MESSAGE	
ADDRESSER	CONTACT	ADDRESSEE
	CODE	

Figure 4.11a Jakobson's elements of communication

He then goes on to link these six elements to the functions of communication by suggesting that within each communicative function a different element is dominant. He then arranges his six functions to correspond to the dominant element in the arrangement above.

	REFERENTIAL	
	POETIC	
EMOTIVE	PHATIC	CONATIVE
	METALINGUAL	

Figure 4.11b Jakobson's functions of communication

- **The emotive function** communicates the sender's emotions, attitudes and status.
- **The conative function** prompts the receiver's response to the act of communication and encourages participation.
- **The referential function** communicates the relationship between the text and the wider reality, truth and fact.
- **The poetic function** communicates the text's formal and stylistic qualities.

- **The phatic function** establishes and maintains channels of communication.
- **The metalingual function** identifies the significant codes of the text.

Jakobson argues that whilst all the above functions are co-existent in any act of communication, their importance varies according to the character of the individual act of communication being considered. A chat show guest's reminiscences of their childhood would be principally emotive; a stand-up comedian would hope to be chiefly conative; our experience of the news is likely to be referential; our enjoyment of an adaptation of a classic novel ought to be poetic (otherwise described by Jakobson more broadly as 'aesthetic'); much embarrassed communication on public transport with strangers is phatic; whenever we enquire of the geographical origin of an English speaker we are engaged in the metalingual function of communication. Jakobson offers a structuralist insight into the character of communication in a linear context and offers us as readers a useful and, in terms of the two approaches, a largely non-partisan approach.

In this context the 'three hearts' might be more usefully 'addressed', at least at the level where there can be a fairly open debate about which element is most significant. Here, for example, is one way of looking at the candidates:

- One response is to the **sender**, Benetton, and their **emotive** labelling of the hearts as 'white', 'black' and (most controversially) 'yellow'.
- Equally the **receiver** is absolutely vital to the active, **conative** decoding of the text.
- However, the focus might also be on the hearts themselves (and their realism), on their **context** and their **reference** to the 'real' world beyond the advert itself ('They can't be real, can they?' we partly ask ourselves).
- At the same time this is also an **aesthetic** issue (related to the form of the **message**): we respond to its bleak 'poetry'.
- Yet some would say that the text has little more than a shock effect: a **phatic** opening of channels (and our mouths), a form of vigorous **contact**.
- Finally there may be those who would argue that engaging with any Benetton campaign at this stage of their journey/notoriety is to have a knowing and nodding engagement with the particular communicative **codes** that this company have made their own. Thus we are working **metalingually** with Benettonese.

ACTIVITY

Identify Jakobson's six elements and six functions within the Benetton advertisement opposite. Which do you personally consider especially significant in this example?

Figure 4.12 Benetton *Mafia* advert, February 1992

The semiotic school

As we have seen, the strengths of the process approach lie principally in its focus on communication as a way of getting the message from sender to receiver. The semiotic approach takes a rather different view because it is concerned with understanding communication as a cultural phenomenon, rather than being able to measure the success or failure of individual acts of communication. The emphasis here shifts from the *information content* of messages to their *meaning*. Meanings are not simply transmitted along a line which notionally connects the brain of a sender to the brain of a receiver, they arise from interactions between communicators in all sorts of different cultural contexts. Be warned! We are entering a world in which meanings are no longer simply labels attached to signs. Meanings here are seen to be slippery, problematic – and fascinating.

In summary we can see the semiotic argument in this way:

- ■ It sees communication as the generation and sharing of meanings.
- ■ It is concerned with how messages and texts interact with people.
- ■ It sees the study of communication as the study of text, context and culture.
- ■ It does not see misunderstanding as evidence of communication failure.

In this part of the chapter we will be addressing, in a practical way, the insights offered on Communication and Culture by the semiotic approach (or school). This will involve a consideration of the following:

- The composition of signs and their organisation within codes.
- The operation of signs as elements within syntagms and paradigms.
- The different levels at which signs can have significance.
- Peirce's ideas about the sign categories: icon, index and symbol.

In simple terms the semiotic approach is concerned with our use of and response to various kinds of signs which themselves operate through a variety of codes or meaning systems (see Chapter 2 for a fuller discussion of codes). These signs might be spoken or written words but they might just as easily be images, garments or gestures. Thus if we take a still image from a film such as the one below, before we ever get to consider the way in which the piece is artificially constructed, we are able to identify a multitude of signs potentially working through a number of common 'interpersonal' codes, such as clothing, hairstyle, gesture, posture, orientation and facial expression. This chapter will do little more than refine this view by offering ways of getting at the underlying structuring of such 'collections' (and selections) within specific cultural contexts because this is principally what the semiotic approach offers.

> **CODES:** meaning systems consisting of signs. Signs are anything that has the potential to generate meaning, to signify. When a sign has generated meaning, it is said to have achieved signification. This is fundamental to the semiotic approach to the study of communication.

Figure 4.13
*Summer of
Sam*, 1999

What do you consider to be the most significant 'signs' operating in the image opposite? In simple terms, which 'bits' of the picture are most important in forming your interpretation of what is going on/what is meant?

As we have seen, the semiotic approach also suggests a crucial role for us as 'readers' of texts. The act of creating (rather than correctly identifying) the meaning of a communicative 'episode' or text is seen as a matter of an active 'negotiation' between producer, reader and the text itself within a specific cultural context. It sensibly suggests that the meaning of the text above is not fixed and depends on the context in which it is received. This context might be personal (conditioned by your attitude to folks with Mohican hairstyles) but it will also be social and cultural (conditioned one way or another by prevailing attitudes to such hairstyles). Clearly the mildly risqué content ('you can see her bra') of the image becomes deeply offensive in some, usually religiously defined, contexts.

> **NEGOTIATION:** this concept is at the very heart of the semiotic approach to the study of communication, implying as it does that texts do not have meaning except through the process of negotiation between text and reader.

Very much in the manner of the logical approach we used in the previous chapter, the semiotic approach is concerned to consider systematically those elements that constitute communication texts. This activity is sometimes referred to as textual analysis. Textual analysis involves the breaking down of a text into its component parts so that we can see the relationship between different signs and different codes. For example, we might recognise that the film still opposite is constructed from elements including setting, costume, lighting and actor performance.

Identifying the contributing codes of communication is a very useful step in the analysis of any text; it is very like discovering the spectrum of colours from which all others are made. Codes are the languages of communication; they are the systems through which communication operates. John Fiske (1990) argues that it is important to distinguish between two types of code, which he calls representational codes and presentational codes. Representational codes are those that produce texts such as the one above; they are used to create messages with an independent existence. On the other hand, presentational codes are used to provide information about senders and contexts; they are primarily concerned with self-presentation. Clearly, the still opposite theoretically has examples of both types of code, though its very presentation as a still makes it essentially representational rather than presentational. The presentational elements – notably the non-verbal communication offered by the above characters' posture, appearance and facial expression – are all explored in detail elsewhere in this text (see pages 36–53).

It is enough here that we take on board that at the heart of the semiotic approach to the study of communication is the recognition of codes as the organising systems of communication. Implicit in this understanding is the notion that all communication is encountered and interpreted in a social and cultural context; in other words, through interaction with other human beings. Systems and structures, like the conventions of a language, make the generation of meaning possible, but it is at the level of interaction and context that individual meanings are made.

Codes are, in essence, convention-governed systems that are agreed to by members of a community or culture. Codes may be behavioural, signifying, technical or cultural; in other words, they might be used to determine how we behave, make meaning, use media or even maintain our way of life. They organise what we do, what we see and what we say. They constitute our lives and are the various languages in and through which our lives are expressed. An understanding of our subject, Communication and Culture, is an understanding of codes.

ACTIVITY

Identify and list the codes likely to be active in a simple activity such as walking to college or school and partaking of the delights that these institutions offer. Classify these codes in terms of (a) those that condition or control our behaviour and (b) those that affect the way we make meaning or communicate. You may wish to start by considering the code that determines which bits of the built environment we walk on and which bits we generally avoid. It is also interesting to contrast the codes of your different subject choices.

If our lives are literally described by a network of codes, the next useful step might be to look at points of intersection. Codes are all very well as organising principles of communication, but to us as students of Communication and Culture, interested in the interaction of text and reader, the particular will always be more important than the general.

Let's think about the CD, the cover of which is reproduced in Figure 4.14. Although it is quite interesting to see this CD in terms of a set of coded conventions – representational and technical – we are always likely to be more interested in what it particularly is and, in this case, how it particularly sounds. What is encoded here is a piece of communication that works through a number of codes, some of which we are unable to access in this format, except in our auditory memories if we have the knowledge and inclination. The CD in Figure 4.14 is not a CD but rather it is a representation of one. It is an idea given concrete form. It cannot be played.

Figure 4.14 McFly, *Motion in the Ocean* CD

ACTIVITY

Make a list of the elements (essentially signs) that make up this text. What does each element add to the overall communication? Which codes do we need access to in order to understand these signs?

A code is a system of signs agreed by the users. Given signs are selected from within given codes. There is, therefore, clearly a code within which *Motion in the Ocean* can generate meaning and another which can distinguish between the name 'McFly' (which for some of us has connotations of the *Back to the Future* films) and the stylised version of that name, complete with a possibly symbolic star which appears to dominate the CD's surface. The background, too, is a significant sign, a foundation onto which other signs are locked.

Without needing to access the musical content, we are aware that communication is taking place: an encoded message is being offered for decoding; an invitation to negotiate meaning has been posted; a collection of signs is doing all it can to signify. Whichever way you choose to describe this situation, this is the essence of all text-based work. Of course in the real world of texts this piece of technology is contextualised by its 'box' and particularly the cover design which both advertises and protects it. In other words the round object in Figure 4.14 is covered (in a number of ways) by the square thing in Figure 4.15.

Figure 4.15 McFly, *Motion in the Ocean* CD cover

Before we go any further, it might be important to register your first impressions of and personal response to this text.

ACTIVITY

What is communicated by the McFly CD cover? Look at every component and comment.

While the approach we are adopting here is essentially semiotic, it does not differ that much at this point from the process approach. Do not see these approaches as mutually exclusive (as a matter of either/or). At a practical level, let them both inform your critical work. Process simply puts much greater store by the role of the encoder and what his/her intentions are, whilst semiotics tends to privilege the receiver and his/her context(s).

Moving from the CD to its cover, we can take another step towards understanding how codes operate and how signs are selected and combined. This arrangement of signs (group members, facial expressions, costumes, setting) is clearly a selection from a vast number of possible selections and combinations. The number of different ways four people can be arranged in a simple square is staggering. The signs that appear can only be understood in terms of their relationships both with one another and with all the selections that have not been made: the choice of a light (and watery) background, for example, precludes the choice of a dark (and dry) one. These relationships are what the Swiss linguist Ferdinand de Saussure (1983) called the syntagmatic (or horizontal) relations and the paradigmatic (or vertical) relations of a code, a language, a set of signs. A syntagm is a set of choices (for example the clothes you are wearing at this moment) and a paradigm is a set from which a choice has been made (one pair of shoes/footwear from a choice of, hopefully, more than one).

INFORMATION BOX – SYNTAGMS AND PARADIGMS

SYNTAGM: in semiotics, a chain of signs, a unique combination of sign choices. Units may be visual, verbal or musical. The scale of the units in syntagms may range from the very large (the nine planned episodes of the *Star Wars* triple trilogy might constitute a syntagm) to the very small (as in the syntagm *I like noodles* which consists of the signs 'I', 'like' and 'noodles'). The important point is that syntagms invite negotiation as a whole; they are bigger units of potential meaning. The signs which comprise a syntagm are organised in accordance with the 'rules' or conventions of the relevant code.

PARADIGM: a set of signs from which one might be chosen to contribute to a syntagm. Paradigms define their individual members with reference to all others in the set. To select from a paradigm is at that moment to reject all other signs in that set, just as by selecting something (or nothing) to cover your feet today, you have rejected all other possibilities; this choice from a paradigm of 'foot coverings' has contributed to the syntagms which constitute the things you are wearing today. When Peugeot's 'lion' went 'from strength to strength', it got its strength partly from the paradigm of 'elite animals' from which it was chosen and partly because that paradigm does not include 'weasel', 'frog' and 'sloth'.

A sign, then is meaningful in the context of the other signs present in the syntagm and in the context of other unselected signs from the paradigm.

ACTIVITY

Look at the McFly cover and identify *six* significant paradigms which have been used to create the syntagms offered.

- How would the meaning of the syntagm change if an alternative choice had been made from any of the paradigms?
- Which of these do you consider to be the most important to the meaning of this text?
- Which choice turned out for you to be the most significant?
- What are the dominant signs in these syntagms?

The important point to remember is that, as students of communication, we are interested specifically in engaging with texts in an attempt to work out their meanings. It is not technical terms which unlock texts but rather the issues these concepts and methods raise.

In the case of McFly, a very conventional text is further clarified by reference to such paradigms as 'settings for bands', which here perhaps directs attention to the expression 'in their element', which is another way of saying 'mad for it' or 'ecstatic'. The 'element' in question is of course water with all its symbolic implications but more important as a medium that allows maximum potential for the band to express its unbridled enthusiasm and youthfulness. For an 'enjoy-it-while-you-can' teeny-pop sensation, this is a snapshot of what 'pop' means: it's about energy and as much sincerity and irony as the sender and receivers will allow.

ASIDE – EXPLORING THE CULTURAL CONTEXTS

No reading of popular cultural conventions can really afford to stop at the generic conventions since these necessarily have a historical and cultural dimension. Dealing with this cover as a text for consideration within the section of this course dealing with cultural contexts and practices would certainly add an extra dimension. While McFly's 'gallivanting' is conventional popstar behaviour, it actually has a fairly impressive heritage, as does the underwater setting. Both of these, but especially the latter are almost certainly being consciously tapped by McFly and their management or at least by a certain portion of the mass audience.

It was an objectively more (in many ways) significant group, The Beatles, who pioneered pop 'zaniness' in their famous album covers such as *Help!*. At that time it was part of a revolutionary shift of power within popular music from songwriters (as a professional class) to artists, since The Beatles wrote their own songs (eventually) and did things their own way. Here the 'larking' was seen as a sincere sign of their independence and originality.

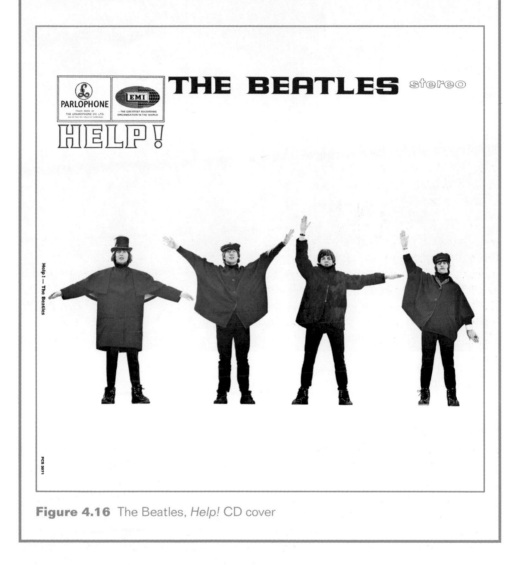

Figure 4.16 The Beatles, *Help!* CD cover

On top of this the other 'lineage' apparent in the *Motion in the Ocean* design is the band and album that every modern 'wants-to-be-credible' band aspires to. In 1994 Nirvana reputedly saved rock with their surprise masterpiece *Nevermind*, which featured this iconic cover design:

Figure 4.17 Nirvana, *Nevermind* CD cover

ACTIVITY

Compare and contrast the three album covers presented in this chapter which span the years 1965–1991–2006. What are the differences in the texts themselves and to what extent are our readings altered by extraneous factors (such as the reputations/status of the bands)?

Given that all the human figures on *Motion in the Ocean* are taken from that specialist paradigm 'members of the pop group McFly', it is their arrangement and presentation that are important. Here, in fact, is an excellent example of the overlapping of representational and presentational codes, where the self-presentation of individuals is set firmly within the representation of the group itself. The individual syntagms that represent the four individuals are in themselves part of a larger syntagm whose meaning is 'McFly'. The male at the top of the cover, for example, is communicating discretely through various non-verbal signs, such as his facial expression and his posture, but he is also himself a significant component of the representation of the whole group. We might intelligently guess that he is the singer, since he is most significantly holding eye contact and we'd be right.

As these lads are all equal in size (a key signifier of importance), then position is almost bound to be the less than subtle indicator of 'hierarchy', which in terms of pop groups is most likely to be a marketing 'tool'. Usually you sell the singer and guitarists more strenuously than the bassist and drummer simply because they are closer to the audience and therefore more 'recognisible'. This notion appears to be at work here since the rhythm section is left and right while the 'frontmen' are top and bottom. In addition to this, in the paradigm of body postures Danny and Tom (top and bottom) are better displayed than Dougie and Harry, who are differently but partially obscured. Thus despite the 'ordinary boy' uniforms which suggest equality and togetherness, there are leaders here at least in the cynical arena of the marketplace. Equally, the massive 'McFly' logo binds them together despite these minor inconsistencies.

In seeing some of this, we are allowing ourselves the opportunity to explore the very idea of a convention, and to see the levels at which formulas work. It also reminds us that blandness and conventionality are neither necessarily neutral nor harmless. Too much public communication plays these games and carries a significant ideological impact simply because it goes unnoticed and unchecked. This is the point the writer George Orwell was making when he remarked of advertising that it 'hits below the intellect'.

In the majority of print advertising, readings of largely visual texts are prompted, supported, privileged, even prescribed by a variety of verbal arrangements: headlines, captions, slogans, titles. Roland Barthes, the French semiotician, devised the term 'anchorage' to describe the ways in which texts, or parts of texts, are anchored to particular meanings (Barthes 1967). In this way the creator of a communication text can steer the reader to the meaning that they prefer them to make of the text. In the crudest sense, this process can be exemplified with reference to the simple illustration in Figure 4.18.

Figure 4.18 René Magritte, *The Treachery of Images (This is Not a Pipe)*, 1929, oil on canvas, 60 × 80 cm, Los Angeles County Museum of Art, purchased with funds provided by the Mr and Mrs William Preston Harrison Collection

In the above example, the caption deliberately contradicts the image, defying our expectations, but at the same time reminding us of how we routinely expect a title to label or elucidate an image; even one which has a relatively limited range of meanings. Magritte's caption should also remind us that the image is not a pipe, but a *signifier* of a pipe (see below).

Assigning any of the animal titles to the drawn animal in Figure 4.19 is tantamount to investing this crudely made sign with meaning. While it is fair to say, with process theory, that at the point of conception, this collection of marks had a

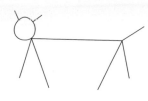

Figure 4.19
Sketch of a dog, cat or horse?

conscious intention, its polysemy (its capability for different meanings) is also difficult to dispute. In fact, the issue is made more problematic and interesting by its context as an illustration from a textbook in a chapter addressing explicitly the ways in which words work upon visual material and in so doing limit the possibility of multiple meanings. Its genuine intention (and therefore one of its readings) is thus 'something drawn that might be variously interpreted' or more specifically 'something drawn that might plausibly represent 'dog', 'cat' and 'horse'.

Perhaps the crudest example of this is the visual joke, where words, a punchline, allow readers to discover something in an image they have not seen. When we were young we might have been presented with this visual puzzle:

What is this?

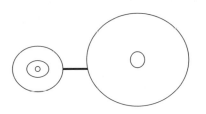

Figure 4.20
Sketch of a Mexican frying an egg

The answer – a bird's-eye view of a Mexican frying an egg – is a classic anchoring statement because it literally activates the given sign and answers our need for explanation, for a meaning. In Figure 4.20 is a series of circles and a line. Words link this to a situation, if somewhat stereotypically and surreally. What we are seeing here – in a very stark way – is the relationship Saussure identified between the two parts of a sign – the signifier and the signified.

SIGNIFIER/SIGNIFIED: according to Saussure, the basic unit of communication is the sign. The sign is composed of two elements – the signifier and the signified. The signifier is the physical form of the sign, for example a written or spoken word or a photograph. The signified is the mental concept triggered by the signifier. When you see the signifier HORSE you think of a horse (the signified). Of course, neither one of these is a real horse. The first is a carefully designed but miniscule quantity of ink on the page; the second is an abstract idea. The signifier and the signified unite to form the sign, but the relationship between the two elements is an arbitrary one, that is, there is no logical or necessary relationship between them. That's why it's possible to change which signifier relates to which signified; there are no absolute rules connecting the signifier and the signified. If you had no knowledge of English or you could not read, then the signifier HORSE would not attach itself to a signified in your mind. If you speak French, you will recognise the signifier CHEVAL.

The process of making sense of McFly in a swimming pool/ocean was clearly about imposing such unity on signifiers and signifieds whilst being massively helped by the conventional nature of most pop group communication. The water, for example, or the bubbles or the shirts are all there to 'mean' something but the connection is not there until you 'receive' the text or part of it and look for the significance.

In the Mexican gag the signifier is anchored to its comic purpose by the words of the punchline and at the same time other explanations (other signifieds) are downplayed or eliminated. The circles and line might, for example, have had a scientific, paranormal or anthropological significance. Anchorage lessens or even removes the 'might' given that its function is, in Barthes' words, 'to fix the floating chain of signifieds'. It is clear that some signifiers, by their character, need far less anchoring than others.

ACTIVITY

What are the 'problems' with the text opposite as far as clarifying the message is concerned?

How effective is the caption in anchoring the meaning? Is the text entropic or redundant? (See pages 113 – 114.)

Figure 4.21 *Is there something you've forgotten?* flyer

Even though there are directive words here, they can hardly be said to be significantly 'anchoring' the text's meaning: unlike the Mexican gag, they don't really provide an answer. Rather they work in a free interplay with the images to stimulate receiver response. Barthes called this process *relay* since that is exactly what the words and images are doing: combining in order to work together towards meaning.

INFORMATION BOX – ANCHORAGE AND RELAY

i

Barthes' approach to meaning-fixing operations is clearly logocentric: it assumes that words are the leading communicative elements. Thus while anchorage is given some prominence within his writing, relay is almost a footnote. They are defined by Barthes as follows:

1 In *anchorage*, 'the text directs the reader through the signifieds of the image, causing him to avoid some and receive others . . . It remote-controls him towards meaning chosen in advance'.
2 Whereas in *relay*, 'the text and image stand in a complementary relationship; the words in the same way as the images, are fragments of a more general syntagm and the unity of the message is realized at a higher level, at the level of the story'.

In the preceding years and with the advent of an increasingly visual culture, relay has become a much more significant semiotic operation. At the same time we might regret that Barthes was not prepared to conceive of a situation where images might themselves dictate meaning. As the Semiotician Daniel Chandler notes: 'He did not coin a term for 'the paradoxical case where the image is constructed according to the text'. Even if it were true in the 1950s and early 1960s that the verbal text was primary in the relation between texts and images, in contemporary society visual images have acquired far more importance in contexts such as advertising, so that what he called 'relay' is far more common. There are also many instances where the 'illustrative use' of an image provides anchorage for ambiguous text – as in assembly instructions for flat-pack furniture'.

(Source: www.aber.ac.uk/media/Documents/S4B/sem09.html)

Relay is clearly evident in the cover designs of the Rockstar Games computer game franchise *Grand Theft Auto*, which feature a patchwork of images that take their meaning from and extend the meaning of the specific version: in Figure 4.22 we are looking at the PSP version of *Vice City Stories*. These words do not so much 'anchor' as imply or open a discussion between the text and the reader. Even so these covers are extremely conventional and predictable; the images clearly do define the context in a way that is expected. This is a potentially open representation of a fictional location, partially closed by the central 'caption'/title. In this way the obvious themes within the images are confirmed both in terms of form (stories) and content (Vice City).

Figure 4.22 *Grand Theft Auto: Vice City Stories. Grand Theft Auto and Grand Theft Auto: Vice City Stories* are both trademarks of Rockstar Games, Inc.

As we begin to consider the potential readings of any image, it is noticeable that images are capable not only of different meanings but also of different types of meaning. Put simply, and with direct reference to *Vice City Stories*, there is a significant difference between the designation 'man on a motorbike' and 'mean and free'. Barthes addresses these different kinds or levels of meaning in his notion of 'orders of signification'. These are levels at which signs might be significant or signifiers may connect with signifieds.

The first order of signification is *denotation*. Connections are made between signs and objects. It is agreed that specific signs will signify specific objects at a general societal level; these are the direct, obvious and straightforward meanings of signs. In the *Vice City Stories* example, what is denoted might include 'a helicopter and gunman', 'the fact that it's a game for Sony's PSP' or perhaps 'a woman with large glasses'.

The second order of signification is *connotation*. If denotation describes the way in which signs signify at an immediate and direct level, then connotation describes the way in which signs signify indirectly and by association. Connotation describes the way in which groups of people share meaning at an associative level. By virtue of the groups we are members of, we share in the connotative use of signs. In the *Vice City* example, the particular ways in which these images have been presented might provoke particular sorts of personal response, connoting aspects such as style and genre. In the same way each individual pictured will have connotations, which derive from our cultural understanding. For example, we may see connotations of criminality, luxury, excitement and danger in the *Vice City Stories* images.

What is the point of distinguishing between these two types or 'orders' of signification? The reason is that connotations are much more dynamic and changing and cultural-specific. The connotations of a signifier can change markedly depending on the time, place and context; we only have to think of the rapid pace of change in fashions for clothes or hairstyles to realise that the positive connotations of 2005 can very rapidly change to the negative connotations of 2009. Denotations, on the other hand, tend to be more stable, though we shouldn't be tempted to think that they are entirely fixed. If this were the case, dictionaries would not have to be constantly updated.

Myths are, according to the authors of *Key Concepts in Communication and Cultural Studies* (O'Sullivan et al. 1994), a culture's way of conceptualising an abstract topic. A myth consists of a collection of concepts bound together by general acceptance and significant in our understanding of particular kinds of experience. The image we have been examining contains within it a very specific kind of myth – that of 'gangster chic', a culturally created 'brand' of 'history'. This is connected to notions of revenge and pride and honour, but also ruthlessness, dishonesty and violence. Myths concern shared beliefs and explanations; we are not particularly interested in whether these beliefs are true or false. Our culture supplies us with numerous myths to explain the world to us. Often these myths are logically inconsistent (e.g. science and astrology), but our interest is in the currency these explanations have within a culture rather than in testing out their claims to truth.

ACTIVITY

Myths, semiotically, are just powerful kinds of connotation: those that, though open, lead us to similar conclusions. What are the key components of the 'gangster' myth perpetrated across the *Vice City Stories* cover?

ACTIVITY

Competing myths

Read the two following explanations of 'the city'. Both are recognisable though mutually exclusive myths that circulate widely in many cultures.

The Good City

This is a vibrant, dynamic and exciting place. It is open for work and play 24/7. It is full of opportunities to meet people and make new friends. It is a centre for arts and entertainment; you need never be bored in the city.

The Bad City

This is a dirty, oppressive and polluted place. Crime is widespread and people don't trust each other. It is very crowded and nobody has time for anybody else. There is a great divide between the haves and the have-nots. It is lonely and alienating.

continued

The third order of signification is *ideology*. Fiske and Hartley (1978) have suggested that myths and connotations are in themselves evidence of a deeper, hidden pattern of meaning which they label ideology. This is ideology as a description of the various ways in which society, or those controlling it, organise and control the ways in which meanings are generated – what Marxists would call the intellectual means of production. A final visit to our *Vice City Stories* example will reveal that part of the meaning system in which the text is active has to do with gender. It is hard to avoid understanding this collection of images without reference to the connotations of the male and female, not to say myths about masculinity and femininity, and this is partly a response to the text's implicit ideology. Here the women are prominent but only in the ultimate context: as decorative objects supervised (literally overlooked) by men and passive rather than active.

ACTIVITY

Consider the levels of signification at which the text in Figure 4.23 operates.

Conventions are also at the core of the relationship between signifier and signified, as one of the principal influences on the ways any reality can be represented. For example, if we want to communicate the idea 'boy', we might choose a conventional way of representing this by speaking or writing the English word that is formed 'b-o-y' or 'B-O-Y'. In fact these are only two of the vast number of ways this idea might be represented in written or printed form. Others include 'boy', 'Boy' and 'BOY', each of which carries its own particular connotations. What must be grasped, however, is that, whatever the typeface, there is no logical or necessary connection between this sign (these signs) in its physical form as signifier and any idea or reality we might associate with it, that is, any signified. The connection is artificial and arbitrary, a matter of agreement.

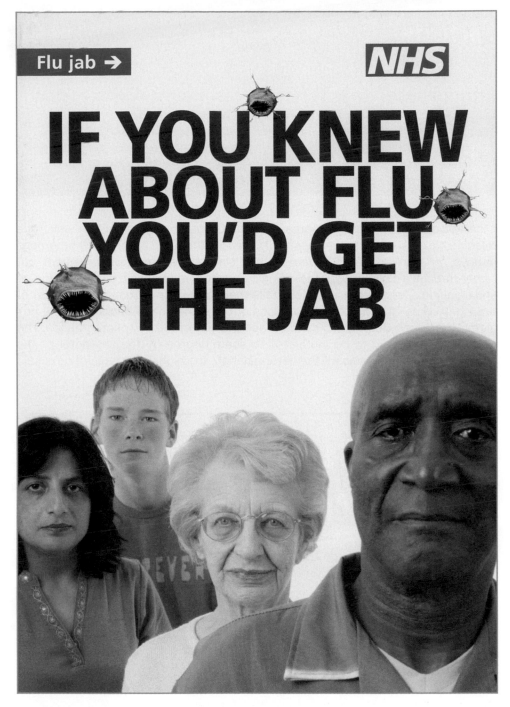

Figure 4.23 'If you knew about flu, you'd get the jab' NHS leaflet

Collect or suggest *ten* different ways or forms of representing the concept sometimes signified by the word 'boy'. These representations may be made by you or collected from outside sources. Arrange them in order of greatest convention, in terms of the degree to which their meaning is dependent on 'outside' knowledge of the language, society and culture in which they were made. A word is therefore highly conventional whereas a photograph has a low degree of convention.

Clearly, you will have found representations (signs and syntagms) in which the relationship between the signifier and signified is other than arbitrary. Photographs of boys, for example, do not represent 'boy' simply by a matter of agreement, but rather through a closer (albeit technologically aided) relationship between signifier and signified. These representations take their form largely from the character of the signified. In the case of photographs of boys, the shape and size of the boy pictured is largely determined by the shape and size of the boy photographed. The signifier is thus said to be motivated to some degree by the character of the signified: the more significant the determination, the higher the *motivation* is said to be.

MOTIVATION: in semiotics this refers to the relationship between a sign and what it represents. Specifically it describes the degree to which the form a sign takes (word/symbol/drawing/photograph) is determined by) the subject being represented. Thus the horse in a colour photograph is said to have high motivation simply because, as a sign, its form (what it looks like) is very like the horse it is representing. Similarly a word sign has very low motivation because its form/shape/appearance usually has next to nothing to do with whatever it is representing. Spoken words sometimes have a degree of motivation when they sound like the thing they stand for; for example, cuckoo, splash and woof.

Figure 4.24 Boys, boys, boys: a) schoolboys; b) Fall Out Boy; c) Boy George; d) boy scouts

ACTIVITY

Try to make sense of the representations of boys in Figure 4.24 in terms of the degree of motivation and convention they contain.

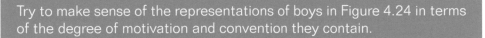

No representation is free from convention, for no sign is totally motivated (though some are totally conventional). In any representation, even photographic, there is room for the sender to impose perspective, focus, distance; in other words, there

is room to conventionalise the representation. The more consciously the images are being produced for specific contexts, the greater the degree of convention bearing down on the motivated image. Many texts use the contrast between the 'naturalism' of motivated images and the 'artificiality' of conventional signs to productive effect. Take a look at these images in Figure 4.25 from a mobile phone information booklet from The Carphone Warehouse.

Figure 4.25 Carphone Warehouse icons

These images clearly involve motivated and conventional elements. Examine the degree of convention here and suggest what sorts of meaning are delivered in this way. Another way to do this is to look at the level of redundancy or predictability of them as messages.

If we now look at the front cover of the booklet which featured these images in Figure 4.26, we can see more precisely – owing to the anchorage provided by words – the context for these images. We can also identify a number of significantly more conventional and significantly more motivated signs. This is useful up to a point, but it does leave a rather large grey area somewhere between highly motivated and highly conventional. Whilst Saussure was content with the dichotomy of signifier and signified, of motivation and convention, Charles Peirce went further. Rather than a dichotomy, Peirce (1966) proposed a trichotomy – three elements in the composition of the sign, three different types of sign. He labelled these three types of sign as icon, index and symbol.

This cover contains good examples of Peirce's three sign categories which, he stressed, were tendencies and not mutually exclusive designations.

Peirce first identified those signs that communicated their signified through resemblance; in other words, by looking like their signified, or in certain cases by sounding like or smelling like their signified. These are essentially motivated signs and he labelled them *icons*. The representation of the Sony Ericsson mobile phone is clearly in this category but so too are each figure's 'props' to some degree.

Figure 4.26 Carphone Warehouse 'Your phone, your way' leaflet

Second, Peirce talked of *indexes*: signs that communicate their signified by association. In other words, because one thing exists, another thing is assumed to exist. We see smoke, we assume the existence of fire. Therefore the character of the relationship between indexical signs and their objects is said to be existential. The cover in Figure 4.26 provides a range of examples – from the briefcase and collar and tie as indexes of business to the baseball cap and bling which are indexes of 'youf culture' and 'chavdom'. A briefcase does not resemble business; rather it is in some sense a part of business as a broad concept and cultural practice. Notice also that 'props' such as the collar and tie have been described as both iconic and indexical, reflecting the different ways in which they are communicating.

Peirce's third sign category, *symbol*, was reserved for signs where the relationship between sign and object was a matter of agreement. There is no logical or necessary relationship between the sign 'phone' and the object we recognise from the picture; it is a matter of social convention. If we follow the social convention, we will get along with fellow human beings. If we don't, we will not get along, we will most likely be shunned by them. All the words on this cover and the 'The Carphone Warehouse' logo are typical examples of symbolic signs.

In uncovering the categories of sign we find we are, in fact, engaging with the very act of signification, examining *how* signs mean even before we examine *what* they mean. In the whole of this section we have been trying out explanations of the way texts work in order to find out more about what they might have to say. Our next text carries with it a significant challenge: to communicate your understanding of sign categories with reference to a specific live text.

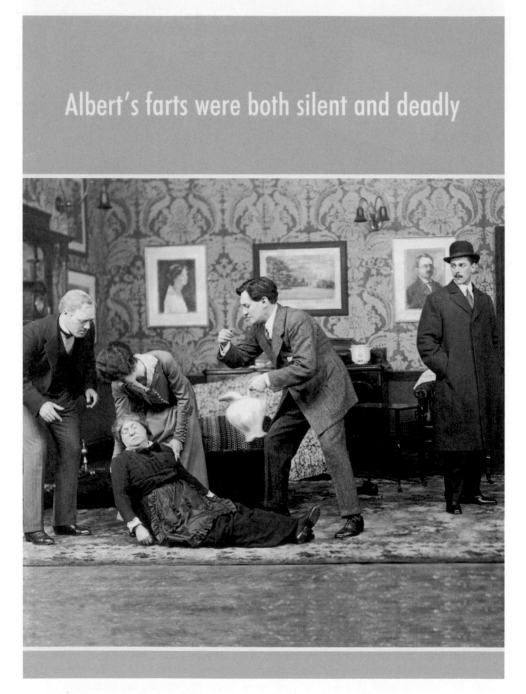

Figure 4.27 'Albert's farts were both silent and deadly' greetings card

ACTIVITY

Plan, in note form, a five-minute presentation entitled 'Icons, indexes and symbols' aimed at your fellow students. Exemplify your explanation with detailed reference to Figure 4.27, paying particular attention to:

- the anchoring text
- the monochrome image
- the characters and their 'costumes'
- the setting
- body language.

References and further reading

Barthes, R. (1967) *Elements of Semiology*, London: Cape

Cherry, C. (1978) *On Human Communication: A Review, a Survey and a Criticism*, 3rd edn, Cambridge, Mass./London: MIT Press

de Saussure, F. (1983) *Course in General Linguistics*, trans R. Harris, ed. C. Bally and A. Sechehaye, London: Duckworth

Fiske, I. (1990) *Introduction to Communication Studies*, 2nd edn, London: Routledge

Fiske, J. and Hartley, J. (1978) *Reading Television*, London: Methuen

Jakobson, R. (1962) *Selected Writings*, The Hague: Mouton

O'Sullivan, T., Hartley, J., Saunders, D., Montgomery, M. and Fiske, J. (1994) *Key Concepts in Communication and Cultural Studies*, London/New York: Routledge

Peirce, C.S. (1966) *Collected Papers of Charles Sanders Peirce*, Cambridge, Mass.: Belknap Press of Harvard University Press

PRACTICAL ANALYSIS
5 AND CASE STUDIES

In this chapter we will be demonstrating the use of techniques of textual analysis on actual texts. This will be geared to the twin contexts of 'reading' that the course demands, which roughly correspond to the coursework and exam work. With this in mind:

- We will take you through an in-depth analysis of a couple of different kinds of texts to reflect the range of what this course is asking you to read.
- We will give you examples of the kind of examined textual analysis work you will be expected to perform on print texts.

We have broken down the communication process into its component parts. It is now time to start putting it all back together again. This chapter will offer you examples of the sort of analysis you will be asked to undertake as a student of Communication and Culture. This section is principally about the demonstration of a method, of a way of thinking, of a critical process. It will deal with a range of texts and the principal tasks you will face.

The process of looking at, engaging with and, ultimately, analysing texts is a logical and straightforward one. It requires you first of all to examine what you are offered in an open, honest and personal way and then to use that information along with the specific knowledge and experience provided by your course of study, and/or this text, to push that response further. It is a subjective and objective approach, usually in that order but most often in an integrated fashion. Having asked 'What do I think about this text?' you are expected to consider 'How else could this text be considered or interpreted?' Sometimes this 'how else' makes you reconsider your own initial position, sometimes not. It is perhaps useful to see this process in terms of a series of actions:

- **Look:** What is it? How does it impact on you?
- **Read:** What does it say? What does it consist of?
- **Explore/analyse:** How is it structured? How does it work?

- ■ **Review:** What do I think of it now? Is it as I originally thought?
- ■ **Respond:** Here are my considered thoughts, feelings, opinions.

first impressions

It is vital to record your first impressions of the texts you are asked to work with. In most cases this initial engagement is all a text has in its original, 'real world' context. This is partly because much of the material produced, for example, by the mass media is genuinely ephemeral (i.e. here today and gone tomorrow), first impressions are sometimes all that a text is intended to receive but it is also due to the fact that so much communication doesn't even leave a fleeting record. When we are reading 'the shopping trip' for example, we are dealing with an event recorded only by its purchases (and the odd snap perhaps nowadays).

Figure 5.1 Poster for *An Inconvenient Truth*, 2006

Examine the illustration in Figure 5.1, a promotion for the film *An Inconvenient Truth*. It is likely that your first impression was some kind of response to the striking, spiralling plume of smoke issuing from the centrally placed chimneys and to the words (particularly 'inconvenient' and 'warning'). This is clearly the intention of the text's designer, given that the chimneys are spewing forth their toxins exactly at the place centrally above and halfway up, which is for most people the focus of a poster's (or any image's) communication. You may also have been struck by the key words, reddened for maximum impact.

At this point it is useful to be able accurately to classify the text with which we are dealing. Lasswell (1948) is useful in this respect, inviting the identification of sender, message, receiver, channel and effect. In the case of the film poster, the responses could be:

Who?	Paramount Pictures.
Says what?	There is this film.
To whom?	Anybody who cares about the planet/is sensitive/is intelligent.
In what channel?	Film poster.
With what effect?	They know about it (the film principally though also 'issues').

These responses can then be supported or challenged with reference to conventional communication practice within the identified medium and/or channel. The confirmation question runs something like 'What makes this a film poster?' (If we didn't know, on what basis would we guess?) In this case our evidence might include: the relationship between images and text; the way in which the credits are presented; the bold title and subheader; the hierarchy of types; the quoted critical approval.

It is not always this straightforward, but the process is always about looking for those aspects of a given text which it shares with other texts you have looked at. Moreover, it is important to remember that the sort of critical analysis you are engaged in is not about producing correct answers but rather about producing meaningful responses.

We are now becoming interested in this poster, given we have engaged with it both in terms of the initial impact and in terms of how it fits into a genre. The next stage is to consider in detail what we are in fact being offered. It is useful here to think in terms of the dominant signifiers, the dominant syntagms and the significant paradigms, and codes that are at work in the text.

In an almost arithmetical way we are considering the different ways in which the meaning of the article might be calculated or totalled. This process might start at a formal level in the equation:

IMAGES + WORDS = TEXT

In the text in question, this bears considerable fruit, for it asks us to see a relationship between the dominant image (full length, colour, dominant) and the words.

This is, in essence, a narrative – a story that transports us from first impressions to the point of provocation or disinterest (depending on how 'green' we are), or crudely from a state of ignorance to a state of knowledge. Having got the formal structure worked out, we can get into the detail: of the significant syntagm which is the first image; of the written text in terms of its register, its vocabulary, its mode of address, its bias, its function; and of the background as an ominous, brooding context for it all. This stage is setting the agenda, uncovering interesting issues of representation, of narrative and of genre. It is also appropriate at this stage to identify the dominant codes, which in this case are largely visual and verbal.

NARRATIVE: the way in which a text reveals information to the audience in order to create a 'story'.

Clearly, this preparatory work on texts requires significant annotation of the texts themselves. Start on a separate sheet and sketch the general relationships; for example, the proportions of text and the positions of images. Once you approach the details of a text, the most appropriate place to work is on and around it, exploding general points to either side, above and below.

Decoding what's there

Paradigms are those collections of signs from which we make selections. The signs chosen are then ordered into chains that we call syntagms. Identifying these paradigms is therefore a useful way of revealing something of the process of construction. This text activates paradigms that dramatise the film's central point (as it turns out): the relationship between the earth and the sky as mediated by the involvement of mankind. Thus we get a kind of sky, a version of the earth and, in between, man's interference. In fact, the preferred reading is probably to see the influence of man (bang in the centre of the poster) as the malign influence since the chimneys are directly connected to both the sprawling industrial darkness at the bottom and the 'eye of the impending storm' above. This argument is enacted in simple terms: arrangement and colour are the significant codes here.

Unanchored this could easily be a simple stereotypical image of industrialisation, an image extracted from an archive that would cover all of the so-called 'developed' world. Here is a factory and some dramatic 'smog': end of story. It is the anchoring text that makes it more than this, which extends its reach in many directions. What this anchor activates is one set of dominant signifiers which add up to 'an inconvenient truth'. This anchor/relay (depending on how much negotiation is involved) shifts the mode of address from a mournful reflection on dirty factories to a direct confrontation of our responsibility in all of this. Also there is a second written text that follows this up with both barrels! 'A GLOBAL WARNING' it proclaims with all the weight it can muster from typeface, colour, play on words and finally meaning. Here the signifiers are supporting their signifieds by representing the weight and horror of their message. While word signs are chiefly symbolic, it is also the connotations of their physical forms which are significant here. The Gothic typeface and boxed reddened 'WARNING' operate at the level of myth, since we all arrive at the same personal response to them. 'Global' sends the whole text in another direction, providing connotations for the 'factory' of 'nuclear power plant' and 'Chernobyl' and of the storm as large scale and terminal. In this way we have activated the text and taken part in its operation. This process is vital but it is your findings that will form the basis of your writing.

ESSENTIAL ARCHIVE

Figure 5.2 Cover of the DVD of *Bart Wars*

In a former version of this book was an annotated analysis of a more irreverent and allusive text which might also be useful:

Rather than labouring a point let's review the process by quickly responding to a new text. Here are the key questions or prompts with a series of my own (and thus not the only) responses.

Look: what are my first impressions? It's amusing – a *Star Wars* spoof; there is that play on words and the Vader/Skywalker duel.

What is it? It's a video cover saying 'Here are some episodes of *The Simpsons*' to a youngish/young at heart audience. It wants us to buy the video. The sender is whoever makes *The Simpsons*.

Read: what does it consist of? Formally, some cartoon art and some words. In terms of content it offers some familiar characters and some familiar mythic film characters. Colour is clearly important: clear, bright, well defined.

Explore: the dominant signifiers are the words and the human figures. A dominant code is intertextuality.

Intertextuality: this is defined by John Fiske as follows: 'the meanings generated by any one text are determined partly by the meanings of other texts to which it appears similar': more simply the ability of one text to refer to another.

Much of the intended meaning of the cover depends on various degrees of knowledge of the *Star Wars* films and mythology; for example, 'the Simpsons strike back' is a variant of *The Empire Strikes Back*. Moreover, and more significantly, the fact that Bart is shown duelling with his father, Homer, refers to the moment in the first trilogy where Luke Skywalker discovers that Darth Vader (Homer in this parody) is in fact his father. This is a scene from the third film, *Return of the Jedi*, and thus the whole trilogy is parodied on the cover.

Essentially the representations are iconic, though with fairly low motivation and this allows a range of visual humour and an informal register. The costumes are exaggerated but recognisable, the facial expressions dramatic but in this context amusing: partly in the context of the style of presentation and partly, to *Simpsons'* cognoscenti (those in the know), in the context of Homer and Bart's ongoing relationship and beyond to the father–son relationships on which both these texts draw.

Review: A clever and amusing text, whose function is principally phatic. It is doubtful if any of the episodes referred to in the lower part of the cover are substantially related to the *Star Wars* phenomenon. The P.G. logo, which is an index of suitability and security, has an irony in the context of a son and father fighting to the death, which can surely be no accident, particularly as Bart is reputedly 10 years old.

Of course these texts are clearly cleverly constructed, whereas most of our analysable communication is more temporary and immediate. Say for example that, prompted by the incredible story about the shopping mall that provides sensitive male shoppers for women attached to insensitive ones (see page 238) you wanted to look at gender and shopping. Perhaps you noticed on a trip to a local mall that the thing most male shoppers had most in common were their uniforms of replica sports shirts and jeans. How can this be analysed semiotically, in this context as text. The fact is you approach it in just the same way:

■ **Look:** What is it? How does it impact on you? *The impact is to suggest a similarity or togetherness, a sense of being comfortable even in a traditionally uncomfortable context for men.*

■ **Read:** What does it say? What does it consist of? *It speaks of identity (sometimes national identity). It consists of colour and texture and tradition. The shirt is an index of commitment and allegiance. It also may have connotations of locality or conversely of brand loyalty which will make some readers see it as a terrible index of the commercialisation of the game of football.*

■ **Explore/analyse:** How is it structured? How does it work? *It operates as the dominant signifier in a common contemporary male clothing syntagm. As such it registers a departure from convention since it differs from traditional male clothing within two significant paradigms: texture and colour. Traditionally females wear silky colourful garments while male garments are more likely to be coarse and plain. The replica shirt offers men, perhaps, a viable alternative to cross-dressing! When women wear replica shirts the meanings are different: the connotations are more straightforward.*

■ **Review:** What do I think of it now? Is it as I originally thought? *I think there's more to it than meets the eye. There are clearly gender issues both ways which indicate both the way in which football has become a significant cultural product and the way in which traditional gender roles are adapting.*

■ **Respond:** Here are my considered thoughts, feelings, opinions. *I think there is definitely some work to do on men and shopping and on the apparent male 'leisure' uniform. Partly this is fantastic marketing and advertising, even better than getting us to traipse around the mall with liveried shopping bags. It is also about male roles changing in a negotiated way with men being allowed to make a small transition in dress and cultural practice whilst still maintaining face (via their commitment to traditional male allegiances). Interestingly, they pay through the nose for this privilege, since the garments they are wearing to shop in are designed in laboratories for optimum sporting performance. This becomes somewhat ironic when you consider these high performance garments come in sizes up to XXL (extra extra large). It would be good to interview some guys and discover their reasons for displaying their colours.*

Hopefully you can see from this example how flexible the toolkits are (and how useful). They are a way of interrogating experience to discover its structures and assumptions. The notes above provide the groundwork for a series of potential explorations. Critical reading is at the very centre of all we do and the most efficient way of identifying issues which can then be pursued.

Some print texts and new style questions

In this section you will have the opportunity to respond to a range of print texts for yourself. Each is presented in the style of the new style textual analysis section of the AS Communication and Culture exam (COMM1).

What you will realise, looking across a range of very different texts, is that it is experience of the method, of the specific tools, that is needed and not necessarily experience of the potentially vast range of texts. In other words, it matters that you have looked at texts, not that you have looked at a specific variety of text. What you also need is genuine and honest engagement with texts and this is clearly helped by them being unseen and unprepared. This is nowhere more true than in the new AQA specification with its short question approach, which ought to quell for ever the anxiety about difficult texts. The questions are the drivers, the texts are 'merely' the fuel.

a) Document A: Special K 'Loser' ad

1. Identify the dominant signifiers within this text. (4 marks)
2. Comment on the connotations and functions of the different typefaces used on the document. (6 marks)
3. Explore in detail the ways in which the words and images work to create the experience of the text. (10 marks)

Figure 5.3 Special K *Be a Loser* advert

b) Document B: AQA flyer for new Communication and Culture course

1. Comment on potential barriers to communication in this text.

2. What do you think is the intention of this design? Give reasons for your answer.

3. Explore the levels at which this text has significance.

Figure 5.4 AQA Communication and Culture leaflet

c) Document C: Powergen advertisement

1. At whom precisely do you think this text is aimed? Give reasons for your answer.

2. What might a semiotic analysis tell you about the Powergen logo?

3. Explore the relationship between the words and the size, shape and appearance of this text.

Figure 5.5 *The Gloves Are Off* Powergen advert

d) Document D: Dudley MBC's 'What is culture?' survey

1. What is the relationship between the words and the images here?
2. What are the potential connotations of the image here and how it is presented?
3. What potential barriers to communication are possible here?

Figure 5.6 *What's your culture?* Dudley Metropolitan Borough Council

e) Document E: view of the Seven Sisters

1. What is the intention of this text? Does it succeed in this?

2. The image below is a highly motivated icon but that does not mean it is free from convention. In what specific ways is this text conventional?

3. Explore the relationships between icons and indexes in the image below.

Figure 5.7 View of the Seven Sisters

f) Document F: Halifax Visa advertisement

1. What is the difference representationally between the 'bread', the 'cake' and the '£20 notes'?

2. Examine myth and ideology in this text.

3. Examine the relationship between words and images in this text.

Figure 5.8
Halifax advert

g) Document G: Operation Christmas Child

1. Comment on the key words on this document. What is their collective purpose?

2. Comment on the iconic, indexical and symbolic elements at work in the Operation Christmas Child logo

3. What is the 'preferred reading' of the picture of the child? Suggest an oppositional reading of this same image.

h) Document H: iPod touch (open and closed)

1. What messages are being offered by this product through these two shots?

2. What are the most important components of the syntagm that makes up the product?

3. The iPod is a cultural product that has had a massive impact on the way we 'deal with' music. What is the impact of these cultural contexts on the way we respond to the images above?

Figure 5.10
iPod touch

i) Document I: Jude and Sienna *Once Upon a Time*

1. How motivated do you consider these images to be?

2. Comment on the ways in which ideas about narrative contribute to an understanding of this text.

3. Explore the ways in which non-verbal signifiers operate within this text.

Figure 5.11 Jude and Sienna *Once Upon a Time*

AS COMMUNICATION AND CULTURE: THE ESSENTIAL INTRODUCTION

j) Document J: Real people, real lives

1. Consider the mode of address of each of these images.

2. Use captions to prompt conventional and oppositional readings of each photograph.

3. Which of these best illustrates the title 'Real people, real lives'. Support your answer with evidence from ONE image.

Figure 5.12 Three snaps of everyday life: a) couple; b) family; c) boy in office

further examples

It still seems corny to say so, but if you want examples just look around. Texts are around you and among you – from the cereal packets you absent-mindedly read at breakfast to the books or magazines you read before you go to sleep. All have their messages, their devices, their conventions and their idiosyncrasies. All await the careful reader. A list of places to start might include:

- Leaflets: look at a range from those which inform you about sexually trans-mitted diseases to those which offer you *English Heritage* or *The National Trust*.
- Flyers: from adverts for Dial-a-Pizza to local band promotions.
- Brochures: from college prospectuses to luxury car specifications.
- Magazines: from *FHM* to *The People's Friend*.
- Newspapers: from free papers to 'the Free Press'.
- Advertisements: from matchbooks to billboards.
- Posters: from Che Guevara to Baby Spice.
- Book jackets: from Harry Potter to Beatrix Potter.
- CD covers: from Westlife to *Parklife*.
- Websites: from Ilovecamerondiaz.com to DavidCameron.com.
- Scripts: from screenplays to school plays.
- Storyboards: from *Chicken Run* to *Logan's Run*.
- Postcards: from college promotions to seaside humour.
- Greetings cards: from 'It's a Boy!' to 'With Deepest Sympathy'.
- Packaging materials: from cereal packets to shop liveries.

This is not a list to alarm you but rather to remind you of the vital part played by communication texts in our lives. To be aware of this is in itself a step towards being an effective critic.

further case studies

The illustrated man: the human figure as text

The illustration opposite is recognisibly a publicity shot for a film (though as we shall see shortly 'boys' have rarely, even before the invention of the camera, needed an opportunity to pose with their weapons). Here some people are repre-sented standing in front of the camera. These people are communicating at a number of levels and in a number of ways. They are communicating in the picture and with it but also apart from it as we all do when 'pictured'. In other words, they constitute 'text' in a number of ways: as a crowd/group held together by a common context and purpose; as a group sharing certain demographic variables such as gender, ethnicity and age, uniformed to some extent; as a series of individuals expressing their own identities through subtle modifications of clothing, of hairstyle, of attitude. The frame is containing them but also constraining them, allowing them to be all the photograph allows but no more. This is referenced by

Figure 5.13 *Ali G Indahouse, 2002*

the perfect composition in which this band of 'brothers' is set squarely and skilfully in the centre ground of the photograph and wrapped around the available 'scenery'. The weather too appears to be coming out in sympathy, while the arrangement of 'bodies' and the collection of 'gangsta grins' puts a further pressure on any thought of this being 'realistic'. Of course for many of us the presence of Sasha Baron-Cohen's alter ego, 'Ali G', is enough to reorder our thoughts, to slip over to an alternative mode of reception, as if the pattern of the text almost suddenly became more obvious and conscious. The meaning of this text suddenly becomes less open, less accessible and we are aware perhaps for the first time of the photograph having a maker, a deviser. It is no longer a 'snap' (if it ever was) and the meaning is now directed into a series of creative decisions made by the sender.

ACTIVITY

What is it that gives each of these men their individuality within the limited terms of reference of this image? List the categories (e.g facial hair) and then explore the choices that have been made in each case. If you had to add a further figure to the set where would they go and how would you design them (height, gender, age and so on)? Now add yourself to this image: how do you differ from the pictured 'gang' in each of the categories above?

Now change the background and consider the change in meaning: suggest three alternatives to create three different effects.

In exploring what makes up expressed identity, you are in fact rehearsing the content of much of your Communication and Culture course. This will include a consideration of such matters as domestic architecture, interior design, industrial and commercial design, clothing, hairstyle, body adornment and modification as well as the various sorts of language we use. All these are potentially to be read and that reading process has already started by focusing your attentions on the text in Figure 5.13.

Attention to detail is vital to the business of textual analysis, irrespective of which 'tools' you are going to use. Remember TV's *Catchphrase* and 'Say what you see': without this there is nothing. The Ali G text has some clear 'starting points': what we see are six men at the corner of 7th Street with guns (and one of them is 'Ali G'). You've already attempted the next phase by looking at the men in detail so focus instead on the way you are viewing them and the ways they can be viewed.

ACTIVITY

Consider the significant elements of the appearance of the men in Figure 5.13 and the ways in which they can be read, that is, what are the factors that will likely affect the way they are read? Make two lists: features of the men as text which might affect reading; and features/characteristics of reader which might affect reading.

This is an extreme version of the confrontations that we have every day with 'other people' and we all have our own ways of dealing with this world of 'otherness', that is, with those people who are not us. It is relatively easy to classify those people whom we encounter on a day-to-day basis in terms of the relative depth of our relationship with each of them: from family and intimates through workmates and fellow students to relatively infrequent 'total strangers'. As we meet (to us) new people, we like to think that we judge them according to their behaviour and react to them accordingly. On reflection, however, it is probably truer to say that we judge them according to our behaviour, our experience, our norms and our prejudices.

ACTIVITY

Who are your friends? How long have you known them? Where did you meet? To what extent are they 'similar' to you in looks, interests, gender, ethnicity, or class? To what extent is this 'sameness' extended the closer you get to 'home' (i.e. how far are your best friends especially like you)?

Friendship is a loaded activity, it depends heavily on social experience and therefore is bound to be value-laden. What we communicate to others subconsciously may in fact operate as an informal and unconscious 'invitation to treat', a beacon for potential relationships. In other words, who we are, superficially, might be a significant factor in the relationships we form. After all, what are relationships but exchanges of communication, structures within which codes are employed and messages are delivered? What are relationships, after all, but communication texts framed by cultural contexts?

When the famous Italian semiotician Umberto Eco proclaimed in 1973, 'I speak through my clothes,' he was just identifying one element of a considerable set in which every gesture and intonation, every affectation and attitude is potentially significant. This set constitutes the human figure as communicator, the variety of codes through which this significant text has significance. The tension remains between those elements that are intentional and those that are not: those that are given to be read and those that simply 'leak'.

'We see things they'll never see': Learning to look

As 'textual analysts', our primary concerns are to describe what is there, what is represented in, on and by a particular text. What a text clearly does is to give physical form to a message, a meaning, a set of ideas. These ideas have been conceived, or at least created, in the form of a text: having presented themselves to the author(s), they are being re-presented to us (i.e. presented again, for a second time).

ACTIVITY

Given the issues raised about problematic representations of some social groups, what actions would you take to address what theorist Gaye Tuckman dubbed 'the symbolic annihilation of women'. Tuckman was referring to the trivialisation of women and their reduction to 'mere' appearance within the field of media representation. How is it possible to encourage a broader set of representations of women? Censorship? Boycott? Feedback?

Thus communication texts must be addressed in terms of their representations and the degree to which these leave room for the reader to explore meanings. As we've already begun to look at the representations in the 'six on 7th Street' text, let's move to the 'room for the reader to explore' stuff by offering another. Then hopefully we can use both texts to provide us with examples of the general issues concerning analysis that this chapter is intending to address. In many ways the text in Figure 5.14 is very much like the Ali G text, though in other ways it is quite dissimilar. It too is a picture of 'male friends' posing with their 'dangerous' weapons and they too are collected around their leader and aware of the impact they are making. On the other hand, as a seventeenth-century Dutch oil painting by a genuine Old Master (Rembrandt) this text has a force that derives from context as much as mere appearance. While both texts in this chapter are very much cultural artefacts, they come from very different cultural contexts: one 'high', the other 'low'

Figure 5.14 *Company of Captain Frans Banning Cocq and Lieutenant Willem van Ruytenhurch* also known as *The Night Watch* by Rembrandt

ACTIVITY

Look at the similarities and differences between these representations of men. These may be to do with their physical appearance, the way in which they are photographed or painted, their costumes, or simply their presentation on this page.

You may find that these representations of men fit into a broader social 'model' of how men are usually represented and thus perceived. Men are only very rarely 'captured' as passive surfaces, still and calm before the camera. They make unconvincing pin-ups, preferring activity to mere exposure. Both of these texts are significantly contrived and part of that contrivance is to allow the 'participants' to be seen for a variety of purposes. In both cases there is a credibility issue, which these men refuse to face.

STEREOTYPE: a mould into which reality is poured, whatever its individual shape. A stereotype is a simplified and generalised image of a group of people, which is created out of the values, judgements and assumptions of its creators, in most cases society itself. A stereotype of men might suggest their machismo or manliness as in this case.

More importantly, though, you may begin to ask yourself what are the connections between discrete sets of men. This can be addressed in at least two ways logically (by systematically identifying in detail what is there) and imaginatively (by imagining what kind of story the text is telling).

In the case of these texts, the logical approach is a little long-winded because the message, though potentially simplistic, is easy to understand. We know where these texts are coming from and have an inkling as to whom they are speaking. In simple terms they share the following:

1   Guys
2   Guns
3   Costumes
4   Attitude
5   A public context (they are both publicity 'pieces'/PR).

The imaginative approach to textual analysis would suggest that we engage with the form, style and content in an unaffected and open way, but even this gives little significant extra information. What we know about these texts are heavily dependent on the way they function within the conventions of genre and mode of address.

> **GENRE:** the subdivisions of the output of a given medium (e.g. television, film, in this case magazine publishing). A genre is a type, a particular version of a communication medium. For example, soap opera is a television genre, for it represents a particular approach to theme, style and form.

> **MODE OF ADDRESS:** describes the way in which a text 'speaks' to its audience. The text incorporates assumptions about its audience. If you can answer the question 'Who does this text think I am?' you are on the way to identifying its mode of address.

Both of the texts considered here are very much genre pieces and largely their modes of address are established by their generic identities. The 'Ali G' text is a publicity shot (one of many) taken to promote a film and printed in a brisk technocolour. *The Night Watch* is an example of seventeenth-century Dutch portraiture (these were pictures of living persons, often painted to order): in this case sixteen of those depicted paid Rembrandt 100 guilders each to appear in the work. This fact in itself begins to cast doubts on the naturalness of the picture, on its 'realism'. Like the presence of the character Ali G in the first text, it is a piece of information that influences our perceptions of the text.

Of course this is partly to do with an exploration of the content of the text (Ali G is a significant part of what's there) but it is also to do with a growing appreciation that all texts have significant contexts and, to misquote John Donne, 'no text is an island unto itself'. It may be possible to engage with both of these texts in a free and open way but even that would not excuse you from a consideration of the broader cultural contexts and the extent of their influence. The first text is highly conventional and dominated by its star, everything else is decoration. The painting is so busy being a famous painting that it puts off the casual observer and forgets that to lose your name is to ultimately lose your meaning. The painting's official title is *Company of Captain Frans Banning Cocq and Lieutenant Willem van Ruytenhurch*, a merely descriptive label to accommodate all who were paying, perhaps. *The Night Watch* was conceived as a title by viewers, in response to the relative darkness of the setting. This, it turned out, was nothing more than the impact of time, and when restored, the fact that Rembrandt had painted in the brightest day had the press dubbing it 'Day Watch'. Suddenly the whole meaning of the painting was in question (and some would argue it always will be) since without significant guidelines we are left to our own devices and that will never do.

Concluding that our original text is highly conventional is not to deny other interpretations but rather to identify the most likely intention of the piece. In terms of the possible things the text could say, one stands out as most likely, as most desired by the text itself. The conversation a text offers is called a discourse. This is conventionally referred to as the 'dominant discourse', MacDougall (2000) explains it like this: 'What the text tries to do is offer a winner – a discourse that is privileged over others.' Clearly, all readings of these texts are being made in relation to the dominant discourse; even if we reject it out of hand, we can't ignore it. These are classic examples of what Eco (1979) has called *closed texts*, texts in which one reading is significantly privileged. Other readings can be offered but they do not enhance the experience of the text, rather they are likely to frustrate readers and/or lead them to reject the text. *Open texts*, by comparison, are those in which individual readings are not significantly 'preferred' and in which the potential polysemy of the text is emphasised, even celebrated.

> **POLYSEMY/POLYSEMIC:** the capacity of a text or part of a text to be read in several different ways. For example, a red rose might communicate love, a fondness for horticulture, a political allegiance or Lancashire.

It is difficult to talk in the context of the Rembrandt about 'dominant discourse' because beyond the bogus interpretative title, which sort of 'wrongly' tells you what is going on, there are few clear clues. This text is open in the way that most mass media texts are not; it has no clear editorial position. This text has alternative readings but it would be difficult to categorise or even explain them in the way that Stuart Hall, among others, has done for media texts.

In their 1980 book *Culture, Media, Language*, Stuart Hall and his co-authors present three main types of reading of media texts, each of which has to do with the reader's social context (i.e. where the reader is in social terms). These are:

- **The dominant-hegemonic**: the reading that the text prefers; the dominant discourse; the reading that relates the text to society's ideological norms.
- **The negotiated**: the reading that broadly accepts the dominant discourse but which modifies it according to personal circumstances.
- **The oppositional**: the reading that contests the dominant discourse and takes some alternative and opposed meaning from the text.

Hall is interested in the ways in which communication media reflect particular social and cultural views, which he argues are those of dominant groups and classes in society. The adjective 'hegemonic' is chosen to reflect this perspective, since hegemony, a term used by Gramsci, represents the way the ruling classes maintain their power by manipulating the way we think about ourselves and our world. In simple terms, Hall would argue, for example, that our 'harmless' movie promotion is implicitly promoting all manner of social and political propaganda – about the desirability of consumerism, about social and intellectual elitism, about the position and value of women. This is not just about what the text intends to say but about the ways in which all texts fit into a pattern of social communication, which on the largest scale is about society talking to itself.

INFORMATION BOX – HEGEMONY *i*

The Italian writer Antonio Gramsci explained why the majority of people in a culture do not adopt the values and beliefs of their own class. He argued that the dominant minority within cultures present the values and beliefs of their own class as somehow 'natural' and thus universal. In this way people end up promoting the values and beliefs of the dominant or ruling class rather than of their own class.

It is possible to see *The Night Watch* in these terms, with the dominant-hegemonic as the need to see the text as a work of art (and thus in some unspecified sense valuable) and an oppositional reading as one that rejects these notions of cultural value. Most practical readings of text are negotiated, a compound of the two previous positions mixed with significant personal response.

PREFERRED READING: the reading a text's producer would like receivers to make. The producer will compose the text in a way which ensures this occurs.

Suggest oppositional and negotiated readings for both the texts featured in Figures 5.15 and 5.16.

Figure 5.15 Lelli Kelly, *Shoes for Girls* advert

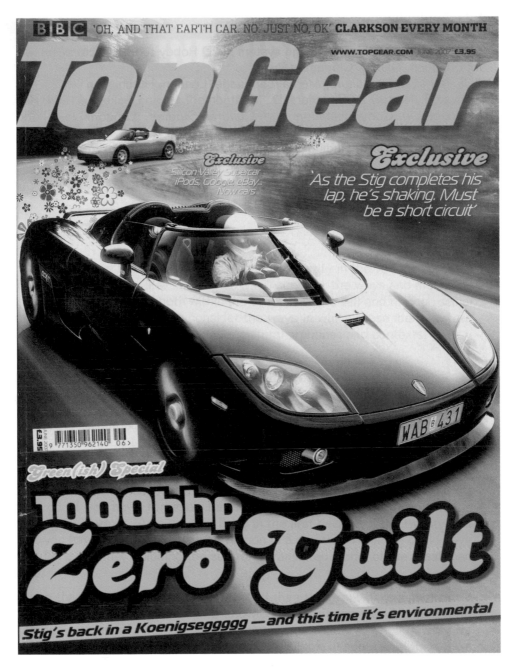

Figure 5.16 *Top Gear* magazine cover, June 2007

Figure 6.1 Phone box vs mobile phone

Figure 6.2 Floppy disk vs USB

At one time university students phoned their parents once a week from a phone box to let them know they were OK. Now instant communication is taken for granted and those who leave home without their mobile phones describe themselves as feeling 'lost' and 'naked'. Where once there was a single terrestrial television station, then two and three, then four and five, now more than seven out of ten people have access to more than 100 channels. All of these add to the complexity of contemporary life, they are all additional issues that we must address, factors in the increasingly complex negotiations about who we are.

The anthropologist Clifford Geertz (1973) memorably described man as 'an animal suspended in webs of significance that he himself has spun' and went on to identify culture itself as those webs. He concludes that the analysis of culture is 'therefore not an experimental science in search of law but an interpretive one in search of meaning'. Here, Geertz is reminding us of the difficulty of our task as we set out to analyse and understand our own cultures; the vary nature of culture is complex and interwoven, but, like a spider's web, a thing of delicate beauty.

Figure 6.3 Culture: a web of significance – complex, delicate and beautiful

It seems clear that contemporary society is essentially multicultural and not in the conventional sense of multi-ethnic or multi-faith but in a far more wide-ranging way in which the interests of groups designated by social class, gender, age and ethnicity are creating a sophisticated multidimensional matrix within which we must find definition and meaning. In some senses this bottom line outcome is the one thing that has not changed. In lay terms we have always needed to grow up and know where we fit in. Theorists from the 'uses and gratifications' tradition who see communication as servicing basic human needs would label these two as examples of 'personal integrative' and 'social integrative' needs.

What has significantly changed and is progressively changing is the complexity of the processes involved. It seems reasonable to assert that historically identity was very much more preordained and stable. In 1900 for example, where you fitted into society depended in a very predictable way on the social class and gender into which you were born. The process of getting there, of growing up was for most people simple and efficient: an all too brief childhood, minimal education and then work as a fully fledged adult. This pattern continued well into the twentieth century. In fact it was not until the late 1950s and early 1960s with the 'invention' of the teenager and the raising of the school age to 16 that things significantly shifted. Recently, the government announced that the school leaving age will be raised again. By 2013, it will be a formal requirement that young people stay in full-time education or workplace training until the age of 18.

ACTIVITY

'Growing up'

How do we make the transition from childhood to adulthood? To be sure, there is no one clear cut age or event which marks this transition, but there are many formal markers and informal rituals that mark the advent of adulthood. Informal rituals may include an eighteenth birthday party or buying your own clothes for the first time. Formal markers include the age at which you can get married or vote. Additionally, there are the biological markers of adulthood such as the deepening of voice and the physical changes of puberty.

Make a comprehensive list of these transitions and link each one to an age in years.

What does this list tell you about your culture? Can you identify contrasts with other contemporary or historical cultures?

Perhaps the extension of the formal period called education, or at least extending the expectation of the time people will be spending at school and college, is making these designations more difficult. We often hear it said that people are getting younger (that '40 is the new 30', for example), that growing up is taking longer. The extension of formal education is all very well but if it does not coincide with an extension of the scope of education, then we will merely take those disengaged by school and force them into two years of further disengagement at college. With more and more people staying on and considerably more of them going to university, it is perhaps not surprising that those left behind without even the option of an old-fashioned factory job feel disenfranchised. These 'kidults' are even denied the simple status of adults. In formal terms and by anyone's measure, these young people are not being effectively or appropriately socialised, inducted into our contemporary multicultural society.

They are, however, being socialised (and have been since the process is continual and continuous). Bernstein (1971) described socialisation as 'the process whereby a child acquires a specific cultural identity' and continued 'whereby the biological is transformed into a specific cultural being'. It may be that 'kidult' is a specific cultural identity in the way that 'British Muslim' is or 'white working class' or even 'Emo'. Clearly they are states that the biological human part has cultivated, acquired and negotiated in communication with others (individuals and institutions). The identities described above are not active at birth, they are contexts in which we become ourselves. It is these contexts which must be our focus here since if we are properly interested in who we are (i.e. who we have become) we must take an interest in where this becoming has taken place.

Becoming and being: six contexts in search of an actor

What are the major influences that affect us as we grow up? Here we will examine these so-called agencies of socialisation and explore in some greater detail the ways in which they work to earn us 'safe passage' into the broader culture.

One of the first problems with trying to address these processes, called variously socialisation and enculturation, is that hindsight is a wonderful thing. In retrospect these influences (the family, friends, community, religion, education, work, media) seem entirely discrete and responsive to analysis. Even though the process of socialisation is ongoing and arguably lifelong, it is clear by sixteen or thereabouts that we have reached Bernstein's goal of a specific cultural identity. From this position it is relatively easy to evaluate the influences: the relative importance of religion in your 'story', for example, will often be very apparent. It is also relatively easy for theorists to offer their models, for example, to see the agencies as crudely bridging the gap between selfhood and the world, between the individual and the wider culture. This is essentially a linear model since it sees socialisation as a journey from 'pure self' to 'social self' via a series of stages or stations.

Figure 6.4 The influences on our development: family; religion; friends; community; education; work; media

AS COMMUNICATION AND CULTURE: THE ESSENTIAL INTRODUCTION

The order in which these 'filters' appear is a matter of some debate and may differ from individual to individual. This is not a statement of rank order but rather of chronological sequence. But which comes first, religion or the media? And has one replaced the other?

A sequence like this can be categorised in many different ways. For example, in simple terms, it might describe the process by which we have our 'edges' knocked off, a process of filtration by which we are refined and improved. Psychologically it can also reveal in some detail the confrontation that Freud describes between the 'pleasure principle', which dominates our earliest experiences, and 'the reality principle', which insists that the world demands compromises. At the same time it allows for a less antagonistic process to be described in which the agencies act as donors, each providing us with something that we need.

Whatever the specific details of what it says it clearly tells a certain kind of story, which is in essence a 'quest narrative'. The supposition is that we go out into the world to find ourselves and on the way encounter experiences and characters that either help or hinder us. This is a classic folk tale with substantial villains (usually the media and religion but with the odd evil stepmother into the bargain), individual courage, drama and the greatest prize of all, in modern terms: 'self-knowledge'.

Figure 6.5 *Lord of the Rings: The Fellowship of the Ring*, 2001. A story with all the ingredients of a 'quest narrative'. But does our life story have a similar structure?

In fact, whatever the depth of experience, this process simply does not operate in the way implied by the 'model' since rather than being 'organised' stages these agencies are colours perpetually woven into the design, codes contributing to that ultimate chain of signs: identity. All this means is that, whatever we choose to do for convenience in a book like this one, the relative demands made on our identity by these various sources cannot be separated out. They are interdependent, not only filters of and perspectives on identity but also filters of and perspectives on one another.

This interdependence is hardly unexpected. If the purpose of socialisation is to make us 'fit in' (in Bernstein's words to sensitise us to 'the various orderings of society and various roles [we] . . . are expected to play') then one tension will always be the point at which these different roles (son/daughter, friend, student) coincide. This 'role conflict' is very much a part of the process through which identity is negotiated since it makes us acutely aware of 'audience' and of the essentially dynamic relationship between the various agencies.

This turns the simple linear model on page 101 into something that is much more like a Hall of Mirrors, where we see ourselves reflected, refracted and distorted in the crossfire of metaperceptions (views of other views). This creates something much more complex than the following diagram suggests:

All that this confirms is the ways in which the agencies of socialisation embody attitudes towards the world which necessarily include the other agencies. In simple terms we learn about families from being in them but also from our experiences of observing a broad range of other families within contexts such as the mass media (though equally by observing and interacting with our friends and neighbours). In the same way attitudes towards education are fostered not only by our experience of it but also in the views of family and friends. Identity is created in these intersections, what Geertz earlier called 'webs of significance', since they become 'sightlines' against which we can measure and establish our own personal responses. In the multitude of these measurements we are described and defined.

Not that this is an abstract process, in fact it is essentially pragmatic and material. Raymond Williams famously wrote:

> **Culture is ordinary: that is the first fact. Every human society has its own shape, its own purposes, its own meanings. . . . The making of a society is the finding of common meanings and directions and its growth is an active debate and amendment under the pressures of experience, contact and discovery, writing themselves into the land.**

(in Gray and McGuigan 1993, p. 6)

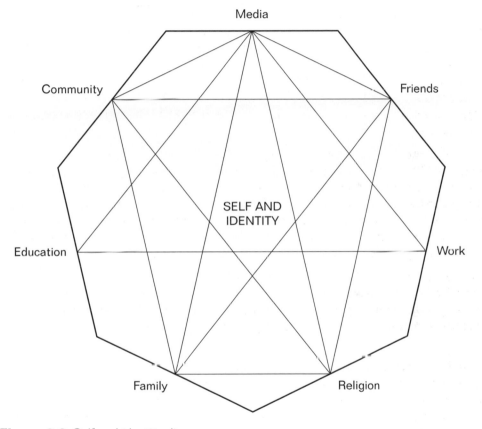

Figure 6.6 Self and identity diagram

We may talk of 'intersections' and 'perspectives' but identity is accessible only as far as it is represented or, in other words, communicated. Identity must be read in our appearance, our activities and our behaviour; in actions as well as words. Communication and Culture describes these as 'sites' and here there are principally two: 'the individual' and 'cultural contexts and practices'. To get further we need to examine each of these through the codes of communication which enable them to be expressed, perceived and analysed.

Communication, culture and the individual: dressing the human text

Codes (see Chapter 2) are the means by which we represent our identities, be they verbal or visual, primitive or technological. As we have already implied, Communication and Culture encompasses all we say and all we do and all of this is potential evidence of who we are. In a sense we are constituted from all our choices: form and style as well as content (not just what you say but also the way you say it). This is nowhere more true than in our concern with appearance. Appearance is literally 'that which appears', all there is to see. However, what is also implied is an awareness of a 'surface' (the human body) which can be adorned or prepared to deflect and impress.

ACTIVITY

Expressing identity through appearance

When Umberto Eco proclaimed in 1973, 'I speak through my clothes,' (quoted in Hebdige 1979, p. 100) he was just identifying one element of a considerable paradigm: a set in which every gesture and intonation, every affectation and attitude is potentially significant. This set constitutes the human figure as communicator, the variety of codes through which this significant text has significance. The tension remains between those elements that are intentional and those that are not: those that are given to be read and those that simply 'leak'.

How specifically do you express your own individual personality?

List the most significant *ten* ways and comment on each.

PROMPT: your clothes, hairstyle, props, accessories or make-up.

Here you are creating a map or model of yourself as communicator with an implicit understanding of the communication theorist Paul Watzlawick's much-quoted formulation 'one cannot not communicate'. And just in case you're disputing this and wilfully challenging anyone to detect any communicative intent in your defensive posture and emotionless face, be aware of Abercrombie's observation that 'some signs are given, others are given off'. This means that we can communicate a great deal without really intending to – our bodies are complex texts. The subtitle of this subsection is 'Dressing the human text' to which we might now add 'inside and out'. Perhaps what is needed is an *Operation*-style diagram.

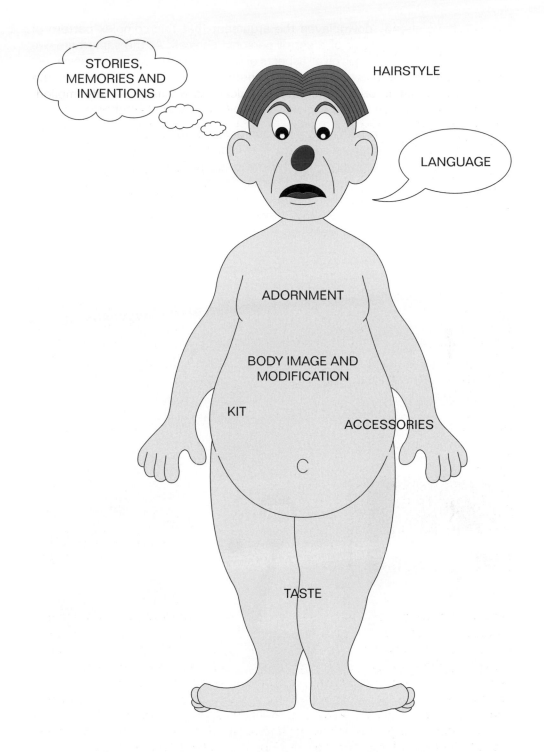

Figure 6.7 Dressing the human text diagram

Now we have already downplayed the argument that this complex pattern of features is merely a matter of a set of personal choices. At the same time, we have identified key influences on all aspects of our appearance and communication. The job now is to put these two aspects together to examine the details of self-presentation and its revelation of identity. In doing so we are principally involved in analysing the human text to explore the significant paradigms of identity.

Perhaps we should start with a warm-up and one step removed from the realities of life in contemporary cultural contexts. Television favours a dramatic style which works naturalistically showing characters who resemble real people. This is not as easy as it seems since drama also demands interesting backstories and the potential for development, whereas that's only what we (as real people) would *like* to have. However, in some ways devising and reading dramatic characters does reveal much about how identities are established and what the conventions are.

ACTIVITY

The following activity has two distinct parts: first, we are reading the characters created by others, then tentatively devising ones of our own. Consider each of the three images below and identify the key elements of the communicative syntagm (the chain of signs which define each character). What other elements (unseen) are also part of this significant chain?

Figure 6.8 Brian Potter, David Brent and Russell Brand. a) Peter Kay performs as Brian Potter b) Ricky Gervais plays David Brent in *The Office* c) Russell Brand

BONUS: Despite the fact that two of these were 'written', they are all in their own ways extensions of their creators (*personae* as some would call them). How much of the performer in each case is being seen? (Answer as a percentage.)

The above creations are comic but our newly devised characters will take their place in the following texts:

- *Eastenders*: member of a prominent new family
- *Dr Who*: new human assistant
- Central character from 'interesting' new detective show.

In devising your character, please use the categories listed below:

- Language (idiolect)
- Stories/memories/inventions
- Hairstyle
- Body Image (modifications)
- Clothes and other adornments
- Technological 'kit'
- Taste.

It's also then worth briefly considering the distinctiveness of the characters pictured in Figure 6.8 in terms of these categories. What is the significance of each of these categories for each of the characters? Are some categories more influential than others?

'Speak that I might see you': into the idiolect

So much of this course asks you to investigate and explore, to hunt down the connections between different kinds of phenomena, to attempt a reconstruction of everyday life from its residual evidence. In doing so it presupposes both that the evidence is available and that the cultural contexts in which the receiver reads are also important. Language seems indisputably to meet these demands. This is partly because it is principally in its spoken form the most significant means we have of addressing two of the most basic communication needs: self-presentation and affiliation. At the same time it is entirely acquired by inhabiting the various contexts within which we are active: the family, the community, education and so on.

An individual's personal language register, or idiolect (idiosyncratic dialect), encompasses all our experiences and knowledge of language. The idiolect consists not only of vocabulary but also of the conventions of performance: all our words in all the forms, contexts and with all the differing emphasis we have given to them. It is therefore part archive, part linguistic fuel tank, part magazine (in the sense of a place where bullets are kept) and in all cases dynamic and alive. It exists in time and so is being continually renewed yet at the same time nothing is ever forgotten or removed. Perhaps it would be useful to liken it to a palimpsest, one of those old reused medieval manuscripts where writing new texts never quite obliterates the old. In this way the language of one stage of our lives only largely replaces the language of a previous stage since we are not improving our language as we progress, we are merely altering it.

INFORMATION BOX – SLANG

i

While Ambrose Bierce's *Devil's Dictionary* defines slang as 'The grunt of the human hog (*Pignoramus intolerabilis*) with an audible memory' you might find a more useful version below:

Nonstandard vocabulary of extreme informality, usually not limited to any region. It includes newly coined words, shortened forms, and standard words used playfully out of their usual context. Slang is drawn from the vocabularies of limited groups: cant, the words or expressions coined or adopted by an age, ethnic, occupational, or other group (e.g., college students, jazz musicians); jargon, the shoptalk or technical terminology specific to an occupation; and argot, the cant and jargon used as a secret language by thieves or other criminals.

(*Britannica Concise Encyclopedia*)

ACTIVITY

'All slang is metaphor, and all metaphor is poetry'

One of the easiest ways to look into the layers of our idiolects is to fondly remember yesterday's slang. Slang changes especially quickly and is particularly sensitive to influence from the surrounding cultural contexts, particularly popular cultural contexts. It also develops as we get older (and supposedly more adult). An interesting contemporary slang word is 'txt' which no one possessed ten years ago yet which has seeped into everyone's usage today. Consider the list below (provided by Helena Platt) as a starting point for attempting a reconstruction of some of the key phases and phrases of your 'development'. Here's to the language we have (thankfully in most cases) lost!

Helena's Timeline		
Year	The Language Report[1]	My Word
1978	Satellite dish	Birth
1979	Karaoke	
1980	Nip and Tuck	
1981	Stepford	Insecurity
1982	Kissogram	
1983	Liposuction	
1984	Shopaholic	
1985	Full Monty	
1986	Britpop	
1987	To email	
1988	Rollerblading	Minogue
1989	Doughnutting	
1990	Twocker	Press gang
1991	Ethnic cleansing	
1992	Off-message	Friendship
1993	DVD	Endurance
1994	Metrosexual	Achievement
1995	Chuddies	Failure
1996	Viagra	Loss of confidence
1997	WAP	Enjoyment
1998	To Google	Difficulty
1999	Blogger	Lost
2000	Bling	Contentment
2001	9/11	Challenge
2002	Metatarsal	Reaching Goals
2003	To sex something up	Disappointment/Enlightenment
2004	Chav	Confidence
2005	Biosecurity	Development
2006	Bovvered	Change

1 The words listed here are taken from the publication 'The Like Language Report for Real', Susie Dent, 2006, London: Oxford University Press.

continued

Slang is edgy and controversial, that's one of its functions. The American poet Carl Sandberg described it as 'a language that rolls up its sleeves, spits on its hands and goes to work'. It includes the changing ways in which we linguistically deal with taboo subjects such as criminality and sexuality. This is why Shakespeare's comic scenes involving low-born characters are today so incomprehensible. When they were written they provided comic relief by offering crude jokes in the base language of much of the audience in contrast to the high poetry of the noble characters and their lofty lives. Three hundred years later the lofty language remains largely unchanged but the slang has moved on many times and seems like a different language (because it is). Is it likely that 'cowabunga' is going to have any resonance in ten years time? Does it even now?

This image of language as a multidimensional store is of course only that, an image, a metaphor. Language is also instinctive, subconscious and creative. Using words is rarely the same as choosing words: the latter is far too systematic. Of course when we have the need to be precise, such as when we are attempting the impossibility of describing what language is, we are especially aware of the process of selection. In semiotic terms we are consciously identifying and engaging linguistic paradigms. More often though we are dealing with language in a much more instinctive way, negotiating contexts that change in mid-utterance rather than which present themselves as neatly defined linguistic challenges. This text is a suitable example – for though the general context is clear, each sentence, and at times each word, brings with it its own dynamic. The problem as ever is that being involved in the process makes it difficult for you to recognise the extra linguistic elements – the elements other than words.

ACTIVITY

'Pure and simple every time'

Rank the following activities in terms of their focus on 'pure' language, or if you prefer 'purely on language'. What other factors are involved in these activities?

- Spelling the word 'procrastination'
- Writing a history essay
- Writing your diary
- Writing a story
- Txting a family member
- Txting a potential date
- Chatting with a friend
- Making a presentation in class
- Asking someone out.

What there is of course is context – that most important of Communication and Culture concepts. Just as the idiolect is deep and wide, it is also tuned to the different demands of different contexts and audiences and purposes. At one level this is pretty straightforward. It is about selecting or accessing the appropriate register (literally a contextualised language). The difference between writing a history essay and asking someone out is about using different languages not selecting different words. The influential British linguist M. A. K. Halliday suggested that registers have three dimensions:

- Formality
- Technicality
- The tendency of the register to be spoken or written.

These are all fluid and active tendencies not mutually exclusive choices but they do help to clarify the difference above. A history essay will tend to be formal, technical and consciously adopting the structures of written language whereas asking someone out is pretty much the opposite.

ACTIVITY

'Taking the register'

Which registers would you expect to employ in the following situations:

- Txting a mate about going out
- Writing a blog about your favourite TV show
- Giving a presentation about your 'culture'
- Emailing a request for a job application form
- Writing an investigation into the use of registers.

These registers are part of your idiolect's repertoire, to be practised and prepared for future use in the same way that your irregularities of grammar or idiosyncrasies of spelling or pronunciation are waiting there to trip you up. Your idiolect is your personal dialect and a dialect is a language variant fully formed. Your language is intimately and personally yours, a storehouse of your experiences, your relationships, your values. Much more than what we eat, we are what we say and as importantly the way we say.

Figure 6.9
Alphabetti spaghetti – we are what we eat, we are what we say

If your idiolect could be removed and examined (seen and heard), it would provide a unique guide to the person you are and have been: your interests, your relationships, your relative status, your history and your ambitions for the future. Language is never neutral, it occurs only in active human cultural contexts where it is given value according to both its qualities and the context's expectations. Our idiolects, containing performance (how language is delivered) as well as competence (how it should be structured), will necessarily contain accents and other dialect elements. At the same time they will involve an awareness of the status afforded to different kinds of English accent and dialect just as much as we are aware of the effect of certain kinds of words which we know but in many contexts never use.

ASIDE

Just a couple of discussion points . . .

a) Former NUM leader Arthur Scargill once remarked in an interview 'My father still reads the dictionary every day. He says your life depends on your power to master words.' Is knowledge of words or the way they are pronounced a greater 'power' in our lives?
b) The extract below from Tony Harrison's poem 'National Trust' talks about the fate of those who have no voice:

> The dumb go down in history and disappear
> and not one gentleman's been brought to book:
> Mes den hep tavas a-gollas y dyr
> (Cornish-)
> 'the tongueless man gets his land took.'

What do you consider most important: fluency in speech or in writing?

One thing that has a profound affect on our language is education. It floods the idiolect with new words but also new attitudes towards language. It often challenges the linguistic forms into which we have been socialised at home, particularly if those forms are regional, even if they are not fully fledged dialect forms. We learn for example that being educated conventionally implies certain kinds of language and language use and that bad language will only lead to badness of other kinds. The further we go on in education the more likely it is that these pressures to recognise the value of a Standard English will be felt (see Chapter 2 for a discussion of Standard English). This is a major part of the argument that suggests that middle-class children do better than others in education. They do so because the language of education is their language. Children who bring regional dialects to the classroom have a lot more to learn before they can effectively begin to learn.

Mary's story

Consider Mary's story:

Mary has a strong sense that being at university is particularly difficult because of who she is, a black working-class woman. Language is central to her concerns and raises particular issues for her when she sits down to write. In a discussion about writing in academia she compares the difficulties she faces to the experience of a white middle-class student on the same course:

> He doesn't have to make a switch. It's him you see. Whereas when I'm writing I don't know who it is (laughs). It's not me. And that's why I think it's awful, I think it's awful you know. It's not me at all. It's like I have to go into a different person. I have to change my frame of mind and you know, my way of thinking and everything. It's just like a stranger, it's like I've got two bodies in my head, and two personalities and there's conflict.

(Lillis 2003)

Meanwhile we are continually reminded of the ways in which our language and language use contains our attitudes towards the world at particular times and more generally. It contains for example attitudes towards males and females particularly and generally and our attitudes towards being male or female. This necessarily means having the capability to express attitudes that you do not consider to be your own. Taboo or forbidden words make for an interesting case study since the censorship that is involved is imposed both by social conventions and by personal filters and is always revealing. Those who bemoan the spread of Political Correctness, the awareness that the act of labelling can often be the first stage of negatively representing groups of people, often accuse these meddlers of restricting freedom of speech. Often their complaints are couched in the following terms 'We are not allowed to call them xxx any more' where xxx refers to a derogatory term for some commonly misrepresented group. Actually it was never meant to be about banning words, but rather about increasing awareness and sensitivity and addressing thoughtless discrimination. It is therefore alarming how uncomfortable everyone seems to become with the range of these politically incorrect terms as if recognising that branding travellers 'gyppos' or the mentally ill 'loonies' has made the words themselves radioactive. I suspect that banning words is about as misguided as banning breeds of so-called dangerous dogs: it's not so much the breed as the breeder.

The recent controversy over a *Big Brother* contestant's use of the word 'nigger' and her subsequent and summary 'eviction' is a case (study) in point. First, it confirms the importance of context since it followed on from Channel 4's public pillorying for 'allowing' the racist bullying of Bollywood star Shilpa Shetty on the previous *Celebrity Big Brother*. Without this context perhaps the decision would have been different. Either way Emily's casual 'me nigger' directed at her confounded, but not offended, new friend Charlie brought an immediate and direct response from Channel 4. Emily was marched in her nightie from the premises, protesting her innocence (not of the act but of the implication that it suggested she was a racist) and Channel 4 had yet another bumper crop of complaints. However, while literally thousands had complained about the offensively racist nature of the treatment meted out to Shilpa by Jade, Jo and Danielle, the calls and emails about Emily almost unanimously criticised Channel 4 for their 'overreaction'.

The response to the Shilpa Shetty incident was genuinely and heart-warmingly staggering, surely an optimistic sign of Britain's continuing racial tolerance. For consciously provocative programming (with offensive language – for example the film of Tony Harrison's *V*) Channel 4 might expect complaints in their hundreds. The defenders of Shetty numbered 45,000.

ESSENTIAL ARCHIVE

An interesting case of language and representation can be found in the *A2 Media Studies: The Essential Introduction* (Bennett et al. 2006a, pp. 88–9). It concerns the sign language used by the deaf:

> This is what is particularly interesting about a debate in 2004 involving deaf sign language which was featured in all the prominent news media and even made Jonathan Ross's Friday night chat show. Users of British Sign Language, which despite more users than Welsh or Gaelic was not recognised as a language until 2003, were called upon to 'renew' (for renew read 'clean up') some of the signs they used to represent some minority groups: chiefly the sign for gays/homosexuals and the sign for Orientals. In each case they were thought to promote stereotypes in a negative way: they were highly iconic signs, a limp wrist and pulled eyes respectively.

continued

In fact further investigation produced an even more interesting demonstration of the issues since the 'story' was some ten to fifteen years old, which tells us something first of all about the media news agenda. It also provides a context in which these issues of representation can be examined and debated. When called on to respond to this (outdated) charge representatives of the deaf (themselves a significant minority 'interest') argued that these attacks were themselves prejudicial to their sense of identity which, as with national groups, is enshrined in their language. In other words they argued that the tools of their representation of the world contained more than simply a set of counters which might be used in place of, for example, the idea 'homosexual'. It was in fact an index of their intrinsic values, which is also of course what their opponents were also arguing (and that these values were prejudicial).

Cath Smith, a widely published author of sign books including sign dictionaries, has suggested that these issues are at the heart of many of the problems faced by the deaf community. The very fact that BSL was so recently acknowledged by the government is an indication of a situation where often those who can hear and vocalise spoken language make decisions for those who cannot. Smith acknowledges that even at the time that signs were being recorded there was a tendency for those recording to have a greater sensitivity to issues of offence than those using the signs and in many cases new signs were 'proposed' to replace the more insensitive (blunt) ones.

'Gay' and 'Oriental' are two apposite cases in point. The former transformed itself more than ten years ago from the camp limp wrist to the version below with no significant protest.

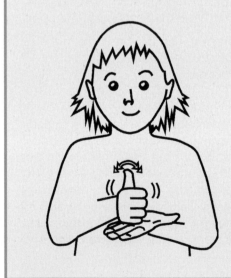

Figure 6.10 Gay deaf sign from the *Let's Sign* Dictionary, www.deafsign.com

Cath Smith compares those who still use the 'limp wrist' to those who persist in language with terms like 'poof' and 'poofter' rather than the generally acceptable and uncontroversial 'gay'. The oriental revision, on the other hand, was rejected out of hand and the pulled eye remains the conventional sign in a victory for practice over theory. Incidentally the oriental deaf sign for Europeans similarly traces the eye shape only this time with a circular motion.

One of the questions raised here is about to whom language belongs and who is responsible for monitoring its use. In a country that prides itself on its freedom of speech it is about a recognition that all freedoms come with responsibilities. However, it is also about recognising the subtleties of human communication in which nuance is often as important as formal definition. This means that the ill will and intolerance is not so much in the words themselves but rather in the performance/delivery.

Perhaps this is easier to understand if we consider pragmatically the way that language works. Linguists talk of three levels:

- Reference (propositional): where language makes statements about specific people, places and things.
- Force (illocutionary): where language engages us in communication with particular purposes.
- Effect (perlocutionary): where language has an impact on us.

This is really a model of linguistic and semantic 'follow-through'. We use language primarily to have control over the world: we name things so that we can own and use them (this is very like the Americans putting a flag on the Moon or the Russians on the sea-bed). In other words we have the word 'chair' so that we can more effectively dispose of them (fetch them, arrange them, get them counted and so on). In this example, the word 'chair' is uncontroversial. It references the world in an unproblematic way (with no particular force or value judgement) with the effect that communication can take place. However, we can give even a simple word such as 'chair' force. If, for example, we were to describe the royal throne of state or the Holy Papal throne as 'chairs', then the force would come from the purpose and context. Here the 'chair' would be an ironic comment on those who are seated on these thrones and their relative unimportance and irrelevance. The effect of this is to set ourselves against these so-called authorities.

Thus when we reference 'women' as 'girlies', 'birds', 'bits of stuff' or simply 'skirt', we are doing so with force and effect. They are, in this way, actively diminished by this rather than described. Similarly describing hardened professional soldiers as 'our lads' seeks to say something about their vulnerability and innocence with the intended effect that we are even more positively disposed towards them.

ACTIVITY

In this way what we call ourselves and how we describe ourselves is very important. Try to find words to describe different aspects of yourself, prompted by the categories below. For each category try to identify a) an uncontroversial generic term, b) your best attempt at a personal label, c) a term which misreads you in these categories (I'm not . . .).

- Gender (e.g. man, guy, I'm not a geezer)
- Social class
- Appearance
- Taste in music
- Attitude to school/college.

Good taste/bad taste: I know what I like!

If your idiolect provides long-term evidence of where you've been, your taste provides clues to 'where you're at'. Your taste is a set of preferences negotiated first within yourself and then judiciously gate kept – often now via the various filters of your personal website. The colonisation of personal taste by MySpace, Facebook and Bebo has considerably raised the profile of 'my music' and 'my films' but let's not forget they were always important, both psychologically and socially. Moreover the issues always have been the same:

- How to decide what we like? (What are the processes and how does identity fit in?)
- How does what we like affect who we are? (And how others perceive and interpret us?)
- Can taste be developed (cultivated) and should it be? (Or does it develop anyway as part of growing up? Does 'develop' imply 'improve'?)
- What is the relationship between personal taste and the 'Taste' (or 'good taste') which education seems keen to develop in us (appreciation of classical music, art and literature).

Here the focus must be on personal taste and the ways in which it contributes to the development and clarification of identity. This must mean that we start psychologically with the need for a stable self-concept, in other words for a harmonious relationship between self-image, ideal self and self-esteem. Taste appears to be intimately involved with the natural negotiations between 'image' (self as I see myself) and 'ideal' (self as I would like to see myself) with 'esteem' as the reward for a productive relationship. Knowing what you like and ultimately value in the face of significant contextual pressures is an extremely strong position to be in. However, in the face of so many pressures from fashions of all kinds, very few of us feel entirely confident in the expression of personal tastes and values.

Taste is a metaphor, which transposes the natural sensory process by which we judge what in the world is good to eat to anything else that might be ranked in this way, be it films, clothes, guitars, men. This is why the following exchange between Stephen Fry and Hugh Laurie is potentially funny (go on, laugh!). The scene is a mock SAS recruiting interview:

STEPHEN: Any particular disabilities?
HUGH: I've got no sense of taste.
STEPHEN: In what? Films? Music?
HUGH: Food. I can't taste food.

Figure 6.11 The SAS sketch from *A Bit of Fry and Laurie*, first series

There are two connected points to make here, both of which relate to the way in which this transfer from the domain of the senses to the intellectual and cultural sphere brings with it assumptions. Enjoying the taste of food is an experience more significantly biological (of the palate) than 'tasting' films, though clearly they're not entirely different. More significant though is the evolutionary tendency to associate a 'good' taste with something that is beneficial; there are no sweet-tasting natural poisons. To see taste in books as a matter of such natural selection would be hazardous to say the least, though having no taste in films and music can be as socially dangerous as lacking a discriminating palate.

ACTIVITY

Book and film tasting

Imagine your favourite meal and then try to describe the qualities of it that make you choose it (qualities of the food itself perhaps and of how it makes you feel). How does this notional favourite compare to the best meal you've ever had?

Now consider films or books or TV that make you feel this way or have these qualities. Are they necessarily your favourite films or books? If not, what are the other factors?

It seems clear that taste in films or clothes for example is a less direct form of feedback than getting pleasure from food. In both cases we are employing our senses but the perception we have of films is primarily 'cognitive' (to do with the brain), we are thinking through an aesthetic (a theory of what makes films good) which, even if entirely personal, is the product of more than pleasurable sensory experience. Alternatively, these judgements are then mediated at least in public by the judgements of your peer group, friendship group, even of the wider culture. However, let's stick with the core: the relationship between your taste and your identity.

It seems clear that psychologically and intellectually we attempt to build identities which are both coherent (they make sense at least to us) and effective (they serve us well in everyday life). Taste is arguably at the core of this process since it is basically a provider of support to our developing sense of self. These key texts (narratives, role models, styles, fantasies) are vital to our understanding of who we are since they are an important way in which we define our values – first, and most importantly, to ourselves. Taste is to some extent, then, our 'secret' and as such is difficult to fully interrogate, analyse and discuss. It offers an intimate commentary on what we value, since developing an aesthetic (a theory of what is beautiful) inevitably means developing a philosophy of life (and particularly ideas about what is good and desirable).

If you wish to enquire further into the meanings of taste without being expected to bare your soul, there's a mine of information on suitable cases on a host of fan sites on the web. Fans are those who wear their taste like a badge of honour and largely whose sincerity cannot be questioned. Fans build identities around a commitment to bands, cult TV programmes or film genres and play out the significant relationships for us all to witness. Theirs (like ours) is not a passive commitment but rather an active, dynamic interaction in which they are themselves defined.

ESSENTIAL ARCHIVE

Fandom

The conventional view of fans as 'sad cases' and 'anoraks' has been challenged in recent years, notably by Henry Jenkins as the following extract from *Film Studies: The Essential Resource* (Bennett et al. 2006b) describes: It is interesting to note that the connotations of the word film buff carry no such negative charge. The film buff is erudite and informed and worthy of respect. Henry Jenkins gets at many of these issues in his influential book *Textual Poachers (Television Fans and Participatory Callers)* (Routledge 1992). Jenkins is interested in the various ways in which fans make their own meanings from apparently superficial, ideological and manipulative texts. He sees this as a kind of subversion, a semantic guerrilla warfare. In fact he uses military language to sum up the 'war' between a controlling media and individual consumers, suggesting that we have 'tactics' to deal with their strategies'. Jenkins is also keen to explore the supposedly gendered nature of fandom as this female reader/reviewer implies

> When most people think of a *Star Trek* fan, they imagine a young man with glasses and a polyester uniform stretched tight over his paunch. In this book Henry Jenkins explodes that myth. The typical television fan – of *Star Trek* or any other show – is female, educated, and often caught in a job that doesn't make full use of her abilities. In media fandom, she finds a social and intellectual world that is a rich complement to her mundane existence. Jenkins also discredits a more pervasive myth – that of the TV viewer as an addicted idiot passively receiving broadcasters' ideology of consumerism. In truth, fans appropriate material from TV shows, making new meaning. They write stories and folk songs, and even make videos from re-edited programs. Not all viewers are as active and creative as fans, but it's clear that we need to rethink basic ideas about the viewing process.

> For readers like myself who are involved with modern interactive technologies such as The Well, Internet multimedia, and virtual reality, this book is an important reminder not to view more traditional media forms as 'passive.' – Amy Bruckman

ACTIVITY

To what extent do you think fandom is gendered? For example, do you think specific genres and specific star/directors have more appeal to one gender than the other?

Is 'being a fan' a significant part of your identity?

Of course, taste is also a public commodity which demands the right answers in the right contexts. Whether you're demonstrating to your friends that you know the difference between thrash metal and death metal or proving to a potential employer that you are 'well-read' by confidently naming your favourite Shakespeare play, the game is pretty much the same. Set piece decisions on favourites are rarely more than tactical plays in a social and cultural contest rather than anything significantly to do with core personal identity. Hiding your *Daily Mail* from so-called radical colleagues or your *Heat* magazine from your college tutor are merely physical versions of the little deceits we indulge in every day in the arena of self-presentation.

Figure 6.12 Our real favourite magazines may be hidden under more acceptable publications

Having read Chapter 2, you will now have 'cultural capital' to add to 'street credibility' when it comes to the issue of the values of cultural products and practices. The credibility that cultural capital gives you is far less immediate and exciting than 'street cred' but it is likely to be longer-lasting and more beneficial. It marks out those who are educated and/or have access to respected knowledge and wisdom. It heavily privileges the practices of the upper and middle classes and ignores the equivalent working-class practices. It can be acquired through education (as can the ability to fake it) and it still defines pretty much what we understand as 'cultured' in the way that 'beer', 'bingo' and 'tattoos' define somebody uncultured and uncouth.

INFORMATION BOX – CULTURAL CAPITAL

The idea that knowledge of certain topics can confer similar benefits to monetary wealth. People who possess lots of money and wealth have *economic capital*. Those who are able to converse knowledgeably about (say) philosophy, music, art or literature have *cultural capital*. We could also extend the concept to the realm of expert knowledge in subcultural groups: *subcultural capital*.

ACTIVITY

The final activity of this subsection has a number of stages since it is attempting to remind you how complex an issue taste is. The table on page 204 has five columns in which you are invited to record a number of different kinds of responses to a simple taste test.

Having answered each question in the 'first answer' column, you are asked to rate your answer (marks out of 10) in terms of its honesty, street credibility and cultural capital.

continued

Question: what is your favourite . . .?	First Answer	Truth Quotient	Street Cred	Cultural Capital	Better Answer
Opera					
Ballet					
Novel					
Play					
Film					
TV programme (now)					
TV programme (all time)					
Film genre					
TV genre					
Artist (visual)					
Artist (musical)					
Album					
Song					

AS COMMUNICATION AND CULTURE: THE ESSENTIAL INTRODUCTION

Sixteen, clumsy and shy – that's the story of my life: life narratives

One of the essential ingredients in any coherent and effective personal identity is its guiding narratives, the stories we tell about ourselves which help explain who we are and where we've been. These stories are first told to and for yourself as a crucial part of your negotiation of your identities. Invariably these narratives are shot through with psychological material: thoughts, feelings and memories. Without a guiding narrative, or set of stories, we would all be overwhelmed by incoherence.

ACTIVITY

Recent research has suggested that those events we identify as our earliest memories are more often than not constructed from accounts given to us by our 'nearest and dearest'. Try to think of your earliest memory and tell it to another person. What story characteristics does your memory have? How sure are you that this is how you remember it?

Now recall something that happened yesterday and tell your partner about it. What differences do you notice?

Perhaps the difference between these two sorts of memories is akin to the difference between documentary and feature films. One tries largely to accurately recall an event whilst the other, using the techniques of storytelling, attempts to make sense of those events. Sometimes it seems that this is what committing to memory really means: restructuring experiences into narrative forms so they might be stored and so might continue to be effective. Thus they become what are called in character-based dramas, 'backstories': important contexts in which characters operate. Creating your backstory is essential to the process of negotiating your identity since it provides roots, foundations, depth. What is being assigned here is significance; we're in the process of giving our lived experience some kind of structure and priority. At the same time we're listening to the competing and complementary models offered by our families and friends (and some extent the residual evidence). The stories told about us are as important as the stories told by us.

To some extent when we consider the prominent members of our peer group or class group, for example, at secondary school, they are those people who have the most stories associated with them. Whatever designation they have achieved (class clown, nerd, rebel or Mr/Ms Popularity), these all come with the accumulated evidence of significant events, recorded and embellished (developed) by their telling. This is why, even now, the stories of Year Nine are available for the retelling: they are structured to a degree that is clearly beyond the scope of individual memory.

There are clearly ways in which this cannot be a single reminiscence; it is rather an accumulation of all the informal (and relatively unreliable) eyewitness accounts which have created a kind of myth to some of those involved. The need to record and exaggerate the drama of the occasion has probably informed the narrative, but there are also perhaps shades of Lindsay Anderson's 1968 film *If*, where schoolboys get guns and ambush their teachers. In the media-saturated world we live in all perception is to some extent coloured by these bigger stories.

ACTIVITY

High school musical

Think about some of the key shared stories of your secondary school years. You may find it easiest to track these by the significant characters of your school life. Find a character and a story and then consider what the story has to say about the character or what the story does or did for the character?

The word 'character' is a telling one and exactly the word we use about those who attract stories. It is also tempting to see ourselves as characters in the drama of everyday life, on what Shakespeare described as 'this great stage of fools'. However, perhaps he nailed it better (and more famously) in *As You Like It*:

> All the world's a stage
> And all the men and women merely players:
> They have their exits and entrances;
> And one man in his time plays many parts,
> His acts being seven ages.

Shakespeare goes on to detail the roles we might play in a lifetime. Modern communication theorists have concentrated on the roles you might play in the course of a week: daughter, student or friend. Goffman, whose dramaturgical model (see Chapter 3) enables a significant analysis to take place, took Shakespeare's dictum as a starting point: 'all the world is not, of course, a stage', he said, but adds, 'the crucial ways in which it is not are not easy to specify'.

Communication for Goffman is pitching our different selves (personae) into different contexts (teams, roles) with differing degrees of intention (performance) and skill (staging). In other words being yourself means acting yourself with a dash of personal style to celebrate the individual, though this is the least important component. This at least has a face validity for surely that is our experience of playing roles and the reason why we often experience 'role conflict' when these roles collide.

ACTIVITY

The three common teenage roles below are often prone to conflict. Consider the differences between them as:

- parts to play
- the different kinds of stories told through them and about them
- the degree to which each is scripted (the degree to which you know the role and how to play it in advance).

The roles:

- Son/daughter
- Boyfriend/girlfriend
- Student.

If we are actors playing ourselves in the stories of our own lives, even symbolically, then the question remains as to the identity of the playwright. Some will obviously answer this question metaphysically with answers such as 'Fate', 'Destiny' and 'God'. However, when you get to look at the process up close, a far greater influence seems to come from the social and cultural context. When we are playing the roles we've taken and been given, we're very aware of the expectations which other people have of us in these roles, which will often leave little room for ad libbing, playing it entirely our own way. Where the archetype is very strong and clear, this is a largely an unproblematic process: childhood, for example, offers clear guidelines, its meaning is socially constructed; a collective rather than individual effort. Conversely with a problematic subject such as sexuality, which is far less clearly designated, the script is less secure, more is left to chance. This is further evidenced if we return to the stories we tell. Childhoods which don't provide a set of affirming stories are likely to have been dysfunctional, traumatic and unhappy. The taboo nature of sexuality means this natural recording of new experience is heavily suppressed: there is largely no place for your 'first experience of masturbation' story.

This leads to a different sort of story being manufactured out of desperation and ignorance which claims or denies sexual experience and is necessarily generic rather than particular. The male and female versions of these tales (stories told for a particular purpose) are different but in both cases they are unreliable witness statements rather than fantasies, attempts to sign up to an area of adult life that they only vaguely understand.

It is not surprising that in this bungled semi-silence we place our faith in the sources which do at least provide us with stories. This means we're left to negotiate between the tales of teenage bravado mentioned above ('I did it five times last night') and an increasingly sexualised mass media. In this context we are faced with either the exploitative sexual gymnastics (disturbingly emotionless) or the slick balletic efficiency of, for example, the mainstream Hollywood film where the unbelievably good-looking characters effortlessly pleasure one another in a variety of physically demanding positions which always work. These are not stories which help to mediate our own; instead they encourage us to imagine that our own insecurities and inefficiencies are merely our own, and that to survive we'll need to get some better sex or, failing that, better stories.

Does the body rule the mind or does the mind rule the body? How we look and who we are

Central to our consideration of identity must be an examination of the ways in which we handle and manipulate our physical appearance. This covers a wide range of issues from physique and body image to body modification to hairstyle and bodily adornment but there are a number of prevailing themes. One is the constant tension between what we are given by genes or gods and what we try to do with it and what this tells us about who we are and who we want to be. Another is the issue of who we are appearing for, particularly in the context of broader influences on the way we look.

Figure 6.13 Why must our dressing, as children or adults, be witnessed at least by ourselves in the mirror?

Sociologist Georg Simmel, writing in the early years of the twentieth century, specifically about adornment, was in no doubt about the answer to the second question. 'One adorns oneself for oneself', he wrote, adding, 'but can only do so by adornment for others' (1908). Simmel is acutely aware that appearance implies an audience of at least one and that to be the audience for one's own appearance is often to stand as substitute for the view of others (often significant others) Why else must our dressing, as children or adults, be witnessed at least by ourselves? Whether you are playing tennis racket lead guitar or wearing your mother's clothes (either gender!) you need to see. Mirrors are essential to contemporary existence; without them we would have no idea of who we are.

ACTIVITY

Mirrors

Mirrors appear with great frequency in feature films. Can you think of any examples? Why do film directors use mirrors so often?

List the circumstances in which you would use a mirror in the course of an average day.

How do you react when you catch sight of your reflection, perhaps in a shop window?

Figure 6.14
Why do so many films use mirrors as metaphors for identity? Poster for *The Mirror Crack'd*, 1980

What we're seeing is partly the impression we are hoping to make on others, which means a strange combination of criticism and presentation. At the same time mirrors always give us the simplest, you might say crudest, model of identity – for the reflection *is* our appearance. Whatever else we see, we certainly see that which we recognise as 'us', at least at the level where recognition is possible. This is not a profound experience nor is it unique. In recognising an image as 'who we are', we are sharing in a collective experience, since what we are seeing and saying is exactly what others are seeing and saying when they see us.

Without labouring this point, the issue here is the issue of representation. Seduced by the photographic quality of mirror images, we mistake image for reality, forgetting even that mirrors show everything back to front. Only when we see some significant physical change (and ageing is a particular culprit here) do we begin to think about who we are in this sense. Again this is equivalent to seeing a friend after perhaps a long time and not recognising them. In fact sometimes there's almost a kind of denial: 'That's not . . . it can't be!'

There is enough focus on body image in the media to give us the hint that 'appearance' may not be the most consistent or reliable index of identity whether it be the debate around size zero or reality shows entitled *Can Fat Teens Hunt?* We read a lot about the pressure put on young people (particularly girls) to look a certain way and yet obesity is reaching epidemic proportions. It seems likely that the ideal body image is a good deal more complex than a matter of conforming to society's ideals. However, it is equally clear that for those of us who want to change who we are (for whatever reason) the surface of the body is the easiest place to start. The question is to what extent the progression from 'make-up' via 'makeover' to 'total makeover' is a natural or inevitable process.

ACTIVITY

Body modification

Rate the following ways of modifying your physical appearance in terms of a) impact (what difference it might make on a 1–5 scale), and b) intensity (what this might say about your desire to improve your physical appearance; score – 'low', 'moderate', 'high'). Cosmetic surgery would in this way be a high-intensity activity with a range of potential impacts. Gender is inevitably a factor.

- Washing and moisturising
- Generally grooming head and shaving
- Styling hair

continued

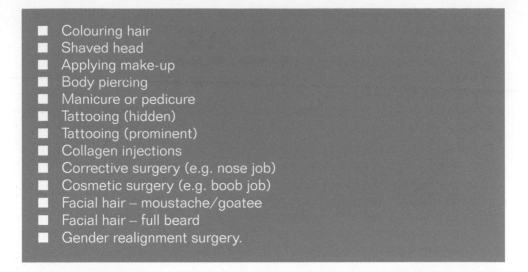

- Colouring hair
- Shaved head
- Applying make-up
- Body piercing
- Manicure or pedicure
- Tattooing (hidden)
- Tattooing (prominent)
- Collagen injections
- Corrective surgery (e.g. nose job)
- Cosmetic surgery (e.g. boob job)
- Facial hair – moustache/goatee
- Facial hair – full beard
- Gender realignment surgery.

The real purpose of this activity is to get you to think about the place that body modifications start, since we're all pretty aware of where it ends. The list you've worked through describes the processes into which we all invest some time but to which most of us also have well-defined positions. We know, at least in theory where we personally draw the line, though often the function of these positions is to make any further progress beyond the line more difficult. The positions we take up and the reasons we give for these positions are especially revealing of the processes implicit in the building and maintaining of healthy sustainable identities and self-concepts.

In the age of the total makeover we're being constantly addressed by the real possibility that we can feasibly change the hand we've been dealt by the genetic lottery. This is a rapidly changing landscape. Only a short time ago substantial cosmetic surgery was an option for only the super-rich or significantly crazed; moreover it was dangerous and, in aesthetic terms, relatively unsuccessful.

ESSENTIAL ARCHIVE

The presence in the market of those who saved up for fifty-plus years to make themselves into Barbie and Ken also means that this issue is kept at a comfortable distance. Consider the story of the Lizard Man from *Communication Studies: The Essential Resource*. What does it say about ideal bodily image?

Figure 6.15 Freak-show performer Eric 'Lizard Man' Sprague

The Lizard Man's story reminds us of the importance of imagination and notions of identity and the dangers of too much: it is clearly to most of us a bad/strange/ludicrous (delete as applicable) idea to want to look like a lizard. However, the contemporary context and a future that promises that anything is possible is asking very different things. If we can get the faces and bodies we want for very little pain and loss, tell me could we? Would we?

The intellectual and perhaps moral bits of us are having none of this and the principles of the argument flow very naturally. The psychological wisdom argues the cosmetic solutions to your problems of self-loathing are unlikely to get to the real problems. Coming to terms with imperfection is an essential part of being human, add the philosophers, while the sociologists remind us that we must not surrender to ideological pressures to conform. Add to this the vanity of not wanting to appear vain, the impossibility of justifying the expense and the simple fear of pain and you have a pretty impressive defence. Also, as the emblematic body modification is a lap dancer's breast augmentation, it is easy to stand back and deride the superficiality of it all.

'Is beauty only to be skin deep?' we ask from our superior positions of those who appear to opt for the knife ahead of real self-knowledge. However, beauty is also proverbially in the eye of the beholder and, as we've suggested, the beholder is also the beholden. Physical attractiveness is one of most difficult issues to seriously analyse within the study of Communication and Culture because it is so sensitive and so central to self-esteem. Yet it is also one of the most significant, since being attractive makes you a more effective communicator; the issue of course, is establishing what being attractive means. Crucially the arguments are compromised by our inability to express our own positions within a flexible paradigm that contains all participants. In simple terms, talking about beauty means drawing down the issue of your own beauty that in turn becomes a contaminating factor. It may be inevitable that the objectively gorgeous want to be known for something other than merely looks, while those of us who lack universal gorgeousness crave the superficiality of such a response, but in between the cliché there's something more than intellectual going on. Perhaps Thom Yorke expressed it best when he wrote:

> When you were here before
> Couldn't look you in the eye
> You're just like an angel
> Your skin makes me cry
> You float like a feather
> In a beautiful world
> I wish I was special
> You're so fucking special
>
> But I'm a creep
> I'm a weirdo
> What the hell am I doing here?
> I don't belong here

I don't care if it hurts
I want to have control
I want a perfect body
I want a perfect soul
I want you to notice when I'm not around
You're so fucking special
I wish I was special

But I'm a creep
I'm a weirdo
What the hell I'm doing here?
I don't belong here
                    (Radiohead: 'Creep')

For those of you whose skin makes others cry I suspect the rest of the subsection is an academic exercise. For the rest of us, modified or unmodified, the trick is in the dressing, the adornment. Adornment covers all the different ways we dress the body from warpaint through crowns and medallions to T-shirt and shorts. Simmel is very clear on its collective and particular function: 'the meaning is to single the personality out, to emphasize it as outstanding in some sense . . . adornment intensifies or enlarges the impression of the personality' (1908). It is this 'amplification' of the personality that is our focus here, though clearly adornment is a set of cultural codes which regulate a conventional set of meanings. All our attempts to amplify the impression of our individual identities are going to be made within these dominant contexts.

Reg Dwight (whose first act of significant 'enlargement' was to adapt the pseudo-nym Elton John) allegedly took to wearing black-rimmed glasses in homage to Roy Orbison rather than as a result of poor eyesight. Since then, and after the subsequent deterioration of his vision, he has spent forty years using an unimaginable variety of spectacles as an index of his larger-than-life personality (or is that persona/stage image?).

INFORMATION BOX – ADORNMENT AND SELF-PRESENTATION

Adornment addresses the six elements that Goffman suggests constitute self-presentation. We adorn our various personae, the versions of ourselves that we deploy and employ to fulfil the roles we have to play both sincerely and cynically. At the same time adornment is essential to the staging and membership of the teams in which we communicate. All this is in addition to the intensification of the impression that personal style might make.

Glasses are an interesting case study since you might instead opt for contact lenses and pass up the chance to make a public statement often in favour of a private one. Surely the most popular reason for wearing contacts is that they are not glasses and as such say little or nothing beyond 'I lack perfect eyesight'. Glasses, at the very least have much more to say than this. Glasses of course have impact which derives from their position, right in the centre of the face. They might be an enforced and unwanted addition to your facial appearance but once installed they're going to be some kind of low-level index of who you are. In other words, a description of you is unlikely to miss them out and were you to be abducted from your classroom by aliens, throwing down your glasses would be sufficient evidence to your friends to know exactly who they'd taken. This is not necessarily the best advice though, since throwing them down would leave you less able to see!

Choosing the right glasses is more important than choosing the right clothes, since unless you are able to have a range of pairs for different occasions and moods, they are going to be a permanent part of your appearance. This puts a good deal of pressure on anyone whose visit to an optician suggests a prescription for lenses (which is not really the point since lenses need frames and that is where the choice lies). The frame is an appropriate metaphor since that's what's going on in and around your face and in most cases the choice is overwhelming. Here is a classic paradigm, a set of significant choices, where only one crucial selection is possible and where selection automatically deselects all other possibilities. Beyond extreme forms of cosmetic or corrective surgery or the addition of facial tattooing it is hard to imagine a situation in which we are more significantly making ourselves, participating in our own representation. As we try out the 'candidates', having already rejected 70 per cent out of hand, we are measuring the degree to which what looks back is that mixture of who we are and who would like to be. In doing so we are at the same time aware of certain kinds of contexts and conventions through which glasses are understood. These are partly generic meanings or stereotypes which Barthes might have called 'myths' (see Chapter 4), such as the association of glasses with being intellectual. At the same time, there are styles which have associations (are indexes of) with particular individuals. A whole generation, for example, was influenced by Beatle John Lennon's decision to sport a version of the simple round frames which were the standard NHS issue of the period, the frames you were issued with if you couldn't afford to choose. There is still a style statement made by the objectively gorgeous (discussed earlier) choosing frames that clash with rather than complement their beauty.

ACTIVITY

The frame game

Figure 6.16 a) teenage boy, b) young woman, c) middle-aged man

Figure 6.17
Different kinds of glasses
say different things about
a person

Consider the ways in which the frame choices above might enlarge or intensify your personality. Which would you choose? Rank them from most likely to least likely and comment on the potential meanings of each both for yourself and more generally.

continued

Now consider the three faces in Figure 6.16. Imagine that they are faces of three extras employed to be used in a major TV production. It is your job to name and costume them for non-speaking roles in and around the main action. Using the frames, offer two contrasting character outlines (including names) for each of the actors pictured.

Having said earlier that when it comes to glasses, lenses are not really the point is a little misleading since tinting the lenses almost certainly changes the meaning as it changes the outlook of the wearer and the perceptions of others. The vast majority of us play this game in the summer or, if shades are an essential part of your rock persona, all year round, when we put on a pair of sunglasses. It's interesting to consider the differences between these two varieties of frames, one of which tends to suggest bookishness and the other the essence of cool. Shading our eyes from the sun might appear pragmatically just as important as correcting impairments of vision but representationally (symbolically) they seem very different. Sunglasses perform very much like other items of clothing in that they often function as part of larger syntagms, or sign chains. They're also more obviously contextualised, either naturally by holidays and sun or artificially by celebrity desire for anonymity at press conferences (or by our desire to imitate such behaviour). In other words, their meaning is more significantly culturally constructed and there's little if any room for genuinely personal expression.

ACTIVITY

Spectacles and shades

Collect images of people in frames and use them to compare the range of meanings generated by spectacles and shades respectively.

When Georg Simmel wrote on adornment he was principally concerned with jewellery and the use of precious metals and precious stones. In doing so he was keen to emphasise the links between contemporary cultural practices (early twentieth century) and those of ancient tribal societies. He particularly wanted to emphasise the use of precious materials in both these contexts as part of the intensification and enlargement ritual. Again this prompts an interesting example since little is written about what is, at both ends of the market, a multi-million-pound industry. Jewellery is interesting because it is not functional, it doesn't do anything but adorn, a quality which sets it one step more removed from even the most fashionable clothing. As such it displays a gender bias, which in itself carries ideological values. As John Berger suggested: 'men look at women. Women watch themselves being looked at. This determines not only most relations between men and women but also the relation of women to themselves' (1972, p. 45).

It may be no longer true to say that those who wear earrings are either women or pirates but male jewellery remains a limited paradigm of limited meanings whereas women have walls full of designs to choose from in any jeweller's or shops that specialise in 'accessories'. What is all this gold and silver stuff for? Are diamonds really a girl's best friend?

ACTIVITY

All that glitters is not gold

Consider the meanings generated by the items below. In doing so it will be useful to address the following questions:

- Where are they worn?
- What variations are there? (size, design, material)
- Is there a symbolic function? (e.g. wedding rings represent 'union 'and 'eternity')

Consider these questions for each of these items:

- Rings
- Earrings
- Bracelets
- Piercings
- Necklaces/pendants.

Now put what you have discovered alongside this passage from Simmel.

ESSENTIAL ARCHIVE

Simmel: on adornment

Adornment intensifies or enlarges the impression of the personality by operating as a sort of radiation emanating from it. For this reason, its materials have always been shining metals and precious stones. They are 'adornment' in a narrower sense than dress and coiffure, although these, too, 'adorn'. One may speak of human radioactivity in the sense that every individual is surrounded by a larger or smaller sphere of significance radiating from him; and everybody else who deals with him is immersed in this sphere. It is an inextricable mixture of physiological and psychic elements: the sensuously observable influences which issue from an individual in the direction of his environment also are, in some fashion, the vehicles of spiritual fulguration. They operate as the symbols of such a fulguration even where, in actuality, they are only external, where no suggestive power or significance of the personality flows through them. The radiations of adornment, the sensuous attention it provokes, supply the personality with such an enlargement or intensification of its sphere; the personality, so to speak, *is* more when it is adorned.

Inasmuch as adornment usually is also an object of considerable value, it is a synthesis of the individual's having and being; it thus transforms mere possession into the sensuous and emphatic perceivability of the individual himself. This is not true of ordinary dress which, neither in respect of having nor of being, strikes one as an individual particularity; only the fancy dress, and above all jewels, which gather the personality's value and significance of radiation as if in a focal point, allow the mere *having* of the person to become a visible quality of its *being*. And this is so, not *although* adornment is something superfluous, but precisely *because* it is so. The necessary is much more closely connected with the individual; it surrounds his existence with a narrower periphery. The superfluous 'flows over', that is, it flows to points which are far removed from its origin but to which it still remains tied: around the precinct of mere necessity, it lays a vaster precinct which, in principle, is limitless. According to its very idea, the superfluous contains no measure. The free and princely character of our being increases in the measure in which we add superfluousness to our having, since no extant structure, such as is laid down by necessity, imposes any limiting norm upon it.

Of course, the meanings of these objects, like everything else in this chapter, are negotiated in the broader cultural contexts and anyway it is an issue to decide when adornment stops and accessories start. However, what is clear is that with what we have and hold not only makes significant statements about us as individuals but is also an important way we build identities and achieve personhood. What we own will carry this home.

Everything I own: what you have and who you are

In 'Imagine', a song often voted an all-time 'favourite', John Lennon asks us to 'imagine no possessions' and adds 'it's easy if you try'. Actually the difficulty of having no possessions does not so much lie, as Lennon implies, in the greed for things and the need to have more than others, but rather in the relationship between our most prized possessions and who we are. We use cultural products as a way to make statements about ourselves – certainly to other people but just as importantly to ourselves. These may be things which we've had for a long time and have sentimental value or things we're preparing to buy anew. The fact is that some things acquire a kind of indexical significance, they become more than statements about you rather they become *part* of you, a component of your identity.

This is relatively easy to demonstrate if we look to the larger-than-life (and less real) celebrity identities constructed by and for the talented and lucky. Reg Dwight's alter ego Elton John, whose glasses were deemed indexical of the man just a few pages ago, is a point in question. Like most musicians his instrument is a key index of his identity, not as 'show' but as 'essence'. The point is that all of us have significant objects which are partly drawn from all the previous categories and beyond: books, DVDs, (records), items of clothing, technological devices or jewellery. Some of these items have stories attached to them, such as Billy Elliot's letter from his dead mother in the film about the boy ballet dancer. Others are simply things that are an important part of how we see ourselves. Some of these look forward, others look back, some are aspirational, such as the model of the car you one day want to own, others are more realistic.

There's already been some discussion in this book of technology and of your personal kit. To some extent this was a discussion about how your kit affected your status and esteem. Here we're more concerned with the degree to which certain items of technology are important in defining who you are. At the same time we are interested in the ways in which your choice of technologies negotiates your relationship with contemporary life and thus defines you within it. This is not only about partaking but also about abstaining. Refusing to invest in the next new-wave mobile for example is going to have a significant impact on how you communicate yourself (in both senses). Here the item becomes a focus for negotiations of who you are and who you want to be.

These negotiations are also evident when it comes to owning your first car. The fact that so many people get very attached to and associated with their cars is interesting, given that few of us are lucky enough to have free choice in this matter. In other words, our fantasy ideal might be a Ferrari on Maserati but we soon associate ourselves with the Clio or Fiesta that we can afford. This is partly a process whereby the significant item is 'installed' within the frame of identity by being given new and personal meanings. Because of the general aforementioned lack of ultimate choice we need to assimilate the car we can afford. We do this by personalising it at the point of purchase or beyond it. For example, we may choose colour rather than style and add significant accessories to impose our personalities on this machine.

ACTIVITY

I'm in love with my car

Think about the ways in which people personalise their cars both inside and outside and by the ways in which they talk about them. What meanings do we assign to our cars and how do they contrast with the broader cultural associations?

Romeo turns sporty

Giles Smith
Saturday December 23, 2006
The Guardian

Alfa Romeo 159 Sportwagon 1.9 JTD
Price £21,495
Top speed 129mph
Acceleration 0–62 in 9.6 seconds
Consumption 46.3mpg (combined)
Eco rating 6/10
At the wheel Gianluca Vialli
Top gadget Start button
In a word Italian

You can tick off all the traditional Alfa Romeo signifiers on the new Alfa Romeo 159 Sportwagon. Like the fact that it's called a Sportwagon, for instance. (You or I would probably say estate.) Does it have macho, stainless-steel trimmings all over the place? Of course. Style to burn? Naturally. Italian words ('acqua', 'olio') on the dials? Goes without saying. Offset numberplate? Does the Pope have a balcony? Alfa Romeo products are nothing if not fiercely protective of their authentic Italian flavour. How it must pain them to fit these cars for right-hand drive. How it must pain them, also, to build estate cars. You can imagine the order coming down from on high and a cringing design and marketing team asking, 'Must we?'

Hence the euphemistic term 'Sportwagon', hinting at a life of skiing, parascending and reckless amounts of outdoor eating in Europe's most vibrant shoreline destinations, as opposed to the term 'estate', which merely speaks of puzzling levels of domestic encumbrance and spirit-taxing trips around the North Circular to IKEA.

And hence the way the 159 hunkers down, low and compact, behind its sleek row of headlamps and the Lord Of The Rings-style breastplate that constitutes its radiator grille. The whole package shrieks that this is a sporty hatchback merely pretending to be an estate under duress and because somebody told it to.

Still, at least it's long enough to incorporate a ski-hatch – a trapdoor-style opening between the boot and the back seats through which you can poke your skis. A ski-hatch! Does any other car accessory more mournfully taunt the British driver with the life unlived? How many people are there in Britain who drive to skiing facilities? And of those people, how many take skis with them, rather than hire them when they get there? Answer: four. Yet those four people get to choose from something like 25 different models of car currently on the UK market with ski-hatches.

Laden with skis or not, most estates corner like trailer-bearing tractors during harvest. The 159, on the other hand, is cunningly girded with structural enhancements, including an 'all-new premium floorpan' that turns out not to be a novelty pizza, but the steel foundation underlying the car's mission to sail rigidly through anything the road throws in its path. And, true enough, the 159 glues itself to the road and burns round the bends, leaving in its trail only dust and a dark tang of aftershave.

But where are you going to put the plastic water butt? Because it stands to reason, surely, that if you're in the market for an estate car, then at some time in the near future you are going to find yourself moving a plastic water butt. Isn't the carriage of plastic water butts, or similar gardenware, ultimately what owning an estate car is all about?

You'll struggle to get a plastic water butt in a Sportwagon, though. Let me rephrase that, lest someone interpret it as a challenge – you'll struggle to feel that a Sportwagon is an appropriate place in which to insert a plastic water butt. Unless, of course, it's a compact, chic, beautifully crafted, Italian plastic water butt.

(Source: http://shopping.guardian.co.uk/motoring/story/0,,1985574,00.html)

ACTIVITY

The clear implication of Giles Smith's review is that this car would be chosen by a driver who wanted to project a particular sort of identity. How would you sum up that identity?

We will return in the next chapter to 'Wheels' as part of a discussion about the ways in which we get around. These cultural contexts and practices are, as we said at the start of this chapter, significant places in which our individual negotiations of identity must take place. In the intersections of self and society, of who we want to be and of who we can be is the struggle for identity. Raymond Williams spoke of a similar struggle being at the heart of all communication:

> **We need to say what many of us know in experience: that the struggle to learn, to describe, to understand, to educate is a central and necessary part of our humanity. This struggle is not begun, at second hand, after reality has occurred. It is in itself a major way in which reality is formed and changed – Communication begins in the struggle to learn and describe.**

(Williams 1962, p. 11)

References and further reading

Beck, Andrew, Bennett, Peter and Wall, Peter (2004) *Communication Studies: The Essential Resource*, London: Routledge

Bennett, P., Slater, J. and Wall, P. (2006a) *A2 Media Studies: The Essential Introduction*, London: Routledge

Bennett, P., Hickman, A. and Wall, P. (2006b) *Film Studies: The Essential Resource*, London: Routledge

Berger, John (1972) *Ways of Seeing*, Harmondsworth: Penguin

Geertz, Clifford (1973) *The Interpretation of Cultures*, New York: Basic Books

Bernstein, Basil (1971) *Class, Codes and Control*, London: Routledge and Kegan Paul

Gray, Ann and McGuigan, Jim (eds) (1993) *Studying Culture: An Introductory Reader*, London: Edward Arnold

Hebdige, Dick (1979) *Subculture: The Meaning of Style*, London: Methuen

Lillis, T. (2003) 'An 'academic literacies' approach to student writing in higher education: drawing on Bakhtin to move from critique to design', in *Language and Education* 17, 3, pp. 192–207

Simmel, Georg (2004) 'Adornment', in Beck et al., pp. 239–41. First published 1908.

Williams, Raymond (1993)) 'Culture is ordinary', in Gray and McGuigan (eds), pp. 5–14. First published 1958.

Williams, Raymond (1962) *Communications*, Harmondsworth: Penguin.

7 CULTURAL CONTEXT AND PRACTICES

It cannot be stressed enough how indivisible are the two sites covered in Chapters 6 and 7, since 'who we are' (our identities) cannot really be separated from 'where we are' (the cultural contexts in which we operate). However, in order to study culture, to explore it, we will necessarily have to take liberties with it since it constitutes the very fabric of the reality we inhabit. Our emergence as 'cultural beings' is by way of cultural codes and practices. This chapter will be about considering these phenomena as influences on and contexts for our emerging identities. If we are, as Geertz suggests, 'animals suspended in webs of their own making' (see page 189), then let us at least examine the strands that bind us there.

The key to cultural practices, those activities that go together to constitute a culture, into which we must be inducted, is that they contain both conventions and values. In other words, they assume/imply that there are ways to behave (bring up children, conduct relationships, have fun) and ways to think (by taking on a set of implicit values). It is our job to identify and challenge cultural conventions but not in order to denounce them but rather to understand. Above all, the processes of enculturation make us aware of the 'language of the tribe' – the various codes, verbal and visual, through which we express our cultural identities.

The writing on the wall: the significance of signage

In the song 'The Sounds of Silence', Paul Simon wrote that 'the words of the prophet are written on the subway walls and tenement halls'. The song offers a nightmare vision of modern city life where the power of neon advertisements over-whelms the reason of those living there so they are imagined bowing and praying to 'the neon god they made'. Simon's point is about communication, or rather the lack of it, and about the city as a place festooned with language but lacking human contact. The streets of any city are alive with messages both commanding and enticing but this language is disembodied and, in Simon's vision, inhuman. He is in fact overwhelmed by the silence, which 'like a cancer grows' being concerned only to be heard: 'Hear my words that I might reach you'. Just as the loneliness of cities seems worse because there are so many people around so, for Simon, the silence is made deafening by the fact that so much is being said.

A common finding of research into issues surrounding illiteracy and adults is that poor readers, not surprisingly, have little confidence in their abilities and place little value on their reading experiences. Part of this profile is to associate reading as a valuable skill only with reading books and not valuing in any sense the reading we all must do when we're out in the world. Perhaps when we imagine illiteracy we make something of the same mistake: we immediately think of the difficulties it would present for our studies or not being able to read the latest Ian McEwan novel or Harry Potter's final outing. We might then come round to the more immediate need to know what's on the telly tonight or who's been evicted from *Big Brother* or what Jordan/Katie Price decided to call her baby. We are still inhabiting a context where reading is done with and to certain kinds of text in order to yield (and store or use) information. However, there's a far more fundamental and pragmatic reason why literacy is essential since it is the key to our participation in social and cultural life. We move in a world which is image-saturated but which still relies on words to provide anchorage (see p. 126); in other words, to suggest and assign meaning. There is an argument to suggest that being unable to access this vast collection of messages leaves you unable to access social and cultural values and, therefore, unable to participate fully in social and cultural life. It is also a situation that leaves you vulnerable to other kinds of danger, not least physical danger, since one set of messages we find in the world are warning us of something or other. These range from the generic and long-term 'Smoking kills', to the much more immediate 'Don't walk' or 'Please look left'.

The language of the street might still figuratively function as a euphemism (a more tactful way of saying things) for bad language, but language in the street goes so much further than that. There's so much variety in terms of typography, register, function, mode of address, effect or impact. Some of these messages address us all; others turn us into audiences and markets.

ACTIVITY

Reading the street

Try to identify the kinds of message we receive which are attached to or printed/written/painted on the physical environment. Complete the following table by also suggesting senders, target audiences and styles:

continued

Kinds of message	Senders	Target	Function audience	Style

Hopefully, somewhere in your table you have found room for those who scribble in the margins of the built environment (interestingly they seem to operate only on the artificial). You may have called them graffiti artists or vandals or listed both distinctively. You may see them as a essentially the same defacing force or see them as allowing some very different kinds of communication. They are also, whether we like it or not, forms of personal expression from 'I love Marge' to the extravagantly coloured images which decorate underpasses and the walls that back onto railway lines. Of course the language 'in the street' is sometimes the language 'of the street'. Daubed obscenities stand towards one end of a continuum of public languages which also includes the formal, ceremonial registers of public memorials. The very fact that we are talking (and let's be fair *thinking*) in hierarchical terms about this language should usefully remind us that language is a cultural institution which contains the values of the 'tribe'. A trip down the high street will confirm this just as clearly as a trip to the library.

This range of public language and the ways in which people take language into their own hands are central to Tony Harrison's controversial poem *V*. Written in the mid-1980s and filmed and broadcast by Channel 4 in 1987 to much acclaim and condemnation, the poem was written as a response to the defacing of the grave of Harrison's parents with sprayed obscenities. The controversy was caused by Harrison's straightforward quoting of the obscenity, thus symbolically defacing the poem which is consciously written in a traditional poetic form to emphasise the contrast. If we want to understand how language works in public, Harrison's poem is a fine place to start since it seriously addresses the relevant issues: identity, power and context.

Figuro 7.1 Graffiti

Harrison leads us from a metrically engaging description of the language of the graveyard – a classically constructed environment endowed with cultural significance – to a consideration of why we need to carve our names and messages anywhere. The language of the graveyard he describes thus:

> The language of this graveyard ranges from
> a bit of Latin for a former Mayor
> or those who laid their lives down at the Somme,
> the hymnal fragments and the gilded prayer,
>
> how people 'fell asleep in the Good Lord',
> brief chisellable bits from the good book
> and rhymes whatever length they could afford,
> to CUNT, PISS, SHIT and (mostly) FUCK!

He then moves on to imaginatively consider the perpetrator whom he somewhat stereotypically dramatises as a skinhead armed with a spray can. He asks with feeling:

What is it that these crude words are revealing?
what is it that this aggro act implies?

In the previous chapter when we considered idiolect, we stated that language is never neutral. Harrison addresses this by contrasting a whole range of uses of language to create a personal impression, not least of his own name 'seen on books, in Broadway lights'. If he can make such a public display with language, then 'why can't skins with spray cans do the same?' he asks.

ACTIVITY

Graffiti: free expression on public sites?

How would you discriminate between vandalism and graffiti? (Or wouldn't you?) What rights should people have to 'write' on the world? What are the rules like at this moment for deciding whether you can put your message up? Does giving people walls to write on change the nature and status of what is written?

Harrison wants us to believe that there is some important connection between the creative writer (poet) and the vandal. In a brilliant imagined dialogue between Harrison and the skin, he plays out the arguments about the public functions of language in language designed to have a public function. In short, Harrison says he is writing this in a book to give the skin 'a hearing' to which the skin bluntly responds:

'a book, yer stupid cunt's not worth a fuck'

Reading this book you might agree or equally you might be profoundly offended. However, as a student of Communication and Culture, you must also concede that language creates its own contexts and those contexts are laden with values. The two words which will most likely cause offence in the skin's line actually communicate certain unease about sexuality and, more disturbingly, a contemptuous attitude towards women and their bodies. This is not where Harrison goes. He wants to find a poetry (in the romantic sense as 'an overflow of human emotions') in the skin's public outbursts. He does this first by suggesting a context but also a skill with an aerosol can.

Vs sprayed on the run at such a lick,
the sprayer master of his flourished tool,
get short-armed on the left like that red tick
they never marked his work with much at school.

Harrison, whose magic also is achieved by penmanship ('this pen's all I have of magic wand') then takes the skin on in a debate about what should be written and where (function and context). The skin is unimpressed, concluding:

Who needs
yer fucking poufy words. Ah write mi own.
Ah've got mi work on show all ovver Leeds
like this UNITED 'ere on some sod's stone.

'Ah write mi own' is a key sentence here in every sense: in its meaning, in its impact, in its dialect form. The language of public places is a language of public senders, the language of hierarchy, of advertisement. Graffiti challenges this order by colonising space often anonymously. The climax of Harrison's poem is the poet's final challenge to the skin: 'If you're so proud of it then sign your name.' It may be, as we suggested, that anonymity is an important part of genuine street communication but Harrison has other points to make. The punch when it comes is hard and clear:

He took the can, contemptuous, unhurried
and cleared the nozzle and prepared to sign
the UNITED sprayed where mam and dad were buried.
He aerosolled his name. And it was mine.

Harrison's poem is a moving and compassionate plea for greater understanding about a universal need to express ourselves but it is also a study in the power of language and the relationships between language and power. It is prefaced by a quotation from then National Union of Mineworkers leader Arthur Scargill:

> **My father still reads the dictionary every day. He says your life depends on your power to master words.**

In terms of signage 'the power to master words' takes on a slightly different emphasis since often the power is economic. The street is above all a marketplace and signage is mostly concerned with advertising in the simplest sense of telling us what is there. However, with this telling come the values of the society which wants to buy and sell things (and those things include us as consumers). The economist J. K. Galbraith described advertising as 'a relentless propaganda on behalf of goods in general'; in other words, it creates a context in which we are naturally consumers. In the same way the language in which we are addressed by the state defines us as subjects or, if you prefer a more positive take on this, as citizens. This is not about brainwashing but it does identify a significant and largely unexamined way in which cultural norms and values are transmitted. Even to reject the values is in some sense to define yourself in relation to them.

INFORMATION BOX – PHATIC COMMUNICATION

The phatic function of communication is the element that concentrates on making contact so the message might be received. Some communication is largely phatic, coughing when you enter a room to show you've arrived, for example. In a competitive communication context, such as advertising, copywriters and designers seek phatic elements that will put their messages ahead of the rest.

The songs that saved your life: music and lyrics

The phatic element of the promotional pop song is the 'hook', the addictive bit of melody that we all latch on to. Once hooked we're all open to three and a half minutes of profundity, profanity or banality delivered directly into our ears and from there very quickly out of our own mouths. Who can ever forget:

Let me tell you what I want, what I really really want . . .?

Moreover, how else could the following words become part of so many recent weddings? No poem could reach so many people:

I sit and wait
does an angel contemplate my fate

and do they know
the places where we go
when we're grey and old
'cos I've been told
that salvation lets their wings unfold
so when I'm lying in my bed
thoughts running through my head
and I feel that love is dead
I'm loving angels instead

and through it all she offers me protection
a lot of love and affection
whether I'm right or wrong
and down the waterfall
wherever it may take me
I know that life won't break me
when I come to call she won't forsake me
I'm loving angels instead

when I'm feeling weak
and my pain walks down a one-way street
I look above
and I know I'll always be blessed with love
and as the feeling grows
she breathes flesh to my bones
and when love is dead
I'm loving angels instead

and through it all she offers me protection
a lot of love and affection
whether I'm right or wrong
and down the waterfall
wherever it may take me
I know that life won't break me
when I come to call she won't forsake me
I'm loving angels instead.
(Robbie Williams, 'Angels')

Of course, some of you are already offended by this analysis simply because this pop stuff has nothing to do with you. What you like is called rock, indie, metal, soul, r'n'b, rap, garage and so on and your music has all the things that commercial pop lacks: integrity, purpose and individuality. The fact is that pop (originally merely an abbreviation of 'popular music') has become reserved as a title for only the most commercial stuff. Pop is the music which shamefully and unapologetically reminds us that the music industry is one of Britain's biggest. This means necessarily that the insights into love-longing which are contained within a three-and-a-half-minute video download have a sincerity which is bought and sold. This is not a cynical or undermining truth about pop music, it is simply a significant bottom line which creates a sometimes ironic context.

Pop music is a set of cultural practices and contexts which are a vital part of contemporary cultural experience. It is vital in the sense that it is a comparatively recent phenomenon: it dates in its present form from about the same time as the invention of the teenager in the mid-to-late 1950s. This means that pretty much everyone alive in Britain today has grown up with pop music as a significant context and soundtrack to their lives. It also means the first teenagers (for whom that label began to mean something) have lived to official old age (somewhere between 60 and 65) entirely within the life of pop – a period which also saw the rise and fall of vinyl (the single record, or '45' being perhaps pop's most significant cultural product). The speed of technological change is such that the rise and fall of the compact disc is likely to be performed in half the time.

ACTIVITY

Retro rock retrospective

This is an exercise in imaginative reconstruction and is best done in groups of between two and twenty-five. 'Retro' is an often applied label in contemporary music, which is partly an indication that popular music now has a past that can be explored (and plundered) and partly reflects the postmodern 'mix and match' attitudes towards cultural matters. The internet is a magnificent archive in this respect as are your parents' record/CD/cassette collections (which are becoming in some cases worryingly credible). Use your musical experiences and tastes to attempt a plan of fifty years of pop.

Decade	Significant artists	Styles	Function of pop music

Decade	Significant artists	Styles	Function of pop music

History is not what happened in the past but rather the attempts we make to represent and record this. Your version of pop history, however historically and musically inaccurate, is still going to provide a defining context for your music messages and meanings. Some of the messages are generic, emerging from the numerous musical subsets from metal to rap. Others appear to be thematic, forming defining principles of this most accessible and popular art form. These are lyrically to do with 'being young' and 'being in love' and 'rebelling': important issues all of them. In this socialising role, pop music may be seen in a much more direct way than television to be exercising what Fiske and Hartley described as a bardic function – singing the key songs of the tribe.

INFORMATION BOX – BARDIC FUNCTION *i*

Bards were the poets and minstrels of their day. They translated the everyday cultural concerns of the Middle Ages into verse. In their book *Reading Television* (1990), Fiske and Hartley argue that television plays a similar role today. Television has its own specialised language and it helps to define reality for us, reinforcing the dominant myths of our culture. The idea of the bardic function stresses continuity; television is playing a role that has always been played.

The idea that pop music also (or even more significantly) delivers this bardic function is attractive on a number of levels. The relationship between the performers and their audience, particularly in the context of large events, does seem at times quasi-religious. Ultimately, a pop concert is a kind of communion which reaches its climax when band and crowd come together for the singing of the anthem. There is also a well-ploughed furrow of pop devoted to the shamanistic nature of the pop artist which is inextricably linked to the use of mind-expanding substances. This chemical romance for some produces the intensity of experience which pop craves, offering inspiration as a way to break on through to the other side.

Shamans are tribal witch doctors who use natural substances (narcotics) to reach states of inspiration in which they claim to be able to communicate with the gods. The drug-fuelled excesses of rock star lifestyles have often been put down to the need to get beyond conventional experience. The writer Aldous Huxley, who experimented with LSD (acid) for this very reason, called this 'cleansing the doors of perception' and in doing so unwittingly provided a name for perhaps the most shamanistic band of all: the Doors. Led by the charismatic master of excess, Jim Morrison, the Doors blazed a trail across America in the late 1960s. Morrison dubbed them 'erotic politicians' and their concerts 'ceremonies'. These ceremonies, which were much more (and less) than concerts, ended abruptly in 1970 in Miami when Morrison was arrested for allegedly exposing himself on stage. His temporary exile in Paris became permanent in July 1971 when he was found dead in the bath following a suspected (but mysterious and debated) overdose.

Figure 7.2 Jim Morrison – showman and shaman

Morrison may have been the ultimate shaman and showman, a rock poet who appealed to both highbrow and lowbrow audiences but his story is a standard rock narrative. Rock casualties are very much a part of the territory: the special ones who live fast and die young so that we don't have to. The meanings are very clear here: it is a classic Faustian pact with the devil. In exchange for the fifteen minutes of what Morrissey called 'fame, fame, fatal fame', they agree to a symbolic suicide which results in either death or obscurity (and sometimes both). If the death is physical, the chances of an afterlife are stronger. If not, there is just a slow decline into 'has been' talent shows or TV gardening programmes. Of course, there's still the money but in so many ways there's never enough.

These symbolic narratives make coded statements about the values of both the music industry and the wider society. The music and lyrics (even the videos) are also significant stores of cultural information whether they're 'about something' or not. They are a record of a period of significant social change, the period in which young people found their voice for the first time. One of the things that popular music does very effectively is to create a sense of time, to make us aware of where we were and what we were doing. It also gives us access to clues about the spirit and character of times we did not ourselves experience.

Music is an important part of any TV drama or film not only for creating the mood and dramatic effect but also for recreating the zeitgeist or spirit of the age. This is often referenced at two levels, both within the action (technically called diegetic sound since it is part of the diegesis or presentation of the story) and as an artificial unheard element of the soundtrack (non-diegetic since it is sealed off from the world of the narrative). The immense popularity of iPods and other MP3 players which have rendered that iconic piece of 1980s technology, the Sony Walkman, obsolete overnight means that now a similar experience can be created in your own story. Very many people are driving, jogging or simply walking through the world with their own onboard 'non-diegetic' sound. Apart from shutting them off from the diegetic sounds of their world, there's also an argument that this direct ingestion of music is tuning their moods and influencing their attitudes and responses to the world.

The tension here is between an individual and collective function or perhaps between a personal and cultural one. Even two friends sharing a set of headphones is as much about isolation as collaboration. In a world which offers fewer and fewer shared experiences, the personalisation delivered by downloaded playlists (and the relative freedom from the excess pressures of fashion and marketing) must be offset against the loss of a collective experience. The decline and approaching demise of the single CD (following on from the famous 45) in favour of a digital download is not merely a change of technological format. The implications are social and cultural since this has changed the way we access music from an essentially social act to one that is technological and individual. Similarly the undermining of the BBC's monopoly of the singles chart and the inevitable demise of *Top of the Pops* (once a popular weekly 'charts' show) reduces the shared experience which once dominated the life of the average teenager. Lyricist Tim Rice was interviewed as part of the thirtieth anniversary commemorations of the death of Elvis Presley and spoke of the impact hearing Elvis had on him. Asked about the impression made by Elvis's 'pelvic' sexuality, Rice admitted that at that time he hadn't even seen the singer. For many years *Top of the Pops* and the limited number of other music shows gave our only real access to the faces that made the music. Twenty-four-hour music TV has certainly changed all that. A download offers music and image without the need to engage in the public act of participation – now no one need ever know you've got the new 'Take That'!

We're S.H.O.P.P.I.N.G., we're shopping: retail therapy in the twenty-first century

It is said that men and women shop very differently. Men go *to* buy things while women go *and* buy things. The inference is that women understand shopping is a cultural practice and men do not. Men think shopping is merely about going to get what you want while women know that while you can't always get what you want, if you try you might just get what you need. Getting what you need means taking your time and immersing yourself in the experience – it's about lifestyle, it's about recreation, it's about aspiration. The proliferation of shopping malls and huge arcaded shopping areas in the last twenty-five years has only served to confirm this.

ASIDE

Find your perfect partner: he shops!

As if to fully validate the gender stereotypes, one British mall started to offer women the opportunity to trade in their husbands/boyfriends/partners for a sensitive male shopper for the duration of that trip. The menfolk are left in a cafe area watching Sky Sports while a more receptive male gives the woman some constructive feedback on her prospective purchases.

Figure 7.3 The modern shopping mall – lifestyle, recreation, aspiration

ACTIVITY

Shopping Survey

Answer the following questions:

■ When do you shop?
■ Where do you shop?
■ With whom do you shop?
■ What do you predominantly buy?
■ What are the pleasures of shopping?
■ How long on average does a shopping trip last?

Which questions do you predict will show a significant gender bias in their answers?

What we are trying to get at here are the meanings of shopping as a cultural practice. In simple terms we are trying to understand and analyse the 'rules' and the meanings associated with and created by the ways we consume. Clearly this is a complex set of issues since the experiences we are offered in a contemporary shopping mall are far removed from any direct model of supply and demand which is based on need. In terms of Maslow's Heirarchy of Needs, the very existence of a shopping mall assumes that the lower-level needs have been met.

INFORMATION BOX – MASLOW'S HIERARCHY OF NEEDS

The basic idea here is that human needs are ranked in order of importance: we are not particularly concerned about our higher-order needs if our more basic needs have not been met. For example, a person who is starving cares little about what others think of them.

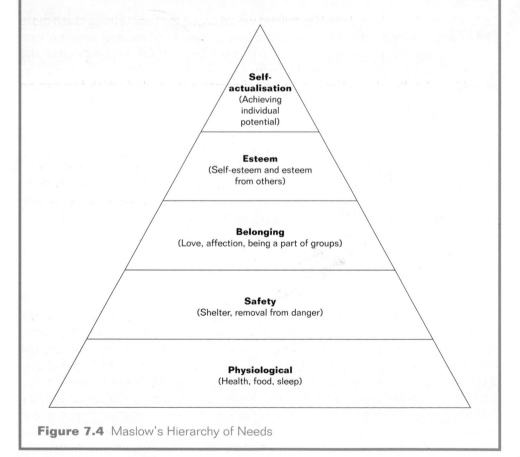

Figure 7.4 Maslow's Hierarchy of Needs

AS COMMUNICATION AND CULTURE: THE ESSENTIAL INTRODUCTION

Shopping in a mall is about esteem needs and self-actualisation (with a dash of transcendence thrown into the bargain). The playful hyperreality of the biggest shopping complexes is a further index of the important place they have in advanced (in the sense of economically developed) Western societies. 'Complex' seems a particularly appropriate term since whatever our take on the significance and symbolism of these places we cannot but recognise that what we do there is far from simple (and not quite the same as what we do in the high street or corner shop).

Some call malls 'cathedrals of consumption', arguing that shopping not religion is the real opiate of the people – the drug of choice. In this model the customs and practices of the great god of money are imbibed by the faithful in their weekly ritual of shopping. This is a complex process so that the subjects are properly laced into the system and unable to see their way through. This view gives a relatively small role to the shoppers, seeing them as ant-like victims in a faceless industrial process. It is very easy to be persuaded by this view if your focus is on the generic complexes which seem to be springing up on the edge of every town. Our focus, however, is not the places but rather what goes on in them. To what extent are we constrained and to what extent liberated by the ability to choose and buy our own things?

Postmodernists such as Jean Baudrillard would argue that something much more fundamental is going on which involves the old authorities and explanations breaking down. An example of this would be the blurring (or dismantling) of the line between superior ('high') and inferior ('low') culture. Without the hierarchy or ranking of cultural practices, a new configuration is needed which focuses on personal choice and individual freedom rather than position and social context. These new models must contain the new order: an imploded culture lacking a significant focus but allowing for a 'do it yourself' and 'pick and mix' approach. This bricolage is, for some, what contemporary retail therapy is really about. In fact, shopping meets the key requirements of what Baudrillard called the 'universalist' model, which simply but efficiently summarises the new demands of contemporary cultural practice. For Baudrillard there are three elements which characterise the hyperreal experience of contemporary reality:

- Entertainment
- Spectacle
- Consumption.

Rather than our day-to-day experiences being controlled by the economic needs of big business, Baudrillard sees the situation as much more complex than that. In an over-stimulated and image-saturated world it becomes less and less possible to discriminate between reality and the 'simulations' of reality such as television. Shopping thus becomes something more than shops baiting traps for consumers; rather it is an adventure in hyperreality. Certainly shops adorn themselves in order to attract attention but the spectacle of the contemporary mall with its temple-like columns and glass lifts creates a context in which consumption is easy and stimulating. However, what are most effectively consumed are *meanings*, which are found at all levels of the process. When we shop we're engaging with all manner of interpretations and fantasies of identity since goods function as adornments and amplifications of the personality.

ESSENTIAL ARCHIVE

Baudrillard's Postmodernism and Hyperreality

Baudrillard is an interesting theorist whose ideas you will meet in A2, but here's a little more courtesy of *Media Studies A2: The Essential Introduction* (Bennett et al. 2006):

> One of the key figures in postmodern theory, Jean Baudrillard, has suggested three principles for understanding contemporary reality: simulation, implosion and hyperreality. For Baudrillard, we live in an era of media saturation in which we are bombarded with information and signs. So much of our experience is in the form of media texts rather than first-hand, direct experience that the signs become 'more real than real'. This is *simulation*; the part of our lives that is dominated by television, computer games, DVD, internet chatrooms, magazines and all the other image suppliers. This is a very big part of many people's lives, maybe, even, the biggest and most important part. Consequently, Baudrillard argues, the distinction between reality and simulated breaks down altogether, we make no distinction between real experience and simulated experience. This is *implosion*. Hyperreality refers to the condition where the distinction between has not only blurred, but the 'image' part has started to get the upper hand.

> Here is an example which may help to explain the rather baffling concept of hyperreality. Let's imagine that I have never visited Paris. In spite of this I have a huge fund of impressions based on the simulations of Paris that I have seen in films and on television, usually to the accompaniment of accordion music. I have looked at magazines, travel brochures and my friends' holiday snaps. I have read about the entertainment, the food and the nightlife. The simulated Paris I know so well is a vibrant, exciting and stimulating city. One day, I decide to visit Paris for the first time. It is drizzling, my hotel room is cramped and dirty, nobody is particularly friendly and I get ripped off in a restaurant. Now I have a fund of rather negative 'real' experiences to add to my very positive simulated experiences. Which of these will win out to form my overall impression of Paris? If Baudrillard is right, they will all merge into one undifferentiated set of experiences, but the image-based simulations will be just that little bit more powerful than my direct experience. My Paris is hyperreal.

Of course shopping is very often a collective activity; we shop with friends and family. This introduces another dimension to the ongoing discussion of meanings and values. This social aspect extends the scope of the exchange of meanings since it increases the range of references. When we shop we are bringing our experience of simulations (media representations) to the partial simulations created by retailers through setting and dressing in conversation with significant others who are involved in a similar process. In fact it could be argued that this is where the real pleasure of retail therapy comes from: the entertainment comes from the active negotiation of identity in a permissive public arena. In other words, shopping is an activity which allows and encourages indulgence and fantasy.

ACTIVITY

Who do you go shopping with?

- Family members
- Friends
- Partner/boyfriend/girlfriend
- Alone.

What difference does it make?

- To what you buy
- To how long it takes
- To the enjoyment of it.

There are places I remember all my life: location, location, location

When very small children are introduced to formal schooling, they do so, in the best traditions of child-centred education, with a topic on 'myself'. In many ways this is an infant version of our work on identity – addressing very similar issues in a less sophisticated, but more direct, fashion. It is also through its focus on family, friends and recreation centrally concerned, as we are, with 'my culture'. One of the seemingly more innocuous activities within this topic is the children's survey of their houses. They are usually given a self-generated questionnaire which asks about the location of their household and especially (because it integrates numeracy), the number of rooms. Responses to these questions offer a thumbnail sketch of the social inequalities prevalent in Britain in a potentially dangerous way since they're presented as merely 'information'. The difference between having four rooms and twenty rooms in this case is not just arithmetical.

Figure 7.5 Home

Home is certainly more than merely bricks and mortar, but nevertheless the concrete is as important as the abstract. Homes are places which allow you to develop, places to which you can return from the world; they are in John Lennon's terms, 'places you remember all your life'. Home contains an almost implicit connotation of 'sanctuary', a place where we should be safe. This is why people who are attacked in their own homes feel particularly violated. The quality of home does not depend on the number of rooms or the presence of a hot tub or a swimming pool. It depends on atmosphere, on relationships, on lived experience. Perhaps as the cliché suggests 'home is where the heart is', where 'the heart' signifies 'emotional truth' and 'the self' as well as 'love'.

However, while not all houses are homes, homes are invariably houses or the equivalent and the place that holds a special place in your affections. The home must also function in other ways, not only as a place of personal intimacy and refreshment after work but also as a place to live in and entertain in. Homes, and houses, are always socially and culturally sensitive texts in pretty much every respect: their locations, their age, their appearance, their 'accessories'. Home may be a very special place but that doesn't mean you want people to share it with you. Once you're old enough to understand this (and who can say what age that is) you realise that inviting people home is not quite as straightforward as it could be. Your home has about the same capacity as your parents or carers to send out the wrong messages: too big, too small, too tidy, too messy (the list works as well for homes as it does for parents).

ACTIVITY

Our house in the middle of our street

The following is a child-like survey of your home, with a dash of irony to keep you interested.

Describe your home.

How many rooms:

- Downstairs?
- Upstairs?

How many:

- Bedrooms?
- Toilets?
- Televisions?

Do you have:

- A separate dining room?
- A study?
- An en-suite bathroom?
- A Jacuzzi, sauna or swimming pool?
- A garden?
- Your own bedroom?

What is your house saying about you?

What are the best features of your home?

Describe your ideal home.

Of course not owning your own house/home, as is the case with most students, you have little choice in the matters addressed (and as a five-year-old you certainly had none). Part of the rebellion which is culturally expected of teenagers is the need for your own space and the negotiation of identity within the family and the family home. What 'you' are allowed to do under 'their' roof is a commonly conceived construction of television drama and of many families. In 'There is a Light Which Never Goes Out', the Smiths' hymn to teenage alienation and resilience, Morrissey expresses it in this way:

driving in your car
I don't ever want to go home
because it's their home, not my home
and I want it no more

Interestingly, while your parents are not expected to be able to understand you, they are expected to maintain the family home, even after you've left it. It is said that nothing offends children more (even in their thirties and forties) than the sale of the family home. It's easy to see how it might symbolically function as a way back from wherever you've gone: a place to run away to. Most significantly though, the home is the site of the inner sanctum: your room, shared or not, the place where you are most yourself as opposed to being mostly yourself.

When people leave home, either temporarily or permanently, the place that most remains to represent them is that bedroom. This is why it is only too easy to understand why the bedrooms of dead children are often left as they were – a set of outlines which at least give a kind of shape to the awful emptiness. Ironically this is almost what those of us who leave in happier circumstances expect: that our rooms will forever be ready to receive us. This underlines the particular importance of the rooms to the sense we have of ourselves in context. Here in the middle of the family, a primary agent of socialisation, and the family home, a representation of family structures and functions, exists a place in which we can rehearse the ways in which we address the wider culture. Here we can play out the roles we are assigned and those ascribed to ourselves. These roles clearly include 'child' and 'teenager', 'boy' and 'girl'. Your room is the one place you are allowed 'early' opinions on decoration, arrangement and accessories. Early on this may be merely a choice between Thunderbirds and Transformers or Barbie and The Animals of Farthing Wood. Later though it is about marking out your little bits of sovereign territory, either with the full cooperation of your parents or in the teeth of significant resistance – or somewhere in between these two extremes.

ACTIVITY

Room Raiders

In the MTV show *Room Raiders* young men and women are asked to select a blind date on the basis of having the opportunity to inspect the bedrooms of three candidates. They are given a metallic 'spy kit' complete with pincers for handling unmentionables. The candidates are apparently marched from their rooms without warning to prevent them interfering with the evidence.

If you were 'Room Raided':

■ What would you ideally like to have time to hide? (This can be answered silently to yourself.)
■ What are the key features of your room that present themselves to be read

   a) subjectively (important to you)?
   b) objectively (will possibly stand out to others)?

■ What information can be gathered from an inspection of your bedroom?

The horror that we would all feel about the invasion of our rooms by strangers comes from the same source that gives us anxiety about any kind of examination. We are anxious that the real (our own) meanings of our work will not be understood without us being there to provide anchorage. As was implied earlier, we are essential parts of our rooms, we are that element around which everything else coheres and just to see us there is to greatly clarify everything else. This is not a process that has much connection with the numerous television DIY shows; it's not about decoration but rather about augmentation (what we add and accumulate) – our rooms are extensions and amplifications of who we are and were. Bedrooms are most often personalised by items brought in rather than the furniture or fittings. Pins, staples, Blu-Tack and sellotape are the significant 'media' here.

If you stay long enough in one place, your room also becomes a record of your development. Like palimpsests, those overwritten medieval manuscripts which never quite remove the text beneath, our rooms offer a sense of the past as a series of layers. Perhaps your latest Fall Out Boy poster is there to cover up the Boyzone stickers that wouldn't come off or that embarrassing Pokemon wallpaper. There are personal items too which escape easy interpretation since they are indexical of people and events long gone: photographs, mementoes or gifts for example (see pp. 144–5 for an explanation of index, icon and symbol).

ACTIVITY

Those were the days . . .

Describe your favourite, best remembered childhood bedroom layout and use it to offer a comparison with what you have now. Which bedroom best described you or represented you?

I guess we'd expect the younger 'you' to be more subject to generic cultural pressures stimulated by mass marketing, which in turn often respond to and confirm cultural values and norms. Here we would expect gender and age (expectations of what girls/boys/young kids like) to be overtly addressed and might take an interest in ethnicity and social class (look for signs of their influence). But what of the way you live now? Is this a clear route to individualism or is that yet another constructed role? How free have you become? Is your room a primal womb or a cultural prison cell wherein your feeble attempts to be free only reinforced the walls?

She's got wheels: she knows how to use them

Cars play a vital part in the popular contemporary imagination. Who would watch a blockbuster action movie which didn't have the obligatory high-speed chase and high-speed collisions? Although their impact is largely direct and pragmatic (one might say metallic), their function within the narrative is more often symbolic or at least indexical. This is true to a large extent of all cars – real and imagined. The primary role of a vehicle is to get us from A to B, but whatever we have or however we use it, inevitably it becomes more than that. In simple terms we drive in a cultural context. Knowing what you are doing in a car is about so much more than gearsticks and carburettors. It's about modelling behaviour learnt by looking since we were old enough to do so.

The essence of driving is attitude. You only have to look at the massive popularity of a show such as *Top Gear* to see that something has been changing. Once it was, like every other motor show, the preserve of a certain kind of bloke (usually sporting a moustache and driving gloves) who could tell you about performance but only in terms of a set of incomprehensible statistics. Essentially it was a series of in-car, in-camera test drives. Now the presenters are just as likely to be racing tractors or trekking to the Pole in eccentric off-road vehicles. The way you drive and the mythology of the 'petrolhead' has become as important as what you drive.

Despite the grave warnings about environmental pollution, learning to drive remains a significant rite of passage. Owning your own 'wheels' becomes a significant adult priority – as important as and more immediately accessible than owning your own house. Our car culture is the real reason for congestion. Sit in any rush hour traffic jam and you are struck by a single thought: here are masses of people making largely the same journey but each has his or her own vehicle; sharing just isn't an option. We don't, on the whole, make sensible arrangements to share vehicles with neighbours and friends because the car is so much more than a practical device for getting from A to B. Like the bedrooms we discussed in the last section, the car is a piece of sovereign territory wherein we have our own full diplomatic immunity: we can be ourselves and don't have to be diplomatic or sensitive to the feelings of others. The smoking ban has, for some, increased the attraction of the car, since it is one of the few enclosed spaces outside the home in which smoking is possible.

This creation of personal space does make the way we behave in cars interesting. When you think about the whole business of travelling in windowed, rolling metal boxes it is, to say the least, odd. What it means is that you're sitting in relatively close proximity to and in view of total strangers; you are on display but at the same time only for short periods. This leads, it seems, to two different kinds of behaviour in response. On the one hand, we feel private enough, for example, to sing at the tops of our voices and talk loudly to ourselves or swear at passing motorists when they can't hear us. On the other hand, we are also aware of an audience of pedestrians and other road users with whom we can communicate in displays of gesture, sounding the horn and flashing lights.

In this way cars function both as a form of adornment, the ultimate 'full metal jacket', and as a kind of movable stage and personal embassy. As a driver you are in control, not only of the car but also of many of the meanings it generates. Of course, cars also have meanings beyond our control. However you drive a Mini, it will never be a Mercedes. So much depends on resources and your creative imagination. You make meanings with the car you can afford and advertising for luxury cars remains entirely aspirational and less and less to do with getting from A to B. Rather like luxury hotels which have to provide you with significantly more than a room and a bed, luxury cars need to find things to add to the four wheels and engine that all cars provide. Often the answer is to accessorise and take further steps away from the core function, transporting the owner into a world of onboard televisions and heated seats rather than getting them home more quickly or safely. The car is a potent symbol of 'freedom', not just the (rather dubious) freedom of the 'open road' but also the freedom of consumer choice. All car manufacturers invite potential purchasers of their products to 'build your own car' by manipulating choices from a huge range of available colours, engine sizes, accessories and optional extras. The creation of an individual vehicle from all these permutations has powerful associations with 'freedom' and 'self-expression'. But are these *really* freedoms? Can we express ourselves adequately simply by making selections from a range of manufactured choices? There isn't an answer, but it is a matter for you to debate.

The MTV show *Pimp my Ride UK* offers a lucky viewer a chance to get a total makeover for their current (tatty) 'ride'. The transformations are extraordinary. These cars are customised according to their owners' recommendations: reconstructed, tuned, painted and accessorised. They emerge as polished chrome and highly colourful creations with backseat games consoles and onboard sound systems that would not be out of place in a nightclub. At one level this merely confirms what we've been saying about the fantasy and symbolic functions of the car. At another it creates a kind of fracture between the world these former banger drivers inhabit and the exotic birds of paradise their cars have become. In some ways, though, we could argue that such personalised and expressive forms of transport, especially if they have been transformed at the hands of the owner rather than MTV, make more powerful statements than the manufacturers' 'build your own' projects described above.

Figure 7.6
A pimped car.
Who would drive
a car like this?

ACTIVITY

Pimp my ride

Speculate on your ideal car not by make but by qualities. Think colour, shape, finish, interior design, the extras. Think also about where your influences might be coming from in this exercise. What is a pimpmobile?

Think of cars (and owners) that you know.

How have these cars been personalised?

How do they reflect or project the identity of their owner?

The way you travel says a lot about your social context and your outlook. This is another area where the medium is largely the message. These messages are not constructed universally but rather in particular cultural contexts. There are a number of popular ways to get about and most of us will use all of them at one time or another. The point is to understand that the choices we make about travelling are not insignificant nor are they always straightforward. They have a necessary cultural context and important personal and political implications. For example, in the face of rising levels of obesity and the threat of global warming and inner-city gridlock, these choices, hedged in by a set a specific attitudes, could be vital to a healthier future.

ACTIVITY

On the move

Rank the following forms of transport listed below in two ways: a) how far you enjoy using them, and b) how much you use them. Now consider the connotations of each means of transport by applying each to the following scenario:

You're watching the opening credits of a film set in modern Britain. The central character, the focus of the sequence, is pictured in transit, travelling. What do you assume about this character when each of the following methods of transport is used?

- Walking
- Driving in a car
- Being driven in a car
- Train
- Bus
- Moped
- 750cc motor bike
- Mountain bike
- Roller skates or blades
- Skateboard
- Bicycle

In Holland everybody cycles, so bikes have no particular connotations of gender, age or social class. Holland is of course mercifully flat but it also has an attitude towards transport and transport policy that provides countrywide cycle lanes. Even without the hills, I suspect heavily congested British roads are a little less attractive to prospective cyclists. It is often said that Britain, like America, is a country that puts the car first. If you consider the inordinate amount of time it has taken for us to invest in city-centre tram systems and congestion charging, you might be inclined to agree. Even more damning is the way our big towns and cities, intersected with six-lane highways, force people into the kind of ill-lit underpasses that foster crime and fear of crime. This is the nightmare world of J.G. Ballard's shocker *Crash*, a 1973 novel that predicts an increasing Americanisation of both our culture and our landscape, and in which the central character, Vaughan, 'the nightmare angel of the expressway', is seen as a sick symbol of our love affair with the motor car.

READING J. G. BALLARD *CRASH* (1973)

'We had entered an immense traffic jam. From the junction of the motorway and Western Avenue to the ascent ramp of the flyover the traffic lanes were packed with vehicles, windshields leaching out the molten colours of the sun setting above the western suburbs of London. Brake-lights flared in the evening air, glowing in the huge pool of cellulosed bodies. Vaughan sat with one arm out of the passenger window. He slapped the door impatiently with his fist. To our right the high wall of a double-decker airline coach formed a cliff of faces. The passengers at the windows resembled rows of the dead looking down at us from the galleries of a columbarium. The enormous energy of the twentieth century, enough to drive the planet into a new orbit around a happier star, was being expended to maintain this immense motionless pause.' (p. 151)

The family life sentence: kith, kin and culture

> In the early 1970s, Virginia Satir wrote a book called *Peoplemaking*. In her introduction she said the family is the 'factory' where the person is made. 'You the adults are the people makers' (p. 3). This is an interesting perspective, in that families do create people not just children. The family structure continues to shape and mould an adult throughout her or his life. As humans we are never finished being made.

(Ivy and Buckland 1994, p. 319)

As we have already noted, the family is a significant influence on the people we are and the people we become. Perhaps Satir's image of a factory is a little strong, since it puts too much emphasis on people being processed. In fact we all become people in families: parents and children alike. Moreover the concept of the family itself is subject to 'becoming' since it too is created and reviewed within a social and cultural context.

ACTIVITY

What do we mean by a family?

Imagine a British family returning from a foreign holiday.

- How many of them are there?
- Who are they? (What roles do they have?)
- Where have they been?
- What is their ethnicity?

Now answer the first two questions for:

- the royal family

Figure 7.7 The British royal family

■ The Royle family

Figure 7.8 The Royle family

■ Your own family.

Which family comes closest to the archetypal average of mother, father and 2.4 children?

It is fairly easy to say what a family is theoretically but when this gets put into practice the fun really starts. This is because families are social structures and primary agencies of socialisation and enculturation. They are essential building blocks of our society and so anyone who has opinions about society will have opinions about the family and its form and function. As with so much of our work, we're confronted with the apparently natural only to discover that our responses to these phenomena are necessarily affected by our cultural contexts. In the same way that a beautiful Lakeland view is conditioned by our expectations of views and the conventions of our understandings of the individual elements, so the family can only be understood within the broadest range of cultural contexts.

In a Communications sense, the family is a specialised kind of group, a network of relationships bound together by the most powerful glue of all: kinship. Blood, they say, is thicker than water. Or is it? This is merely the family of 'family trees', a pattern of dispersed DNA. There is another tradition that defines family much more by its functions, both internally and externally. Thus the 'father', for example, is not so much an ascribed role created by successful impregnation of the 'mother', but rather the role achieved by the demonstration of certain attitudes and skills. This is potentially a head-on collision for those adopted children who elect to find their natural parents. The underlying question is 'does "natural" mean 'real'? The difficulties we have in finding titles for those who perform parenting rolls in modern families underlines the issues. Such titles include carer, caregiver, guardian, parent and step-parent, amongst others. What is clear is that 'family' is a highly flexible concept which embraces all kinds of social and domestic arrangements.

This is in no way to suggest that there is some kind of archetypal family, which will always resist our meddling. It is merely to suggest that every age will have its own conceptions of what a family is and we will be wise to see them as such. One of the classic contemporary political struggles is between so-called traditionalists and progressives. It is useful to see these as shifting positions since the terms themselves are relative. For example, we regularly read in some parts of the media about the decline in traditional family values as if the nuclear family (mother, father and a couple of kids) were an ancient sacred institution. In fact such notions of the family are barely 50 years old and were largely a significant result of postwar affluence and mobility. Traditional models of the family are more likely to be of extended families or in the case of our tribal forebears a collective rearing of children – models still used in much of the world today. It is important to see families as 'of our time' and 'in our culture'.

If we can see the family as an important communication network, we may be less worried about its specific configuration. While vital, families are also on other levels just regular groups. For example they meet the criteria set down below (from the second edition of this volume).

ESSENTIAL ARCHIVE

What is a group?

What is a group? In order for a group to exist, the following must apply:

■ **Individual members must exist in some kind of relationship**.
According to Burton and Dimbleby (1995), 'If there is no interaction between the individuals, then a group cannot be formed'. Hartley talks of a regular pattern or structure of interaction. Judy Gahagan (1975) asserts 'A group should be conceived of as a system whose parts interrelate.'

- **Groups share common interests, goals and purposes**. In *Between Ourselves*, Burton and Dimbleby define a group as 'a collection of individuals who interact in some way and share some common goals or interests'.
- **Groups share common values and norms**. O'Sullivan et al. (1994) define norms as 'Those sets of social rules, standards and expectations that both generate and regulate social interaction and communication.' In most groups these norms are unwritten and unspoken.
- **Groups develop set roes of behaviour which members accept**. O'Sullivan et al. (1994) define roles as 'socially defined positions and patterns of behaviour which are characterised by specific sets of rules, norms and expectation'. To some extent these developed roles are the manifestations of the values and norms of the group; in other words, the theory is put into practice.
- **Group members have an identity**. Hartley (1997) talks about the existence of a group depending on the perception that it exists, logically both inside and outside the group. Turner (1991) categorised this effectively when he claimed, 'A group exists when two or more people define themselves as members of it and when its existence is recognised by at least one other.'

A handy summary of these descriptions of group is provided by Douglas (1979), who declared that a group was 'the largest set of two or more individuals who are jointly characterised by a network of relevant communications, a shared sense of collective identity and one or more of shared goal dispositions with associated normative strengths'. Or as Gahagan (1975) more succinctly puts it, 'a group of people is significantly more than the sum of its parts'. In mathematical terms it is not about addition but about integration.

Of course by these criteria families, like other groups, have the capacity to be both functional and dysfunctional. The descriptions made by Kell and Corts (1980) of group maturity reads like a manifesto for the families we're all trying to maintain. A mature group, Kell and Costs argue, does the following:

- Offers the facility for individual growth.
- Offers an atmosphere of trust.
- Offers equality of membership.
- Adapts to points of disagreement.
- Encourages participation.
- Encourages sacrifice for group benefit.
- Has a good time.

From the list above it seems that group maturity is a function of the attitudes that individuals within the group have towards one another with an emphasis on both those people as individuals and a group identity. This suggests flexibility and is not a particular feature of traditional models of the family which stress fixed roles. Beebe and Masterson (1986) looked at the implications of what they called 'position-centred' and 'person-centred' communication in families – the difference between seeing everybody in a family in terms of the job they do and seeing them all as individuals fulfilling a range of functions. 'Person-centred' families, they claimed, encouraged flexibility in social situations and promoted androgynous communication (communication that is not gender-specific).

As has been stated earlier in the book the models we get of family life are not restricted to our own families. We are surrounded by families and representations of family life and each provides a perspective on the other. The diversity of these representations and experiences is the best antidote to arguments that the family should have a fixed form and purpose. High-profile politicians might well try to defend the image of a happy marriage and perfect family as if their political lives depended on it but even this is a cultural anomaly. The French see little need for looking into the private lives of those in power, preferring to assume these people are muddling through imperfectly like the rest of us.

Figure 7.9 The Simpsons

Probably the most famous family in the world at the moment are improbably yellow and nuclear. *The Simpsons* represent an animated demonstration of the importance of families in which every shred of evidence for the central argument is thoroughly satirised and subverted. The Simpsons are, on the surface (apart from the yellowness), the traditional family with breadwinner dad, stay-home mom and effectively 2.4 stereotypical kids (since Maggie barely functions as a character). Moreover they are a family who conform to the key practices of traditional American family life: they eat together around the same table, they go to church on Sunday, and they watch TV together on a huge settee. Perhaps President

George Bush Senior had not seen the show when he made his famous comments about wanting American families to be more like the Waltons and less like the Simpsons.

However, perhaps Mr Bush had seen and understood (or somebody had done this for him) since *The Simpsons* does exude plurality and tolerance from every pore. The whole show has always been an assault on cant, dogmatism and hypocrisy wherever it is found and takes particular delight in debunking those who have unshakeable answers. Merely to witness the title sequence should be enough. Here the model nuclear family are seen reassembling at the end of day as a radioactive bar (nuclear, get it?) which Homer has unwittingly carried out of the nuclear power plant follows them home. From this point on everything is up for grabs: politics, religion, media, friendship, sex and, at the centre of it all, the family. And yet what persistently, engages, amuses and uplifts us is the spectacle of the Simpsons themselves. Along with all of their friends, relations and neighbours, they go about their business as we go about ours, they muddle through as we do. In this profoundly tolerant human context, the focus is less upon *how* people manage their relationships than upon the fact that they do. Here is a show that for many seasons has addressed the various configurations of contemporary family life but always in the context of interesting human beings and their ways.

ACTIVITY

Conduct a survey on the structure of families on mainstream TV. Is there such a thing as an average TV family? What is the range of different family forms and family relationships?

This is also true of the popular writer of teenage fiction (that most difficult of sub-genres) Jacqueline Wilson, whose central characters more often than not inhabit contexts rarely supervised by pairs of biological parents. With marriage in long-term decline and divorce affecting one in three couples, another way of describing these contexts would be as 'everywhere' and 'anywhere' and 'here' and 'now'. Wilson writes about the challenges of changing and reconstituted families in the same way that Jane Austen once wrote about the rigid social conventions of middle-class marriages in the nineteenth century: with insight and compassion. What she understands is the need for stability if we are to understand who we are, but that this stability can be delivered in many different configurations, and can also fail to be delivered in all the same ways.

Just a brief tabular summary of a selection of Wilson's bestsellers gives the flavour of her exploration of family life. The popularity of this body of work also reminds us how interested we are in the ways that other people live beyond the closed doors of their houses. This is the abiding appeal of television soap opera, fly-on-the-wall documentaries (one of the earliest was called simply *The Family*) and also by reality TV.

Book	Central character	Family
Girls in Love	Ellie	dad, step mum, brother (mum is dead)
Tracy Beaker	Tracy	the lady who wants to foster her, her mum
Best Friends	Alice and Gemma	mums and dads, Gemma's brothers
The Bed and Breakfast Star	Elsa	mum, mum's boyfriend, brother, sister
Love Lessons	Prue	dad, sister
Clean Break	Em	mum, dad, sister, brother
Candyfloss	Floss	mum, dad, stepdad
The Illustrated Mum	Dolphin	Marigold (mum), Star (sister)
Vicky Angel	Vicky and Jade	mums and dads (Vicky is dead)
Lola Rose	Jayni	mum, mum's boyfriend, brother

Table 7.1 Wilson's families

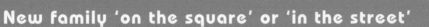

ACTIVITY

New family 'on the square' or 'in the street'

Imagine you've entered a competition to devise a new family for either *Eastenders* or *Coronation Street*. You need to provide the regular writers with material for stories but also to 'reflect the state of the contemporary British family'.

Meet the new boss, same as the old boss: working your way up

We spend, on average, more than two-thirds of our lives at work and the other third is spent either preparing for it or recovering from it. This makes work one of our most significant cultural practices and contexts yet one that is rarely questioned and examined. Two key places we are prepared for work are the family and the classroom but in neither case are we particularly encouraged to say what work is, or to consider why we might be keen to spend much of our lives doing it. It's easy to argue for an economic imperative which overrules the luxury of such considerations but on reflection aren't there other factors to consider alongside the economic: cultural, psychological, and even moral?

ACTIVITY

What separates the human activity 'work' from other human activities? What is the purpose of work a) for individuals, b) for society? What makes the ideal job?

We're prepared for work from a relatively early age. This happens, as we have noted, in two significant contexts: the family and education. A big question in most families for children is 'What are you going to do?' This question has two unspoken components – assumptions if you like. The first is part of the question and is sometimes added. It runs '. . . with your life'. The second, which apparently never needs saying, is part of the answer and is the overwhelming inference that 'doing' here means 'as a job'. Similarly when people identify themselves on a first meeting, beyond name, the first thing that usually emerges is what we do. If identity is a representation of who we are (or think we are), then occupation is high on the list.

Occupations confer status, esteem and suggest means, which is why people sometimes lie about them. In this game of rank order, 'student ' is one of the few answers you can give that puts off this classification since, as a song suggests, 'it's not where you start but where you finish'. 'Student' carries with it connotations which are a mixture of admiration and contempt, but more importantly carries the meaning 'not yet classified' or, in the case of 45-year-old return-to-learners, 'attempting to escape classification'. Thus you can give the answer 'student' even when wearing the livery of a famous fast-food restaurant or DIY retailer. What it does is, whether you like it or not, is to significantly undermine the status of the job you are doing in the meantime, where 'in the meantime' means 'until I can get something better'. In these circumstances you can see why there are sometimes tensions between student workers and those who do these jobs 'for real'. As Jarvis Cocker wrote, in a song about the rich girl who wanted to live like 'common people': 'Everybody hates a tourist, especially one who thinks it's all such a laugh.'

'Common People' has a lot to say about how fragile our civilisation might be for those who through situation or circumstance fail to 'get on'. Education, they say, is the key, but as a greater proportion of people go to university, how much greater the stigma of being unqualified? Perhaps the closest most of you came was in the time between leaving school and getting your GCSE results, when the ultimate punishment for not getting the requisite crop of A–Cs would've been to have to extend your hours at your Saturday job. For younger teenagers, the thumb and first finger popularly functions as the capital L of 'Loser', followed quickly by the M and W, which defines this 'losing' in terms of employment at one of the largest of the American fast-food retailers (McDonald's and Wendy's). This may be amusing enough, but perhaps not so funny for those who are not waiting for their results to come through.

The writer D.H. Lawrence wrote that 'a man should go to work as if to an absorbing game', but is clear that some jobs are going to be less absorbing than others. What we are not invited to think about is the implications of this fact for those who end up doing these jobs. We are vaguely sold the line that it is hard work and concentration that save you from this fate and that everyone has an equal opportunity to succeed, even though we know this to be untrue. It is part of a logic that tries to make us believe that because we don't fail no one has to or conversely that someone has to fail if our success is going to have any meaning. This latter argument will almost certainly be trotted out on the day you get your A-level results, when the relatively large numbers of people failing A levels in 1964 will be called upon to question your success over forty-five years later. As ever, the issue here is about opinions and the way our cultural practices enshrine our values. The debate about what kind of society we want to live in is bound to be an active one and any attempt to hide it behind custom and practice is best resisted. It may be that those of us who succeed in the system are those with the greatest responsibility to challenge the system, if only because we have the greatest access to it. Perhaps we, too, should listen to Jarvis Cocker's ultimate response to the girl whose 'thirst for knowledge' made her seek the experiences of common people. 'You will never understand,' he says, 'what it's like to live your life with no meaning or control'.

The majority of people doing menial jobs in London hotels are first-generation immigrants who often have a limited facility for the English language. Much of the immigration from the Caribbean after the Second World War was as a result of indigenous British workers not wanting to do unappealing menial jobs. We all see the need for clean public lavatories but how many of us want to clean them? The whole of public life is kept bearable by an army of cleaners but this is not a job careers offices give much advice on.

ACTIVITY

Who does what?

How can we address the needs of individuals for fulfilling lives with the needs of society to have dirty jobs done cheaply and well? Is competition the only way to work this one out?

As Cocker implies, choice about work gives meaning to our lives or deprives us of this. Work is the cornerstone of our culture: no country quite prides itself so much on how hard it works or is quite so hysterical about those who dodge work. This is not surprising since Britain was the cradle of the Industrial Revolution, an eruption that created a working class whose labour fuelled a formidable empire. It is an abiding irony that those who worked their daylight hours in dark foundries supported an empire on which the sun reputedly never set. We are now, in the enlightened twenty-first century, committed to work–life balance, though it may take us another century to put life first in these discussions.

ACTIVITY

Which are the best jobs?

Which are the jobs that our society values most?

Rank the following jobs on the following criteria (mark out of ten)

a) Social esteem (respect from your peers)
b) Social worth (value to society)
c) Quality of life (balance of rewards versus commitment)
d) Impact (ability to make you stand out).

- Fast-food crew member
- Doctor (GP)
- Solicitor
- Police officer
- Lap dancer/male stripper
- Bank employee
- Car salesperson

- Lorry driver
- Farmer
- Nurse
- Professional poker player
- Go-kart mechanic
- Soldier
- Air steward (-ess)
- Teacher
- Club DJ
- Rubbish collector

Wired for sound: the medium is the message

At first glance Kranzberg's (1985) first law of technology seems the whole of the story: 'technology is neither good nor bad,' he suggested, 'but neither is it neutral'. Whatever the sci-fi nightmares about superintelligent computers who will 'byte' the hand that programs them, most of us are able to see that the threat posed by computers comes entirely from those who make, maintain and use them. As the old gag says: 'The most dangerous part of the car is the nut behind the wheel.'

However, as was suggested earlier, it is not the technology that matters but rather the impact it has on our cultural practices and in particular the way we think about and view the world. New technologies may appear to be merely improvements on old ones but it is rarely that simple. Digital photography, for example, appeared to merely remove the need for photographic developing (wiping out a profitable industry overnight). However, thanks to digital cameras (and cameraphones) there's been a significant transformation in the availability of visual images of our everyday lives, which in turn has fed and has been fed by internet sites such as *YouTube* and *Flickr*. It's ironic that this massive increase in our interest in photographs comes at a time when cameras are becoming an increasingly redundant item. All this goes to show is that technology affects our lives in unpredictable ways because it may change the ways we behave and the ways in which we perceive the world.

The Canadian cultural theorist Marshall McLuhan saw this process very clearly as early as the 1960s and warned anyone who would listen. McLuhan (1988) understood technology as an extension of human attributes. The mass media he described as an extension of the senses: crudely they allow us to see and hear further. Cars, on the other hand, may be thought of as extensions of feet since they, in simple terms, allow us to do what we'd otherwise do on foot, only quicker and for longer. The downside for McLuhan was that for every extension there had to be a corresponding implication: every gain for one technology clearly meant the loss for another. These losses he called amputations. For example, the invention of the telephone (an extension of the mouth and ear) amputated the art of letter writing. McLuhan believed that we have become people who regularly praise all extensions and minimise all amputations and that we do so at our peril.

McLuhan was alarmed by the process he identified, whereby technology became inevitably overextended having already amputated the alternatives. He saw as inevitable the point where the benefits were reversed and the amputations outweighed the extensions. In the example of the car, we are already seeing something of the beginning of a crisis of congestion and pollution on the one hand and obesity and the creation of a sedentary culture on the other. This is without any consideration of how many die on the roads every year. A further problem, as McLuhan saw it, is that these exterior effects are mirrored by interior effects – the technology also changes the way we think. 'We use the tools,' he said, 'and the tools in turn use us.' Many of us may sympathise with the view that apparently 'labour-saving' devices such as the PC seem to create as much work as they save. On the other hand, most of us would prefer not to think that technology can 'tell us what to do'. McLuhan's way of understanding the impact of technology is usually referred to as technological determinism (see Information Box) simply because its central argument is that technology is responsible for the shape of society and culture.

INFORMATION BOX

i

Technological Determinism

This is the view that technological developments are a primary *cause* of social change and cultural perceptions. It is the underlying principle for historians who link technology inventions to specific timeframes to give us, for example, the Railway Age, the Nuclear Age, the Computer Age and so on.

Alternatives to this approach (sometimes broadly called SCOT or the social construction of technology) tend not to give technology such a powerful role in relation to other factors such as social needs, politics or state control and regulation.

From our Communication and Culture point of view, we are not very sympathetic towards technological determinism because it tends to see technology as somehow *outside* of culture. For us, technology is not at all like a force of nature that 'just happens'. Rather, it is a part of culture. Many of the technological devices we have discussed in this book such as the mobile phone, the digicam or the PDA are not so much inventions as developments. Existing technology is honed, refined and, very often, miniaturised to meet evolving needs as well as to create new markets. This process involves technical research, market research and investment – all of which take place in a cultural context.

In other words, it makes just as much sense to say that culture determines technology as it does to say that technology determines culture. For us, the two have an interdependent relationship which we certainly want to study and understand.

Much of this subsection on technology is based on an excellent set of teaching notes and activities devised by Phil Bury, a teacher at King Edward the Sixth College, Stourbridge, and used with his permission. This extract on how the tools use us, culturally and psychologically, is well worth reading in its original form:

> To this observation might be added the fact that we train children from a very young age to stand within a few feet of high-speed vehicles without being afraid. Less than two hundred years ago a screaming locomotive or high-speed automobile would have caused a person to flee in terror for their lives. We have slowly conditioned ourselves to not be afraid of something that is, in fact, extremely dangerous. Similarly, we know that speed limits of 20 miles an hour would also eliminate most car fatalities, but we also consider the advantages of getting to our destinations quicker to be worth the resulting death rate. Proof of this casual acceptance of the disadvantages of the car could be imagined if one were

to consider the fate of a political candidate who ran on the platform of reducing the national speed limit to 20 miles per hour. We know the advantages, even before implementation, but we choose to accept the disadvantages because there is a privileging of all types of technological extension, even deadly and horrific forms.

Of course the proliferation of new technologies does mean the future remains unpredictable. McLuhan's intention was to make us aware of both sides of the argument; his gravestone bears the legend 'the truth shall make you free'. Things are changing so quickly that what appears at one moment to be a major change in the way we communicate can in the very next moment become a candidate for amputation. (It wasn't that long ago that the floppy disk seemed to be at the cutting edge.) In the very early days of video recording technology, Trevor Horn penned the song 'Video Killed the Radio Star', which not only got to number one but also seemed to have got it absolutely right. However, things are never that straightforward and video has not killed radio, any more than television killed cinema. Perhaps the most important trend to pick out from this is the unpredictability trend. Technological developments have unintended and unforeseen consequences. Equally the amputation of a technology is not necessarily a fatal blow. If the telephone amputated the written message, text and email have to some extent retrieved it at the partial expense of the simple telephone call.

In McLuhan's final published book, *The Global Village* (1988), he offered a model, which he called the tetrad, for looking at the impact of technology on our culture. This consists of four questions we can ask of any innovation in order to examine its potential impact.

- What does it extend, enlarge or enhance?
- What does it erode or make obsolete?
- What does it retrieve that had earlier been eroded or made obsolete?
- What will it turn into if it is overextended; if it is pushed beyond its limits so that its disadvantages outweigh its advantages?

ACTIVITY

The Tetrad

What answers do you have to McLuhan's questions in relation to:

- The internet?
- Mobile communication devices?
- The private car?
- Robots?

Whilst McLuhan's views tend to emphasise the negative effects of emerging technologies, especially in the field of communication, others have been more interested in the different 'ways of seeing' and cultural practices associated with new technologies.

References and further reading

Ballard, J.G. (1995) *Crash*, London: Vintage. First published 1973

Beebe, Steven A. and Masterson, John T. (1986) *Family Talk: Interpersonal Communication in the Family*, New York: Random House

Bennett, P., Slater, J. and Wall, P. (2006) *A2 Media Studies: The Essential Introduction*, London: Routledge

Burton, Graeme and Dimbleby, Richard (1995) *Between Ourselves: An Introduction to Interpersonal Communication*, 2nd edn, London: Hodder Arnold

Douglas, W.D. (1979) *Groups: Understanding People Gathered Together*, London: Tavistock

Fiske, John and Hartley, John (1990) *Reading Television*, London: Routledge

Gahagan, Judy (1975) *Interpersonal and Group Behaviour*, London: Methuon

Harrison, T. (1985) *V*, Newcastle: Bloodaxe

Hartley, Peter (1997) *Group Communication*, London: Routledge

Ivy, D.K. and Buckland, P. (1994) *Exploring Genderspeak*, New York: McGraw-Hill

Kell, C.L. and Corts, P.R. (1980) *Fundamentals of Effective Group Communications*, New York: Macmillan

Kranzberg, M. (1985) 'The information age: evolution or revolution?', in Bruce R. Guile (ed.) *Information Technologies and Social Transformation*, Washington DC: National Academy Press

McLuhan, Marshall (1988) *The Global Village: Transformations in World Life and Media in the 21st Century*, Oxford: Oxford University Press

O'Sullivan, T., Hartly, J., Saunders, D. and Fiske, J. (1994) *Key Concepts in Communication Studies*, London: Routledge

Turner, J.C. (1991) *Social Influence*, Milton Keynes: Open University Press

8 DOING THE COURSEWORK

Education as cultural practice

When Tony Blair came to power in May 1997, he arrived with the catchphrase 'education, education, education' and a belief that this was a way to provide people with greater opportunity. On the surface this is a noble proposition but by this point in the book and the course you will hopefully all be too well 'tuned' to take anything at face value. Education, as a key agency of socialisation, is bound to be a site of tremendous discussion and dispute as well as a significant repository of social and cultural values. Education inducts us into the prominent rituals of our culture but just as importantly it regulates this process so that in passing through, like farm fresh eggs, we are graded.

In a world of league tables and the close scrutiny of academic standards, perhaps what Blair might have meant was 'examinations, examinations, examinations'. We seem to have more of them in Britain than almost anywhere else and we certainly appear to take them very seriously.

Assessments of all kinds tell us an awful lot about the cultures that devise and defend them. The manner of assessment makes a powerful statement about the nature and status of the activity. The formality of an assessment is often an index of its prestige. This is one of the reasons why students at Oxford University are required to purchase formal clothing, including academic gowns, to wear when they sit their exams. The kind of coursework which this chapter supports enters the debate about assessment from a very different direction, but they are both variations on the same cultural practice. Perhaps the issue that really needs to be raised is why we assess in such formalised and systematic ways. What seems to be widely accepted is that we need some way to decide who is educated and, just as importantly, who is not. It also seems that getting people to take tests in order to earn the right to take more tests is clearly the best way of doing this. This is a model not unlike football's FA cup: a vast number enter the competition and at each round many are eliminated while fewer and fewer progress. Then, symbolically, at the end of the process the silverware is given out in the form of better jobs and better salaries.

Figure 8.1 There is no coursework cup

The key to the above model is competition and critics of contemporary education, such as former Chief Inspector of Schools Chris Woodhead, argue that there's not enough of it about. These critics claim that the central weakness of our current system is that not enough people fail at each stage and as a result success has become less meaningful. This may be an argument which has your sympathy but this isn't the only way to understand assessment. If education is meant to provide

three tasks involve reading texts and contexts and presenting your findings effectively. The difference is that while the two readings mean a focus on what is being analysed, the presentation unites presenter and subject in the set topic 'my culture'. It is expected that the readings will serve as a useful, if not essential, preparation for the presentation.

Investigating individuals and writing up your findings

Some of you might look at the 500-word limit for the investigation and be extremely frustrated. You may think how much more you'd be able to write about such matters as body image and taste. You may wonder why there is a need to limit what you write if the point of coursework is to allow you to naturally respond to the course. The answer to this is partly pragmatic, in the interests of making the course manageable both to yourselves and to your teachers (and others) who will need to assess the work but it is also much more than this. It has to do with the nature of the assessment in this unit, which is designed to test the depth of your understanding rather than the breadth of your knowledge (the exam will do this). The 500 words is not the work, but rather it is the write-up: it is not the investigation but rather the findings.

In this way the word limit is in every sense a useful guide to choosing your focus since what you decide to analyse must furnish you with 500 words of findings. This means obviously to some degree it must be 'big' enough, but in practical terms it must also be 'small' enough, in other words tightly focused. It should be obvious that looking at language in general or trying to define taste or body image is doomed to failure but you may need to be prompted with a few good examples before you feel ready to select your own.

ACTIVITY

Potential investigations

The purpose of this exercise is to raise some issues around choosing appropriate focus areas. There will never be a right answer when it comes to selection of areas for investigations, the proof of the pudding is always in the eating. As long as one of the set topic areas is explicitly addressed, there are no further restrictions save for the word limit. Rate the following proposed investigations as one of the following: A interesting and appropriate, B possible but . . ., C non-starter.

- My swearing and how I am perceived in different contexts.
- The language of the tribe: dialect and a sense of belonging.
- Good txt/bad txt and what it says about you.
- Big words and their uses (even when you don't understand them).
- Who defines taste? Senders and receivers.
- Why is taste in music more important than taste in books?
- If you're said to have taste, what does this mean?
- In what ways can bad taste be good?
- How far is the idea of beauty defined by what is healthy?
- Is brawn the opposite of brain? The meaning of muscles.
- Tattoos: how far we are defined by where they are.
- How far is body image mirror image (seen in the eyes of others)?

Whichever topic you choose and however you choose your focus, the challenge is the same: to investigate some aspect of the key triangular relationship between communication, culture and the individual. This overrides all other considerations and creates the arena within which meanings can be generated and contested. Significantly the most important Assessment Objective for the readings and particularly for the investigation is that which requires 'the ability of candidates to apply knowledge'. This knowledge is likely to be of two kinds: knowledge of cultural codes and of toolkits – this is the stuff you must apply.

ESSENTIAL ARCHIVE

Five-paragraph essay

In many ways investigation remains as it was in the old Communication Studies course in that it is:

- 500 words
- Interested in findings rather than process
- Tightly focused on a specific area of interest.

Thus in the crudest terms it is a five-paragraph essay as described below: An A/AS essay is a five-paragraph essay. The paragraphs will normally function as follows:

1 **Introduction:** address key words; set the essay's agenda.
2 First main point and evidence.
3 Second main point and evidence.

There's also a similar need for an opening sentence that both validates the investigation and contextualises the write-up. A formula that works is offered below.

> **My investigation is into the impact of so-called 'bad' language on the perception of identity. I did this by examining TV cook Gordon Ramsey on the appropriately titled *F word*. Here are my findings. (34 words)**

Or

> **My investigation is into the relationship between musical tastes and a person's attitudes and values. I did this by considering how my love of thrash and death metal affects my attitudes towards others. Here are my findings. (37 words)**

Or

> **My investigation is into the ways in which ideas about the ideal male body image impacts on ideas about ideal self. I did this by looking at male responses to male pin-ups in magazines aimed at teenage girls. Here are my findings. (41 words)**

ACTIVITY

Write 30–40 word openings for the following investigations:

■ Elocution and identity: does cleaning your language mean losing your identity?
■ Burberry: high fashion as bad taste.
■ Size zero: better small after all?
■ One of your own devising.

What you have here, for approximately 7 per cent of the word allowance, is a clear steer on the focus, nature and direction of your investigation, or rather, as these introductions explicitly point out, the focus of your investigation findings. You must not confuse the 'looking into' with the 'summing up'. Only the latter is limited to 500 words, though common sense must dictate that the amount of looking into should reflect the space you have for 'findings'.

Figure 8.2 Write up your findings clearly

Thereafter it's just a case of writing up with an eye on the particular demands of this task. This means maintaining a content focus which is at once about individual identity and a cultural context as well as the more specific topics such as 'Language' or 'Body Image'. It also means employing the critical reading techniques we examined in Chapter 4 to interrogate your chosen text. The essence of this exercise (and the whole course) is an investigation of the meanings of significant aspects of everyday life. Whenever you are contemplating, discussing or pursuing meanings you are at the very heart of Communication and Culture as a subject.

In terms of our prototype investigations this might mean:

<u>What the food is going on? Avoiding the F word</u>

- The meaning of bad language (denotation/connotation); relationship to sexuality and taboo
- What swearing says about you: conventionally, subjectively, objectively
- Coping strategies.

<u>'I know it's only rock and roll but I like it'</u>

- Taste and appearance
- Taste and opinions
- Taste and deception (mine and of me).

<u>'Walk like a man': male body image and me</u>

- Male stereotypes and the ideal self
- The eye of the beholder: who's looking at whom?
- The importance of body image to identity.

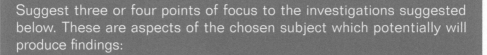

ACTIVITY

Suggest three or four points of focus to the investigations suggested below. These are aspects of the chosen subject which potentially will produce findings:

- Ow bin yow? How we speak and who we are
- Bad taste rebellion: trading trash for independence
- Keeping 'fit': health and beauty.

Exploring context and using secondary resources

An exploration, in this context, is really an extended investigation. It employs the same techniques and address to provide a reading of the chosen aspect of culture experience but it does so in a broader context. From the outset it concentrates on our cultural surroundings rather than our roles within them and invites us to collect the readings of others as well as our own. On top of this it gives us a little more scope for pursuing an area and, as a result, twice as many words in which to record our findings.

The real difference is the focus on 'contexts and practices' rather than 'the individual', though communication and culture remain constant. Whereas the investigations are directed essentially towards 'self and identity', the explorations are interested in the world into which the individuals must travel and its ways: the dance rather than the dancer. Thus while an investigation might focus on individual language competence and use, an exploration might focus on the language of the street, a language which we encounter rather than control or contain. Similarly, an investigation might evaluate how our taste in music impacts on the ways we are understood, whereas an exploration would consider a social function of popular music, such as its ability to create a sense of group identity.

Explorations, then, are extremely small-scale research projects, opportunities to look into interesting areas of culture experience. These areas are defined very broadly by the A-level specification and then more specifically by each of you. The idea is to enter into a dialogue with other writers on your chosen focus area and then to publish findings within 1000 words of engaging prose. However, at the same time, there is a requirement to 'engage with techniques of reading cultural practices and/or products'. The critical analytical reading still remains the corner-stone of this and part of the active choosing is to identify those products and practices that will lend themselves to this kind of analysis.

In addition, there is the requirement, which should best be seen as an opportunity, to 'explore' the views of others. The kind of secondary sources you reference is again entirely up to you but an internet search engine seems a good place to start since it is likely to throw up a range of kinds of text from which you can choose. From fansites, through blogs and wikies to heavyweight academic papers, the idea is that you seek not 'authority' but rather 'stimulus': interesting ways of reading your material. This notion of the equality of sources as potential stimulations and inspirations is central to the intention of the exploration, which is looking to open a conversation or debate about an area of focus rather than produce a definitive statement. To provide a definitive statement within 1000 words should anyway seem inappropriate and once again measuring an area for consideration which will allow a write-up of 1000 words will be a useful skill.

The set topics are deliberately broad since they describe cultural practices which occur across a range of contexts. On their own terms they rule pretty much everything in and exclude little so that it's important for candidates to 'cut' themselves a reasonably sized portion. This is best done logically by identifying the priorities within the task and then by working from the topics to texts. For explorations the following are important:

- 1000 words of 'findings'
- The fact that it is an extended 'reading'
- The need to create a dialogue with others' views
- The need to identify 'contexts' within 'practices'.

The most significant assessment objective across the two readings is that which requires evidence of the 'ability of candidates to apply knowledge'. The upper levels of this mark grid call for 'personal response' and work that is 'thoroughly

The essence of all this work is 'negotiation', in both the lay and the semiotic sense. 'Explore' is meant to give you the licence to go where you like (across three broad areas of cultural practice) and report on what you find both critically and analytically. This is an opportunity not an imposition, a matter of choice, not a chore and a chance to examine an area for yourself and share what you find with others. If this piece of writing needs an audience, it will be best understood as your peers: a group of people who have command of a technical vocabulary and have an interest in how our culture is communicated. Let them dictate the register of your writing, which needs to be determined, persuasive and engaging. Do not let the critical opinions do that: this is about active learning and personal development. The views of others are secondary, they are there to support you, not to impress your teachers (or some invisible moderator somewhere).

Sourcing the exploration: theory in practice

To begin to clarify the question of others' opinions, perhaps it would be useful to consider the earlier exemplary explorations from the point of view of sourcing opinions. First, it is important to understand why this process has not been described as 'research'. We have deliberately avoided using the word 'research' either here or in the AQA specification largely because of the often unhelpful connotations that this idea carries. 'Research' is all too easily understood by students (and teachers) as a process of importing large amounts of often impressive but just as frequently unprocessed work that students have 'found' (which these days means 'downloaded from the internet'). The student is too often merely a compiler, whose voice is crowded out by the overwhelming presence of more illustrious commentators.

This is explicitly not the intention here. The opinions, angles, perspectives and illustrations of and on your chosen focus area are part of the process of 'exploration' and should connote the need to provide depth and context and not the need to find some better opinions. Though it is likely that these sources will be referenced in the writing up of your 'findings', this should be as a result of them helping you to make points and to structure your response rather than the need to prove you've consulted something or someone. In terms of direct quotation, only one rule applies: you quote when others express opinions which better sum up what you have to say than you can yourself or when they simply make points which you wouldn't have thought of (but agree with).

Anyway, enough theorising. In practice the student attempting to place that Britpop thing in some kind of cultural context might (with a little sifting) identify these sources:

a)   Britpop Ten Years On (BBC News24)

BRITPOP 10 YEARS ON

Britpop's birth
How UK music found its voice again

Blur v Oasis
How have they fared in the past decade?

Where are they?
Stars and lesser lights tracked down

'I survived Britpop'
The Boo Radleys' Martin Carr looks back

New wave?
Did Britpop inspire the bands of 2005?

EVENTS OF 1995
Britpop year's highlights

FROM THE ARCHIVE
Battle for supremacy
Blur/Oasis chart result

HAVE YOUR SAY
Your memories of Britpop

(Source: http://news.bbc.co.uk/1/hi/entertainment/music/4136296.stm)

b) Article by John Harris in Guardian Unlimited

Remember the first time

Without Britpop, would we have had hit guitar groups, stadium anthems or rock stars on Newsnight? Ten years on, John Harris looks back on how Blur, Oasis, Pulp and co changed the face of UK music

'It was just a period of time that I felt totally confused by, really,' says Graham Coxon in between gulps of his second pint of Coca-Cola. 'I would do as I was told, but I had a growing resentment about what was happening. It damaged my relationship with the rest of the group and it made my personal relationships very difficult. And there was so much drinking.'

It's a sun-kissed Friday morning in Camden Town, north London. Blur's one-time guitar player – now a happy and productive solo artist, about to release his sixth album – has arranged to meet me in the Good Mixer, the pub that was once a magnet for droves of pop-cultural tourists. The nominal hook for our meeting is the 10th anniversary of the episode that probably drew more people here than any other: the week starting August 14 1995, when Blur's Country House raced Oasis's Roll With It to the top of the charts, and just about every voice in the media felt compelled to express an opinion on the freshly inaugurated age of Britpop.

Coxon dispenses his memories with an expression that somehow mixes disquiet with a wry amusement – not least when he is unpicking some of the period's more ridiculous aspects. When I remind him of how absurdly nasty the Blur–Oasis rivalry became, for example, he expresses a back-handed admiration for the Gallagher brothers. Noel may have provided an ugly coda to the supposed battle by expressing the wish that Blur's Damon Albarn and Alex James would 'catch Aids and die', but Coxon will at least credit him and his brother with an admirable honesty. 'At least they were outright about it,' he says. 'At least they said, 'We hate you, you bastards.' They weren't pretending to like us and then slagging us off, which is what we'd been used to. In that way, I quite appreciated them.' . . .

Most of the alumni of the musical moment that lasted from around 1992 to 1998 are now scattered. Only the Gallagher brothers have remained pretty much where they always were, delivering their strait-laced facsimiles of classic rock to a vast audience whose attachment to the anthems they first heard 10 years ago seems unshakable. Most of the musicians and associates who once shared their company, however, have taken paths that have led them well away from the places they occupied in the mid-1990s.

Damon Albarn, once the most avowed champion of the archly parochial Britpop aesthetic, recently led the charge against Live8's inappropriately Anglo-Saxon lineup, and is currently enjoying international success with his band Gorillaz. Given that that project puts Blur on ice, their bass player, Alex James, is working on a new record under the name of Wigwam with the short-lived 1990s pop sensation Betty Boo, as well as DJing on the BBC's 6 Music digital radio station. Drummer Dave Rowntree, according to his PR, is working on the Transistor Project, a 'digital development label' aimed at helping aspiring musicians. . . .

The world these people built, however, has endured. It's where just about every worthwhile British band aspires to be: that speedy production line that takes promising musicians from their local pub venue, introduces them to the NME, and then – if everything goes to plan – inducts them into the head-rattling world of mainstream celebrity. The idea that there was ever an 'underground', where bands could ply their trade without paying any attention to the world of commerce, seems almost laughable. Less than a year ago, for instance, the Kaiser Chiefs were an unknown, transparently Blur-influenced band from Leeds. Now, their small handful of keynote hits has become inescapable, and their fans include Paul McCartney and Richard Gere.

The best example is provided by the ubiquitous Pete Doherty: on the face of it, a purveyor of the kind of scratchy, lo-fi stuff that once would guarantee musicians nothing more than a regular place on the John Peel show. He is a stupidly inappropriate example of that long-standing showbiz convention whereby fame only arrives when you perform a duet with Elton John. Doherty may not have been invited for canapes at Downing Street, but his unlikely clout was proved by, arguably, an even greater accolade: a half-hour interview on Newsnight with Kirsty Wark.

In the early 1990s, it was all rather different. Daytime radio spurned indie-rock in favour of sedate mainstream stars or productionline pop. The attentions of the tabloids' showbiz editors were similarly myopic. For all their evident talent, Britpop's pioneers were held at arm's length.

In early 1993, it took loud protests from the music press to convince the organisers of the Brit awards to make Suede a last-minute addition (other nominations that year included such cutting-edge attractions as Annie Lennox, Enya, Genesis and the long-lost Curtis Stigers). Blur were similarly marginalised; though Modern Life Is Rubbish was one of the

1990s' most influential records, the highest chart position achieved by its singles was 26. One fact in particular underlines the struggle that once faced those leftfield talents who aspired to push their way into the mainstream: Pulp's Common People made Jarvis Cocker a pop star three months before his 32nd birthday, although he had been mouldering on the fringes for a decade.

Everything belatedly began to align at the end of 1993. Matthew Bannister, the new controller of Radio 1, exiled the old guard of DJs and allowed the cutting-edge to intrude on what the station broadcast during the day. Among the first beneficiaries were the then-unknown Oasis, whose prospects were given a boost when an industry-only demo of Columbia was pushed on to the station's playlists. Blur, meanwhile, had just completed Parklife, the album that would be propelled skyward by the huge success of their watershed single, 1994's Girls and Boys.

'When it happened, it wasn't a shock,' says Coxon. 'It was something that we'd all been half-expecting. It was, "When is the world going to realise that we're making excellent pop music?" And they'd finally twigged.'

He pauses for a moment. 'But in making music that becomes commercially successful, there is some sort of dealing with the devil. You have to alter your art a little bit for it to happen. And I suppose that's when the rot started to set in with me.' . . .

As it turned out, the flashbulbs popping at the first wave of Britpop groups were quickly outshone by the tabloid spotlight on the Gallagher brothers. By 1996, Oasis had nudged their contemporaries to one side, marking the peak of their imperial phase with a two-night stand at Knebworth Park in Hertfordshire when they played in front of a combined audience of 250,000; there had been 2.6 million applications for tickets.

Alan McGee – the one-time president of Creation Records, now in charge of the more compact Poptones label – has little doubt about the episode that played the key role in propelling Oasis to such an elevated place: the week-long battle for the number 1 position that had taken place a year before. The wheeze had been Albarn's idea, and it was Blur who made it to the top: Country House sold 274,000 to Roll With It's 216,000. However, the decisive entry of Britpop into the national consciousness led to an imbalance. Blur, after all, were an angular, arch proposition who had probably reached their commercial limit. The uncomplicated Oasis, by contrast, could now begin working their populist magic.

'Nobody really realises this,' says McGee, 'but at that point, Blur were three times bigger than Oasis. Oasis may well never have wanted to admit that to themselves, but Definitely Maybe was at around 600,000 and Parklife had sold something like 1.5 to 2m copies. They were miles past us. And Damon Albarn, in his bizarreness, decided he was going to have it with these lunatics from Manchester, thinking it was going to be all jolly hockey sticks. And of course, that meant that the spotlight was on Oasis and it brought them up to a new level. In that sense, he probably did Oasis the biggest favour ever.'

As Noel and Liam – replete with Beatles fixation, cocaine habits and designer attire – became Britpop's new dual monarchs, its one-time prime movers sounded a note of complaint. 'The Beatles were always a really adventurous, funny, witty band,' said Albarn. 'But where's the intelligence in this music now?' He had a point, though some of his contemporaries still think Oasis's music was less of an issue than their revolutionary take on wealth and success. Enshrining yet another aspect of Britpop's legacy, the Gallaghers played a key role in ensuring that future generations of musicians would experience very little worry at all.

'I loved their honesty, their openness, the way they treated their success,' says Louise Wener, the one-time singer with Sleeper, now a successful writer whose third novel is about to go into print. 'They weren't embarrassed or ashamed by it. It was, "I'm going to be a rock'n' roll star, I'm going to ride around in a Rolls-Royce, if I make a million quid I'm going to roll around in it." They were the chavs of Britpop.'

Towards the end of my time with McGee, we pull apart one last theory about Britpop's legacy: the idea that, three months after the Blur–Oasis battle, when the latter group released Wonderwall, the rules of British music were decisively changed. From hereon in, the lighter-than-air ballad became obligatory, and the leather-trousers era of rock'n'roll was over. When Chris Martin plays his rapturously received songs of plodding redemption, or Snow Patrol deliver yet another mid-paced example of their anodyne craft, you can hear echoes of the song that made Oasis ubiquitous – can't you?

'No, no, no,' McGee protests. 'I would defend Wonderwall to the hilt. It's an amazing song. None of those people will ever write a song like that in their lives. Ever, ever, ever. They could try for the next 50 years, and they wouldn't do it.'

'cos when you're laid in bed at night
Watching . . . roaches climb the wall
If you called your Dad he could stop it all, Yeah.

Never live like common people
Never do what common people do
Never fail like common people
Never watch your life . . . slide out of view

And then dance, and drink . . . and screw
Because there's nothing else to do

I want to live with common people like you.
etc . . .

d) Wikipedia on Cool Britannia and Britpop.

Cool Britannia
From Wikipedia, the free encyclopedia

Cool Britannia is a media term that was used in the late 1990s to describe the contemporary culture of the United Kingdom. It was closely associated with the early years of the 'New Labour' government of Tony Blair. It is a pun on the title of the patriotic song 'Rule, Britannia'.

Origins of the term

The phrase 'Cool Britannia' was first used in 1967 as a song title by the Bonzo Dog Doo Dah Band, but there is probably no connection between that usage and the modern coining of the term. The phrase 'Cool Britannia' reappeared in the mid-1990s as a registered trade mark for one of Ben & Jerry's ice-creams (vanilla with strawberries and chocolate-covered shortbread). The ice cream name and recipe was coined in early 1996 by an American lawyer living in London, Sarah Moynihan-Williams, as a winning entry in a Ben and Jerry's ice cream competition. Her name for the ice cream as 'Cool Britannia' was meant to presage the era of New Labour, which came about with their election win in May 1997. The phrase was quickly adopted in the media and in advertising, seeming to capture the 'It' quality of London at the time. The election of Blair's government in 1997 on a platform of modernisation and with Blair as a relatively young prime minister gave the idea fresh currency. (There is a strong parallel between this and the catch-phrase

'Swinging London' during the early years of Harold Wilson's Labour government.)

1990s culture

To the extent that it had any real meaning, 'Cool Britannia' referred to the transient fashionable London scene, 1990s bands such as Blur and Oasis, fashion designers, the Young British Artists and magazines. Cool Britannia also summed up the mood in Britain during the mid-1990s Britpop movement, when there was a sudden influx of lively British rock and pop music from bands such as Oasis, Blur, Suede, Supergrass, Pulp and The Verve. Many link popularity of the Austin Powers films and the resurgence of 007 as factors of the spread of Cool Britannia. The movement, along with political factors, saw a renewal in British pride, typified by such things as Noel Gallagher's Union Flag guitar and Geri Halliwell's iconic skimpy Union Flag dress. In March 1997 *Vanity Fair* published a special edition on Cool Britannia with Liam Gallagher and Patsy Kensit on the cover with the title 'London Swings! Again!'. Figures in the issues included Alexander McQueen, Damien Hirst, Graham Coxon and the editorial staff of *Loaded*. By 1998 *The Economist* was commenting that 'many people are already sick of the phrase,' and by 2000 – after the fall of Britpop – it was being used mainly in a mocking or ironic way.

Although 'Britannia' refers to the whole of Great Britain, and not just England, similar terms for Wales and Scotland, 'Cool Cymru' and 'Cool Caledonia' respectively, were also coined[citation needed], but never gained any real popular currency.

Videos

Whatever happened to Cool Britannia? The UK after eight years of Blair Thirty British, US, French and Canadian scholars assess Blair's policies and style after two terms, in May 2005. Links to papers and video.

The internet is also awash with archive footage of this period, which would help to get a 'flavour' (as would films such as *Austin Powers: International Man of Mystery*). The point is to do some 'finding out' in order to give your critical readings some kind of context. There is plenty in the material above to send you in a number of different directions.

Similarly if you decided that 'retail therapy' was your thing and that you wanted to explore some aspect of the apparent gender divide you would likewise find material fairly easy to obtain:

a) John Fiske, 'Shopping for Pleasure: Malls, Power,and Resistance', in *The Consumer Society Reader* (2000, pp. 306–28) or as Chapter 2 in Fiske's *Reading the Popular* (1989, Routledge).
b) Extract from Jennifer Scanlon, 'Making Shopping Safe for the Rest of Us: Sophie Kinsella's Shopaholic Series and Its Readers', *Americana: The Journal of American Popular Culture (1900–present)* (Fall 2005, Volume 4, Issue 2)

This piece addresses young women and shopping via the popularity of a series of 'chick lit' books by Sophie Kinsella (the 'Shopaholic' series).

The Shopaholic books are light reading, beach reading, airport reading. They belong to the genre of chick lit, a phenomenally successful body of girl-centric fiction initiated with the publication of *Bridget Jones's Diary* in 1997. Although there is no consensus on what a book must feature in order to fit into the genre, and although it has subsequently spawned sub-genres such as Christian chick lit, wedding and bridesmaid lit, black chick lit, bigger girl lit, and mom lit, certain characteristics hold the increasingly diverse group of books, often best-sellers, together. They most frequently feature young, urban, professional female protagonists who, while not taking themselves too seriously, work through romantic, career, and body image trials and tribulations. As Red Dress Ink, the Harlequin imprint founded to respond to the enormous popularity of these books vis-à-vis traditional romances, declares, 'Red Dress Ink is women's fiction with attitude! From young and crazy to contemplative and witty, these stories are all about navigating life's little curves' (Harlequin). . . .

Shopaholic readers may relish the escape from the visuals of, say, women's magazines, which provide seemingly endless images of bodily perfection along with directives about how to achieve the body and win the man. Dawn Currie's research on adolescent magazines and their readers found that girls responded most favourably to magazines that acknowledge that real bodies fall short of the manipulated images. Her respondents repeatedly used the word 'real' to describe why they preferred one magazine to another. 'It just seems more realistic,' one writes about *Teen*, while another asserts that the arguably feminist, short-lived *Sassy* 'seems to pride itself on being more realistic than the other magazines' (Currie 245). While many chick lit novels help women negotiate, as Red Dress Ink puts it, 'life's little curves,' the Shopaholic books assume that Becky's bodily curves are of lesser importance than other elements of her life. The Shopaholic series, in fact, suggests shopping is an utterly enjoyable, even passionate experience for any body and every female body. Wedding planning offers opportunities for obsessions about the body, but in Becky's world they are short-lived:

> As I hover at the entrance (to the wedding cake studio), a skinny girl in jeans and strappy high heels is being led out by her mother, and they're in the middle of a row. 'You only had to taste it', the mother is saying furiously. 'How many calories could that be?' 'I don't care,' retorts the girl tearfully. 'I'm going to be a size two on my wedding day if it kills me.' Size two! Anxiously I glance at my thighs. Should I be aiming for size two as well? Is that the size brides are supposed to be?'
>
> (*Shopaholic Ties the Knot* 139)

Becky's brief mention of weight is expressed as a puzzle, as a question, not as an expression of solidarity with such an obsession. Moments later, inside the cake studio, Becky voraciously tastes cake samples and allows her indulgences to apply to her appetite as well as to her wardrobe.

For Becky Bloomwood, participation in consumer culture, rather than staying attractive for a man, provides a way to remain exciting and young, regardless of marital status or other life changes. It's a curious post-feminist existence, one in which there are always new consumer markets to exploit, new consumer choices to explore. It must be said, though, that although chick lit in general, and the Shopaholic formula within that genre, may challenge traditional romance, and may liberate women from the visual demands of television or magazine images, they hardly liberate women from the dictates of contemporary heteronormativity. What Currie argues about adolescent magazines for girls certainly rings true for the world of chick lit: 'the text determines the range of possible readings because it contains implicit assumptions about womanhood and therefore defines what kind of life can be taken for granted and what is open for struggle and renegotiation' (243–44). In the case of the Shopaholic books, and to date most of the literature in this genre, although hetero-sexual relationships may be open for struggle and negotiation, and in the Shopaholic books they may play second fiddle to shopping, the protag-onists' heterosexuality is a given. In this case at least, a postfeminist desire not to police sexuality the way second wave feminists did arguably fails (see Read, Karlyn). . . .

From Minnesota to Manila, from Canada to Chile, the Shopaholic series has a wide following. One quarter of the survey respondents live outside the United States, in Europe, Southeast Asia, Latin America, and the Middle East. The majority of respondents are single, childless, and under thirty years of age. Most read every day and between three and eight books a month. Their reading preferences vary, although over one third identify chick lit as their preferred type of book. When asked what they find most appealing about the Shopaholic books, almost all of the fans speak about the humour in the books; the books are 'fun', 'funny', amusing', humorous', 'silly', and 'hilarious'. Like Currie's respondents about adolescent girls' magazines, many also cite the 'real-ness' of the series: 'The humour and the realness of Becky. She has embarrassing things happen to her and she has a lot of problems and a lot of people can relate to that,' states one fan, while another asserts, 'I love that the main character is so REAL.' Yet another states, 'What I find most appealing about the shopaholic books is that it really could happen. I know it's fiction, but I find myself in the same financial mess. It's good to know sometimes things get better.' Readers of the Shopaholic series, like Currie's adolescent magazine readers, find refuge in the escape from the visualised perfect body. We never learn Becky's dress size, shoe size, or weight. 'I like it because for once the media is not talking about how (women) should be getting married or how they look,' writes one fan. 'They're not simplifying on how a woman's body SHOULD look. It talks about how she loves to shop.' Another states that Becky's 'craze for shopping is easier to achieve than having a perfect body, perfect hair, perfect nose, and perfect man.'

In much romance fiction, the reader identifies with the protagonist in terms of her romantic difficulties, ability or inability to help Mr Right act like Mr Right, the essential qualities that make her female and heroic. In the case of the Shopaholic books, however, few readers identify Becky's boyfriend Luke as significant at all. 'I LOVE LUKE,' one writes, but overall he garners few mentions. Almost every reader, however, identifies with Becky's love for shopping. 'I am not obsessed with finding the perfect man,' writes one respondent, 'but along with Becky I LOVE shopping.' The Shopaholic series provides its fans with a space in which to acknowledge, confess, or celebrate the role of shopping in their own lives. As one puts it, 'Everything is secondary to shopping.' Another writes, 'Like Becky, I think more about shopping than men!' One argues that Luke must be measured against shopping: 'Shopping was her one "true love" up to the point that she met Luke, and she can't bring herself to abandon it just because she met a man.' Yet another reader argues that Becky helps other women move in this direction: 'It gives a little bit of confidence to women who still think that their lives should revolve around pleasing the opposite sex.' Shopping, rather than romance, may fulfill women's needs: 'Shopping,' one fan argues, 'is the ultimate high.'

Reader identification with Becky is strong, and again it is most often linked to her habits of consumption. 'What I find most appealing about Sophie Kinsella's books is that I can relate them to my everyday life. Rebecca Bloomfield thinks and acts very similar to me,' states one fan in what is a common refrain. Over ninety percent of the respondents see some of Becky in themselves, although they express it in different ways:

> 'The character is, essentially, me.'
>
> 'Becky is just like me; we both LOVE to shop.'
>
> 'Becky and I were separated at birth.'
>
> 'I tell you it's like a mirror image.'
>
> 'Becky is so similar to me, except that I can't afford Prada at all!'
>
> 'The character was similar to myself. I am addicted to shopping.'
>
> 'Every woman can read it and say 'I am Becky Bloomwood.''
>
> 'When I read the first page of the first book I thought it had been written about me.'

Importantly, then, almost every respondent reports identifying with Becky not because of her romantic exploits, career changes, or dreams and ambitions, which are considerable, but rather because of her shopping habits. Becky Bloomwood shops compulsively but also shops, for the most part, not to compete with another woman, or to look a certain way to attract a man, but rather to please herself. Her fans acknowledge and celebrate this. 'Shopping is a form of self-fulfillment,' writes one fan. 'When you shop, you let go, you feel like you've earned what you've bought because you bought it using the money you have made.' This fan and others may conveniently ignore the degree to which Becky's spending habits ultimately benefit from the fact that her boyfriend/husband is a millionaire, but certainly the impression one gets is that Becky retains her independence and shops as one measure of that independent identity. Fans indicate that this particular focus, shopping, hits a nerve with women tired of endless directives about the importance of romance. Readers suggest that shopping provides a compensatory exchange for the pressures of contemporary life:

> It's annoying to constantly read books where a woman's only ambition is to find a man. The focus on shopping – and also finances, career, and friendship make for a more interesting reading experience, and also make Becky a more relatable person. A lot of women want to find a husband, but most have other priorities as well.

> The absurdly pressuring push from society and books alike, to get involved in a socially acceptable relationship and to be accepted by friends and family, is just so overplayed and has been portrayed much (too) much already. This series has the most minute (element) of this which simply makes it a refuge from normality.

> I may not be able to find the perfect man, but I can find the perfect clothes.

> Because everything is secondary to shopping.

> It makes Becky more modern, more independent. She's looking for a new pair of shoes not a husband – though she ends (up) finding that along the way as well.

Several respondents reduce the romance, ultimately, to shopping, and do so with pleasure. 'Shopping is what romances her,' one fan writes admiringly. 'There are so many amazing descriptives about all the shops she goes into and everything is so detailed and you would think she is with some amazing man but she is actually just shopping.'

In fact, as Becky deftly realizes, and her fans explain in their own words, shopping provides Becky with a unique form of cultural capital (see Bourdieu). For a contemporary woman, identity may come less from the man whose arm she drapes than from the designer whose shoes she dons. As consumer culture scholar Sharon Zukin writes; '[O]nce we have developed a fine eye for differences among the goods, we can make distinctions among the people who use them'. What marks Becky and her readers as postfeminist, perhaps, is that they transfer their primary interest from a lover to the fruits of their engagement with capitalism. 'I can remember times where eating Ramen noodles for the rest of the week was a great sacrifice to be able to buy a fabulous pair of shoes, purse, etc,' writes one respondent. Arguably, feminism has not failed the modern woman, but romance continues to do so, and in exchange for a postfeminist reality, in exchange for the relationship with the still inattentive or out of touch male love interest, Becky and her fans gets the goods, literally. 'Me and my friends drool more over purses and shoes than guys,' writes one fan, while another explains, 'Becky is not consumed with finding and marrying the perfect man, but only with locating the perfect Manolo Blahnik and Jimmy Choo shoe sale.' Again, these books and their readers, through Becky and her shopping adventures, negotiate the romantic, the compensatory, and the resistant: shopping is seductive, it meets women's needs in ways traditional romance does not, and it provides something of an alternative to cultural expectations of womanhood.

Interestingly, too, in a postfeminist world in which gender boundaries are allegedly more permeable, shopping reinforces essentialist differences between women and men. On a trip to New York, Luke suggests that Becky visit some museums, unless of course she has shopping she wants to 'get out of the way'. Readers share Becky's incredulity that anyone would want to get shopping out of the way, and they also share her sense that shopping is a female practice: 'When my boyfriend and I go shopping,' one writes, 'he sits on the benches and I get to work.' Another argues that 'Men view shopping as a chore, women often view it as a necessity,' while another states simply, 'I think it's an evolutionary trait.' Whether respondents equate shopping with female heterosexuality or not is unclear; however, several argue that heterosexual men dislike shopping while gay men enjoy it.

(Source: www.americanpopularculture.com/journal/articles/fall_2005/scanlon.htm)

c) No Gender-based Shopping Gap.

No Gender-Based Shopping Gap
By WSL Strategic Retail

Young Men Now Shop Like Young Women

Today's men 18 to 34 shop more like women their age than like older men. There is no longer a gender-based shopping gap between younger men and women, according to WSL Strategic Retail's study, *How America Shops™ 2002*.

Shopping Gap Key Findings:

- Younger men make 3.6 shopping trips a week, compared to 4.1 by younger women.
- Younger men visit an average of 1.6 stores, nearly as many as visited by younger women (1.9).
- 29% of these men report that they are shopping more in malls than a year ago, well above the 18% of younger women who do.
- 22% of men 18 to 34 shop more in department stores, in comparison to only 16% of younger women.
- 37% of both groups say that they are shopping more in specialty clothing stores than last year.

The Key Question

Whether or not younger men will maintain their new behaviour and attitudes towards shopping as they mature. If they do, the retail landscape will change forever.

Young Men Are the New Generation of Untapped Shoppers

These young men were the first to grow up in households with working, liberated moms who did not have time to do all the shopping for them. Mom sent them to the mall to get their own jeans and sneakers. Mom delegated grocery shopping and errands. They received shopping gift cards from Old Navy and Gap.

Men are marrying later in life and shopping for their own apartments without female help. When they do marry, they are active participants in the selections that go into the bridal registry. Stores see couples more than moms and daughters at the registry.

Young men are the target for Abercrombie and Fitch, Express for Men, Hot Topics, Burberry, and the new and improved Brooks Brothers. They choose their own hair gel and shampoo. L'Oreal Feria hair colour targets them. Neutrogena and Nivea have launched skin care for men into mass retail outlets.

Young men now shop like young women, given their heritage this makes sense.

(Source: http://retailindustry.about.com/library/uc/02/uc_wls2.htm)

d) References to the photographic sequence 'Shopping' by artist Merry Alpern.

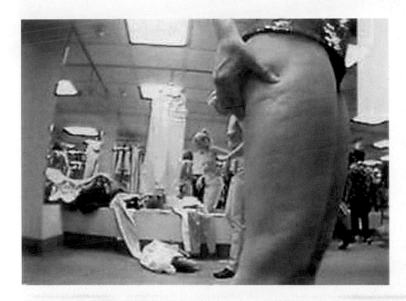

Figure 8.3
Shopping no. 20,
1999

Commentary on Alpern's work from Dörte Zbikowski, Merry Alpern in: *Crtl [Space]: Rhetorics of Surveillance from Bentham to Big Brother*, exhibition catalogue, ZKM Center for Art and Media/Karlsruhe, edited by Thomas Y. Levin, Ursula Frohne, and Peter Weibel, MIT Press, Cambridge, MA, pp. 296–299.

Merry Alpern

by Dörte Zbikowski

When she sets out in pursuit of subjects Merry Alpern takes a hidden camera with her. She captures absolute strangers in intimate situations. Her quest is the unadulterated, immediate moment and not a pose struck by someone aware they are being photographed. The persons captured in her camera's viewfinder do not become suspicious, nor do they later discover their role in Alpern's photographs. But then these are not portraits or photographs of persons but rather pictures of actions. Alpern's final shots are such that her subject's face – and thus identity – remains concealed. The only face that occurs now and then in her *Shopping* series is her own. Yet she regularly has to face charges of breaking taboos and producing voyeuristic, illegal photos. 'I don't go out looking for something in particular,' comments Alpern. 'What you see are things that just happen. In the way, you can view photography as maybe voyeuristic – and I guess by extension I am, too. But that is not my intention. For me, it is isolating a moment in time that will never happen again. A photograph allows you to examine that moment without any distractions so that maybe you can understand what is happening just a little better.'([1])

For her *Dirty Windows* series (1993–4) Alpern took up a fixed observation post. For weeks she sat behind a darkened window in Wall Street watching the goings-on in an apartment opposite where a short-stop hotel had recently opened. Looking through a vertically divided, dirty window she was witness to such intimate scenes as undressing, kissing and sex, counting money and taking drugs. Alpern's photos convey an excitement, a sense of being an initiate of something private or even forbidden combined with her constant fear of being discovered. However, the pictures also exude a specific elegance: the grainy black-and-white film, the sectional shots, the blurring induced by the dirty window imbue a certain tenderness. Not least of all the symbolism and aesthetic attached to viewing through a window heighten the enigmatic quality, which ultimately eludes us behind the window, and only ever hints at the story.

Her next series, *Shopping* (1997), consists of video stills for which Alpern used a hidden camera. Her own shopping experiences provided the idea. At the time she relentlessly hunted through one fashion store after another, without being able to decide on a single item of clothing. The realisation that she no longer knew what she wanted to look like after having tried on so many garments, made her wonder what special attraction shopping holds for women. In spring 1997 she began to record her own shopping habits. By fastening a small surveillance-type video camera into a handbag made of eyelet lace, she was able to film both herself and other women in the fitting rooms. This method produced arbitrary, unplanned shots, some via a mirror. They show shopping as an experience, but the scenes are at odds with Alpern's own recollections. The handbag perspective is also unusual and roughly corresponds to that of a child.

This voyeuristic observation of others made Merry Alpern think a lot about male–female relationships, but above all to question her own behaviour. She sees the morally reprehensible compulsion to look at something which is forbidden as a basic human weakness. Ogling is an attempt to understand oneself better. As regards how she sees herself she says: 'I had a totally different perception of myself in the (*Shopping*) film: my expressions, my body, my ageing skin – somehow I had always seen myself quite differently when I looked in the mirror. Suddenly, I no longer knew what I really look like.'([2])

Alpern's work has a sociological background. As a student of sociology (1973–7: Grinnell College, Iowa), she had already wanted to explore her environment and her study topics by taking pictures. In 1987, she produced her first series of photos in which she realised this concept from the perspective of an artist. She accompanied and took photographs of two young homeless people, got to know and understand them. Not least of all the friendly relationship the pictures reflect makes them so immediate and moving.

In violating the private sphere of total strangers, as well as her own, Alpern seeks to expose the concealed aspects of everyday actions. She is interested in the way the camera can isolate a moment and the photo then convey a new image of this moment. The coarse-grained soft focus, on the one hand, and the cropped quality of her pictures, on the other, leave much scope for our imaginations to create the stories behind the pictures.

1 Merry Alpern, quoted from Pat Willard, 'When No One is Watching' in *Brooklyn Bridge*, February/March 2000, p. 72.
2 Merry Alpern, in *Versteckte Kamera mal anders*; quoted from http://www.allegra.de/extracts/archiv/1999/october/special/merry.html

Are you getting the picture? Or does the writing have to be on the wall (or street)? It's not what you find but 'that' you look. It's not about authorities but stimulus. It's not about facts but rather about opinions and ideas. What you're ideally looking for is a starting point: a title perhaps or an understanding to hang your ideas on. Do one yourself?

ACTIVITY

Offer four or five 'interesting' resources for an exploration of graffiti as communication (vandalism or art?) and say briefly in what ways each piece might be useful in guiding, structuring and energising explorations in this area. Try, in each resource, to find something that might clarify an exploration by providing a lead (or even a title). An example is provided below from the week this was being written:

a) Graffiti artist Banksy hits the jackpot!

Banksy's graffiti art sells for half a million
By Nigel Reynolds, Arts Correspondent

Prices for 11 paintings by the graffiti artist Banksy have gone for four times pre-sales estimates at auction, proving the global credit squeeze has yet to hit contemporary art prices.

A stencilled image of two policeman, titled 'Avon and Somerset Constabulary', sold for £96,000 at London auctioneers Bonhams, thought to be a new auction-house record for the self-styled guerrilla artist who refuses to reveal his real name.

The previous record was £57,000, paid last October for his picture of Mona Lisa with spray paint dripping from her eyes.

'Di Faced Tenners', a painted sheet of fake £10 notes bearing the face of Diana, Princess of Wales, was knocked down for £24,000, against an estimate of £5,000–£7,000. His 11 works sold for more than £540,000.

Once confining himself to witty graffiti images which would appear overnight in streets in London and his hometown of Bristol, Banksy has now become a major mainstream painter collected by celebrities.

Last autumn the artist staged a show in Los Angeles attended by Brad Pitt, Angelina Jolie, Jude Law and Keanu Reeves. Jolie reportedly spent £200,000 on his work.

Earlier in the year, the American pop star Christina Aguilera paid £25,000 for three of Banksy's works on a trip to London, including a pornographic picture of Queen Victoria in a lesbian pose with a prostitute.

Gareth Williams, a Bonhams specialist, said: 'Perhaps the most incredible aspect of the Banksy phenomenon is neither his meteoric rise, nor the substantial sums of money that his art now commands, but that as a self-confessed guerrilla artist, he has been so wholeheartedly embraced by the very establishment he satirises.

'We are sure that this irony is not lost on today's buyers.'

(Source: www.telegraph.co.uk/arts/main.jhtml?xml=/arts/2007/10/25/babanksy125.xml)

- Can graffiti survive being made art?
- How does the 'guerrilla artist' deal with money?
- Where dose the value of a work of art come from?
- Who is graffiti for? What purposes does it serve?

Please remember that what you are doing is part of the exploring of an area and that you will then have the opportunity to write up what you find. This is not the writing, it is help with the reading. It may provide some words but it is mostly providing support, prompts and the occasional 'fire of an inspiration'. It's likely, for example, that anyone who writes about graffiti at this time will reference the massive amounts being paid to some graffiti 'artists' (with Bansky as our emblematic figure). This will have little or nothing to do with a specific resource rather it will function as an event which we are checking for details. In other words, it will be (and will remain) 'secondary' in every sense.

Presenting who I am: exploring personal and cultural identity

Where all of this investigating and exploring leads is to a single piece of work which is intended to embody the work of the AS course. Appropriately for a course that has 'identity' as its key concept, this means a refocus on 'ourselves' as the ultimate cultural product (and repository), the 'animal suspended in webs of its own making'. As the writer Ursula Le Guin famously remarked, 'All journeys are returns' and so it is with this one. The expeditions you have taken into notions of, on the one hand, 'the individual', and on the other, 'cultural practices', must now turn decisively to the self and 'identity': 'Who I am in context'.

Once again it is a broad and flexible brief as befits its subject. It offers you discipline in three ways:

- There are four key concept, two of which should be used to aid the interrogation of your focus area.
- You are expected to address 'the place where the personal and cultural meet', which merely means providing a twin perspective which is both personal ('I') and cultural ('they').
- The medium is a presentation, involving 'sound and vision', which means 'orchestrating' material into an engaging show for an audience of your peers.

However, the key to this task, as so often, lies with and in the title. Given that the presentation is meant to offer its audience six to eight minutes of 'consumption' (something attractive to 'chew' on), it should be clear that this task has a title not a question and requires a selective statement, not an answer. The difference between 'who I am' (in context) and the massively philosophical 'Who am I?' (sometimes referred to as the 'meaning of life' question, whose answer author Douglas Adams claimed was '42') is the difference between a moderate challenge and madness. 'Who I am in context' implies a focus determined by the 'I' and her/his contexts and this is vital.

In this respect a model such as Goffman's dramaturgical model of self-presentation can be especially clarifying. Goffman, you will remember, offers an analogy between being ourselves and dramatic performances, suggesting that we 'play' ourselves very much in the way actors play characters. He also usefully breaks down the process into component parts and unwittingly provides an excellent starting point for viable presentations. All of these layers provide interesting angles on the statement 'This is who I am':

- Persona: versions of the self.
- Role: parts we must play as ourselves.
- Performance: how honestly we play these.
- Staging: how we set up the 'immediate' context.
- Teams: with whom we 'play'.
- Personal style: what we idiosyncratically bring to the game.

What the presentation focus adds to this is 'context': to the psychological we add the sociological and cultural. To 'who I am as brother/sister/student/teenager/ shop assistant, horror fan' is added 'how these identities are contextualised by and in British society at the beginning of the third millennium'. This will involve you in opening up but not necessarily resolving the issues involved in the nego- tiations which are an inevitable part of understanding identities. As a crude rule of thumb, it might be useful to see the issue as the relationship between 'self' (who I am) and society ('who I am expected to be/allowed to be') with 'identity' as a kind of synthesis ('who I allow myself to be'/who I am able to be).

Goffman's model is a more than useful prompt here, suggesting aspects of your life which might feasibly form the basis of presentations entitled 'Who I am in context'. If you were a forty-something-year-old author of a Communication and Culture textbook, your response might begin:

- Who I am as an author.
- Who I am as a father (of four).
- Who I am as a Man Utd fan (aka 'glory hunter').
- Who I am as an amateur football manager.
- Who I am as a devotee of riff-based heavy metal.

This crude formula is a very good place to start partly because it allows you to see what the real question is. What is being asked about in the above list is the age-old question of Communication and Culture: the question of meaning. These presentations might be subtitled 'what it means to be (e.g.) a father (brother, daughter and so on)' since these individual identities are the genuine intersections of personal and cultural spheres.

ACTIVITY

Using Goffmann's model as a prompt suggest *ten* individual identities which might feasibly form the bases of presentation.

Thereafter it is really about choosing that aspect of your experience that interests you most (and, of course, that you want to communicate) and acknowledging the twin priorities of the task:

a) to use this 'case study' to explore the key concepts of the course
b) to illustrate the 'case study' and 'bring it to life' in a show.

In other words, exactly like the readings, which embody this way of working, there is a process of critical analysis followed by a presentation of findings. Though all that will be seen (and assessed) is the presentation (seven minutes of sound and vision), preparation is everything.

It is very important that the presentation should be as meaningful as possible to you: something you pursue rather than contrive. This explains why there are no peripheral tasks, asking you, for example, to say how you did the work or requiring you to review it just after doing it. However, this is a test and you must be aware of this. It is an open opportunity for you to demonstrate the benefits of studying Communication and Culture. The specified key concepts are intended to provide explicit support for this and while they do have a certain formality that is lent by the term 'key concept' they are also recognisably the places any consideration of 'self in cultural contexts' must be. Also despite the requirement to apply two, given the context they are going to be overlapping and interrelating. In fact one way of representing the task conceptually would be to see it this way:

> 'The focus is personal and cultural IDENTITY and the VALUE given to cultural activities: their REPRESENTATION by ourselves and others and their relationship to dominant values and POWER in our society.'

This is both substantial and enabling since it is asking serious questions about experience that is important to you, ground that has been chosen by you. It also means that if you are doing the task set, you will necessarily 'apply' these concepts (in many cases all four of them). There should be no need to bend over backwards to force them in. It is, for example, hard to see how 'identity' as a concept can be avoided, though perhaps it is always going to be a matter of principle. Thus any list of examples must be offered with a 'warning': that the concepts identified in each case represent only one way of seeing each 'topic', that the four concepts are equally viable whatever the focus.

Presentations: focus and structure

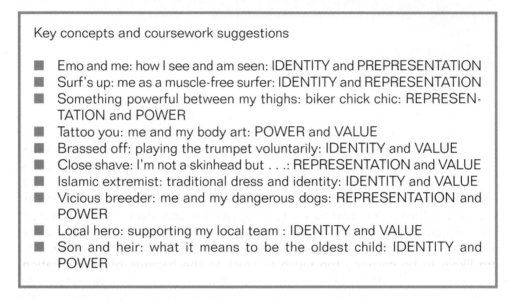

Key concepts and coursework suggestions

- Emo and me: how I see and am seen: IDENTITY and PREPRESENTATION
- Surf's up: me as a muscle-free surfer: IDENTITY and REPRESENTATION
- Something powerful between my thighs: biker chick chic: REPRESEN-TATION and POWER
- Tattoo you: me and my body art: POWER and VALUE
- Brassed off: playing the trumpet voluntarily: IDENTITY and VALUE
- Close shave: I'm not a skinhead but . . .: REPRESENTATION and VALUE
- Islamic extremist: traditional dress and identity: IDENTITY and VALUE
- Vicious breeder: me and my dangerous dogs: REPRESENTATION and POWER
- Local hero: supporting my local team : IDENTITY and VALUE
- Son and heir: what it means to be the oldest child: IDENTITY and POWER

ACTIVITY

Take three or four of the individual identities you identified earlier and turn them into presentations by adding a working title and suggesting the two key concepts in every sense.

Having established the character of your content focus, you can begin to move towards devising your 'show'. The choice of format is left deliberately open so that you can focus on the opportunities offered by the content rather than the limitations of the medium or format. The requirements are merely for there to be visual and verbal components. This means, in ideal circumstances, you can allow your content focus to dictate the direction and shape of your presentation. For all of the proposals above, for example, it is likely that the very act of choosing is based upon the candidate having thoughts in one or more of the following forms:

- Ideas
- Images
- Stories/incidents/anecdotes.

It is then for you decide the best way to 'tell' them. In many ways this is a classic report back, an old-fashioned 'show and tell', exploiting the opportunities offered by new technologies. Whatever your focus you will have something to 'show' so the first decision is about the relationships between still and moving image. Crudely you can have:

- Still images only
- Moving image only
- A mixture of both.

You then need to decide how to 'anchor' these 'floating signifiers' with the sound elements (and most importantly words). Again the choices are fairly simple. Is the sound fully integrated as in, for example, a video diary format or a live presentation with audience or is it essentially a discrete component, a separate commentary as in an illustrated podcast (the modern equivalent of a tape/slide presentation). Perhaps more importantly, given that the sound is to carry much of your under-standing of the content and concepts, is to say that this element should, almost certainly, be scripted. Shorn of the paraphernalia of process (the previous version required you to submit a sheaf of preparation notes and a review), the words are likely to be carrying too much to trust to the hazards of improvisation. 'Presentation' implies performance and audience, and even if they are not present at the 'reading' it is for them that the script and visuals are loaded: loaded with ideas, loaded with analysis, loaded with key concepts, loaded with opinions, loaded with interest.

This probably means that the model of presentation which simply sees the words providing a commentary (or the visuals illustrating a verbal argument), such as the website or illustrated podcast, are likely to be the easiest to accomplish (and be accomplished in!). What these formats allow is a kind of audio-visual essay, where a knowledgeable and engaging guide gives us a tour of the issues. Live presentations merely add to this the potential transfer of energy that comes from a meaningful interaction with an audience so that the 'telling' becomes potentially more telling. It is important that self-devised formats which include, for example, 'live' film (made on location) or consist of montages of 'made' and 'found' material retain (or find an equivalent for) this central interpretative, analytical and to some extent narrative element. This will happen most often, and most safely, through 'script' (though other elements such as sequencing visual language will also have their parts to play).

Perhaps a planning formula would help to clarify this:

Who I am in context: 'Show and Tell'

FOCUS AREA: Me as . . .

(What it means to be . . .   )

KEY CONCEPTS: Identity   Representation   Power   Value

FORMAT:

Visuals?

Verbals?

'SHOW'

What am I going to look at (content, themes)?

How am I going to show/illustrate this?

What evidence/support/resources am I going to look for?

What am I going to create?

How will I combine these elements?

'TELL'

What do I have to 'tell' (big ideas, argument)?

What do I have to say (more specifically) about the stuff above?

How can I sequence the elements I have identified for best effect?

How can I deliver the technical/theoretical analysis?

And this is what it might look like in action:

Who I am in context: 'Show and Tell'

FOCUS AREA: Me as . . . *Marilyn Manson fan (and lookalittlelikey!)*

(What it means to be . . . *different*)

KEY CONCEPTS: *Identity*   *Representation*   **Power**   **Value**

FORMAT: *Short film*

Visuals? *Montage of made and found material*

Verbals? *Voice-over and natural sound of clips, interviews and so on*

'SHOW'

What am I going to look at (content, themes)? *How sub-cultural identity can be a dominant factor in your life, determining how you look (two ways: appear and 'see') and are seen.*

How am I going to show/illustrate this? *By showing myself, others responses to me intercut with my celebrity/anti-celebrity role model in action and reflection.*

What evidence/support/resources am I going to look for? *Sharp interview and concert footage of Manson, interpretative writing about him for sharp quotes.*

What am I going to create? *My own Manson-esque interview, shots of myself touring the college and POV shots of other people's responses.*

How will I combine these elements? *Effectively a montaged documentary with voice-over to provide coherence.*

'TELL'

What do I have to 'tell' (big ideas, argument)? *Books are most often judged by their covers, despite the warnings. Also a subculture (like any other culture) is a way of life: it feeds on and off itself.*

What do I have to say (more specifically) about the stuff above? *Listen to this guy Manson: he makes an awful lot of sense. Listen to me too.*

How can I sequence the elements I have identified for best effect? *Lots to play with here. Two obvious places to start: with the 'real' Manson (his persona, his name OR with exaggerated passer-by responses to me.*

How can I deliver the technical/theoretical analysis? *Through a concentrated analytical voice-over script.*

Do two of these generic topics using the formula before you try one of your own:

- Emo and me: how I see and am seen
- Surf's up: me as a muscle-free surfer
- Something powerful between my thighs: biker chick chic
- Tattoo you: me and my body art
- Brassed off: playing the trumpet voluntarily
- Close shave: I'm not a skinhead but . . .
- Islamic extremist: traditional dress and identity
- Vicious breeder: me and my dangerous dogs
- Local hero: supporting my local team
- Son and heir: what it means to be the oldest child

9 PASSING EXAMINATIONS

In this chapter we will look at how your communication skills and experience can be used to help you prepare for and to sit examinations.

- We will explore approaches to revision.
- We will look at how you can be more personally effective when preparing for, and sitting, examinations.
- We will offer you useful techniques to assist you when taking examinations.

The purpose of this chapter is to offer both general and specific advice on how to improve your chances of gaining high marks in the examinations you may sit in Communication and Culture (and elsewhere). Its rather clumsy title is a deliberate attempt to develop this process from the start. Communication and Culture is a discipline which encourages effective communication and a personal critical response to all manner of contexts and texts. Examinations, and particularly examination advice, cannot be immune to the need to be both rigorously criticised and effectively communicated.

The skills we need in examinations will of course include reading and writing, speaking and listening, drafting and dealing with questions. It is equally important to practise critical skills to deal with the examination as yet another text, and to plan in both a general and a specific sense. There will also be a need for common sense. This is not a skill but all too sadly and too often it isn't demonstrated in the examination room.

It is easily said but examinations should not be feared. It is likely that you will have worked hard all year on your Communication and Culture course. In truth it would be very frustrating if the knowledge you acquired there was never tested or called upon. Exams are merely the rather artificial opportunity you get to demonstrate what you know and to receive some, hopefully much, credit for it. They are a time- and money-saving alternative to having a visiting examiner come to your house to quiz you in depth on your knowledge of the subject. Positively, examinations usually ask you about what you know rather than what you don't know: after all, to 'examine' means 'to look at in detail', not 'to catch out'.

Examinations

Figure 9.1 Sit and think for a few minutes when you first open the exam paper

There are lots of places to go for advice on examination preparation and technique: study skills guides, websites, your teachers/fellow students, Radio One's annual series of radio and television revision programmes. What common sense tells you is that there can be no single definitive answer any more than there can be a single effective general model of communication. At the centre of the examination process is the examinee, just as at the centre of the revision process is the reviser – in other words, you! What helps is whatever helps you to be relaxed, to be confident, to be clear-headed and clear-sighted. If, for you, this means eating garlic harvested at a full moon with a platinum sickle, then so be it!

What follows is a debate between received wisdom and an individual approach: not a contest, but a conversation. It partly rehearses the advice which everybody knows to give to prospective students; it is largely the advice which you would give to yourself if you were writing this part of this book. It also challenges that advice to suggest that there are a large number of potential 'negotiated' readings, or even 'oppositional' readings, of this advice. This is partly meant to function as a viable alternative to the all-too-common position of knowing what you should do both to revise and to prepare for your examinations and equally knowing that you will never actually do this. Too many students buy into the self-fulfilling 'prophecy' which begins with despair, moves to an unrealistically extensive revision plan, and ends with no revision (and despair).

Some of the advice that follows is deliberately provocative because its very purpose is to make you all as individual learners think about how you learn best and how you might best prepare for examinations which judge your quality as learners. Nothing here is advocated, save the need for individual students to make rational and personal decisions about their own revision and preparation. All too often the most important lesson of education is that 'you shouldn't let other people get your kicks for you'.

Communication and Culture is not a subject that lends itself to 'right answers'. You are mostly asked for analysis and evaluation in contexts where the choice of evidence and treatment is yours. Much of what has been covered in this textbook remains a matter for debate, and it is your job to join these debates rather than attempt to bring them to a satisfactory conclusion. What is often being marked is your ability to fashion a convincing argument and support it with relevant evidence: it is the quality of your argument not the character of your argument that is important here.

Advice on examination practice, or rather examinations in practice, falls into three phases:

1   **Revision**: which looks at the various ways in which the knowledge gained from a course of study can be recalled, marshalled and reorganised so as to be useful in the examination.
2   **Preparation**: which covers the period from the arrival in the examination room to the first time your pen is used.
3   **Technique**: which deals with how different forms of question might be approached – from design to realisation.

Let's look at these three phases in more detail.

Revision

Literally 'the act of seeing again', revision is a taboo word for many students, describing a process they only vaguely understand and one that, even when done thoroughly, offers questionable results. Revision has a dubious reputation – stereotypically it involves sitting still for long periods of time and suffering. There is a profound moral dimension to this. In fact it is treated by society at large and by the educational community specifically as a kind of moral performance indicator. Good students do revision in the same way that they don't do sex or drugs. Bad students on the other hand spend their time doing the last two and thus have no time for the former. For, above all things, revision takes time.

Every institution, whether it be school, college or self-help guide, has its own timescale: 'start at Easter', 'at least three months' or 'Christmas is a good time to start'. Courses are cut short, curtailed to allow for the 'revision period', the part of the course where the dynamic that is learning is brought to a standstill. At some point the revision timetable must be drawn up – provided by your school or college, or constructed with a sharp pencil and 30cm ruler. This is a statement of intent, an attempt formally to engage in a self-fulfilling prophecy.

A good example is found in our sister volume *Media Studies: The Essential Introduction* (Rayner et al. 2004).

Drawing up a revision plan

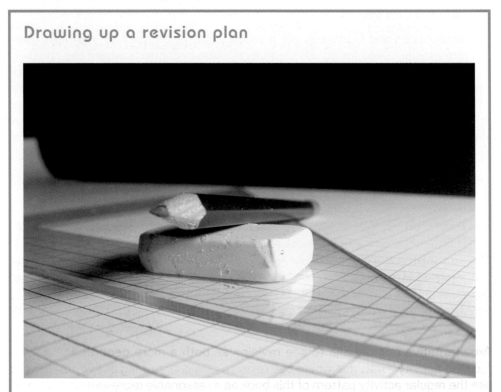

Figure 9.2 Drawing up a revision timetable is easy

A revision plan is the essential first step towards preparing yourself for your Media Studies exam. You may find the following steps a useful way to guide you in drawing up such a plan:

1   Make sure you know what you need to revise. Either check with the specification or syllabus yourself, or ask your teacher what you need to do. In some cases you may find that there is a choice of topic areas and you may have to decide how many of these you are going to prepare for the exam.

2   Make a list of the topics you have decided you need to cover. Check where you can best find the information you need on these topics. Start with your own notes and then look at how textbooks, such as this one, may be able to help you.

3   Draw up a revision timetable devoting a suitable amount of time to each topic. Be realistic about how many hours you can devote to this. There will almost certainly be other subjects making demands on your time, as well as all of those diversions you will have to succumb to.

4   Put together a list of up-to-date examples that you can draw upon to illustrate your answers. If you have made good notes throughout your course, you should have a good range of texts such as films, television and radio programmes, newspaper and magazine articles you can call upon. It is also worth thinking in advance about how you may be able to use these in the exam. Remember, too, to keep an eye on such sources as the Media Guardian for up-to-date information on key media issues and debates.

5   Remember that revision you do at the very last minute may be of little use. Revising is like preparing yourself for a sporting event. A sustained programme of preparation will always be more effective than a last-minute panic.

This is sensible advice but it is not the only approach to revision. One problem with revising in this semi-formal way is that you run the risk of putting unwanted pressure on knowledge that has been organically and contextually acquired. You also simply put pressure on yourself over a significant period of time and stress the skills of recalling information instead of the skills of analysis and evaluation.

An alternative approach is to see revision as both a more general and a more focused activity. First, this would see revision as a course-long activity and would see the regular activity pattern of this book as a reasonable representation of most teaching within the area. In applying knowledge in practical and semi-practical situations, we are in fact revising our understanding of the key concepts of Communication and Culture. This process may regularly lead to topic summary sheets on which you record the key ideas of some topic, but these are merely the regular reminders of how the course is to be assessed.

Do you know how the course you are currently doing is assessed?

- How many examinations?
- How long are they?
- What is the mark breakdown across papers/units?
- What does the mark scheme for each paper reward?

Too often the course is seen as something to remember when in fact it is something to experience. The principle of 'study leave' is well established in this country but not well founded on any significant evidence. Letting students leave school or college to revise reinforces the separation between the course and the examination and stresses the importance of memory over analysis. Examinations need not be viewed like this. They are a small but significant part of the course and one of the 'audiences' that any course must have. Most often the courses we do are defined by the qualifications we seek, in other words by the examinations we sit.

This fact can be approached sincerely or cynically. Partly we must dismiss the need for specific revision altogether, for if we have engaged in intrapersonal communication what question can we fear? More practically we might think early about the amount of knowledge necessary to 'fill' an answer planned and written within as little as 30 minutes. We may in fact 'knock up' our own revision plan which will serve as a gloss to the previous one or perhaps define a continuum within which we all can work.

A substantial engagement with the course, its form and its content, is the essential first step towards preparing yourself for your Communication and Culture examination. Revision is all very well but 'vision' is actually much more important. Make sure you 'see' it clearly first time around so you won't struggle to recall it. The following steps may form a useful guide.

An alternative revision plan

1 Make sure you know how you are to be assessed. Get hold of past questions and mark schemes. Check the range of topics to be assessed and the number of questions to be attempted. Calculate the minimum number of topics to be prepared for the examination and the frequency with which they occur. Give yourself an amount of security according to your temperament (if you are by temperament cautious, revise extra topics).

   (NB: The new specifications at AS and A-Level are by their design easier to predict because they specify not only what you must know but also that this knowledge must be tested.)

2   Consider each topic you cover in terms of a) its most important content and b) the amount of information you could reasonably use, if known, in between 20 and 25 minutes. Compile the essential information, together with quotations and/or notes, on no more than one side of A4 paper for each topic. This is an indication of the amount of knowledge you can need or use in an examination. Given that no examination is longer than one-and-three-quarter hours, and that four questions is the maximum request, revision cannot consist of more than eight sheets of paper or eight sides of A4 paper.

(Psychologically and symbolically the information and content knowledge that you need for any formal examination should be able to be comfortably located on your table/desk. You should end up sitting with no more than six separated and organised A4 sides, perhaps fewer. In this way 'what is to be known' is put in its place and you are in a position to think about what you are being asked and how your response will be structured.)

3   If you have clarified the significant content for each topic and reduced it to a single side of A4, the fixing of content detail is in fact best done close to the examination. If there are things you feel you need to remember, two days is a much more sensible timescale than two months. Try as far as you can to think about one examination at a time and to concentrate your knowledge-fixing on the two days before the examination. This may seem like a heresy but remember we are not talking here about things you don't know but rather about things you do. Obviously other examinations in other subjects will interfere, but ideally you should deal with one examination at a time and not begin to revise the second paper until the first is over.

What this approach advocates is that knowledge of assessment – of what examinations are and what they do – is as important as knowledge of subject. Study at A Level must involve more than the regurgitation of knowledge, and the more that is crammed in, the more likely it is to emerge in an unprocessed fashion. In Communication and Culture in particular there is an established equality between theory as such and the evidence of communication in practice. The latter can be rehearsed across the course but there must ideally be room for 'live' performance – the act of coming to an examination question in an examination room and drawing freshly upon your experience as a communicator. This is the first lure of the subject: we are all experienced and mainly skilful communicators.

This subject asks us to draw on that experience and skill. The more that we try to learn this 'experience', the less like experience it becomes.

Knowledge of assessment begins with the classification of your exams which you attempted earlier. Different kinds of examination require different kinds of preparation as well as different kinds of skills. However, there are simple statements to be made which cover general features of the examination experience.

Preparation

However much good advice you're given and take, the problems of the examination room come down to a simple problem: you need to be calm, relaxed and clear-headed – and you're not! However cool you are in the face of a formal examination, by the time you've stood around for 10 minutes outside the exam room with twenty-five to fifty fellow students who are bombarding you with trivial questions about the coming examination, you are likely to be a little wound up. The way you behave in the first 5 minutes of the examination is therefore vital.

Unfortunately it is not uncommon to find candidates filling this vital opening 5 minutes with frantic writing. No sooner has the invigilator's 'The time is 9.30, you may now begin' died in the air, than the first task response is finding an introduction. This is simply an impossibility if you are interested in maximising your achievement. Clearly, the first 5 minutes are for reading, for getting to know the paper, and for discovering across a couple of readings at least the opportunities that the paper offers. Better not to open the paper at all for the first 5 minutes than attempt an immediate answer to the first question.

You are partly allowing yourself time to acclimatise to the examination environment, making yourself familiar with the overall picture before the real work begins. This may give you ideas, albeit crude ones, about which questions are most demanding and about which questions should be tackled first. Often in this initial assessment, questions are clarified and what appeared easy and attractive at first sight now seems problematic and confusing. This is not the only safeguard against poor question selection but it is the first of a number of filters.

You are also moving into 'examination time', the medium of examinations. Being asked to perform to time is the essence of the examination experience and thus nothing is more important than keeping to time. Do not be fooled by the theory that two good answers are better than three mediocre ones; siphoning time from one question to another rarely allows a significantly greater performance. Unfinished papers simply and literally wipe marks and thus grades off a candidate's achievement. Your performance in the questions you attempt can never compensate for the question you have missed. In fact the latter dilutes the former. Hear this loud and clear: you must attempt the number of questions you're asked to. This is the ugly reality of examinations: if you attempt a four-question AS paper but in fact only manage three questions, the level of performance required in these three answers, just to reach a basic pass mark of, say, 40 per cent, is in fact 66 per cent (this may be the difference between a B grade an an E grade).

The great myth of examination time is the suggestion that, to arrive at your time allocation for each question, you divide the number of questions to answer into the time allowed.

This in fact overlooks all the other advice that we are giving about the psychology of doing examinations. In the new 1¾ hour AS examination you should allow at least 10 to 15 minutes for examination management time – reading the paper in a considered way; moving from one topic area to the next; and checking that all words have been successfully transferred from your head via your pen to the page (and that most of them are spelled correctly). Make a note of the mark allocation for each question before you start and then make sure that you leave enough time to give the questions with the most marks you full attention, even if they come last. Don't forget that you can answer the questions in any order you wish.

Scoring and exploding: paper vandalism approved

The other thing you must do, and this can start pretty much with the first reading, is to make the examination paper your own. You do this in a primitive way by defacing it, leaving your own marks on it. These marks are the evidence that you have ruthlessly explored the questions' potential and have identified any potential problems with them. If you do not do this, you have not justified your entry. If your paper can be handed back and reused, or even effectively photocopied, you really haven't made the examination your own – it still belongs to the examiner and the examining body.

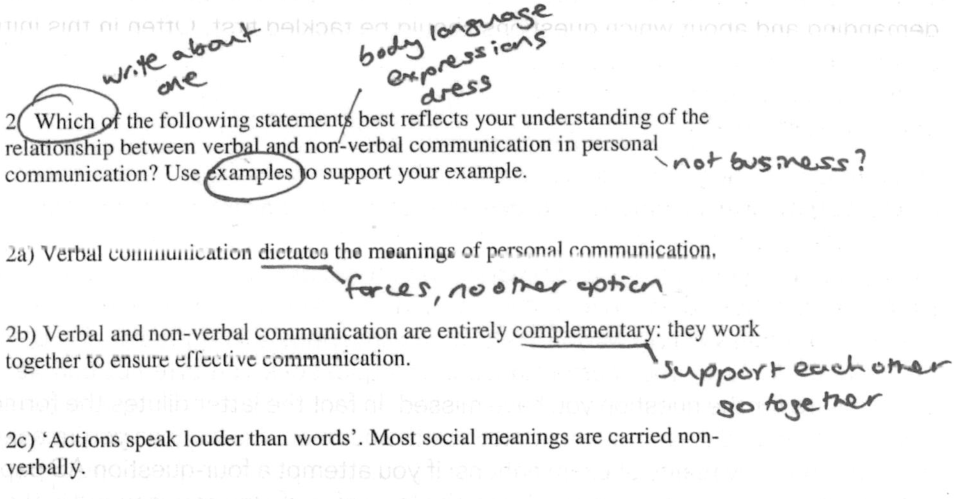

write about   body language
one   expressions
                dress

2 Which of the following statements best reflects your understanding of the relationship between verbal and non-verbal communication in personal communication? Use examples to support your example.   not business?

2a) Verbal communication dictates the meanings of personal communication.

        forces, no other option

2b) Verbal and non-verbal communication are entirely complementary: they work together to ensure effective communication.

        support each other
        so together

2c) 'Actions speak louder than words'. Most social meanings are carried non-verbally.

Figure 9.3 Defacing your exam paper

The longer you stay in the examination system the more likely you are to have a tragic examination story – about the friend of yours who read 'First World War' when it said 'Second World War' or answered eight questions when the instructions said 'choose ONE'. These stories are told up and down the country in the lead-up to examinations, and much fun is had at the expense of these buffoons who could not be us. Yet the catalogue is added to every year without fail. Candidates answer on books they haven't read, attempt six hours' work in three hours or even sit the wrong examination. If defacing the paper does nothing else, it reduces this risk. Educationists and psychologists frequently assert that the most effective learning is active – and not passive – learning. Taking your pen to the examination paper is a sound extension of this principle. You claim and maintain your status as an active examination candidate; you will not settle for being a passive examination candidate for whom examinations are something that happens to them.

Underachievement in public examinations is in fact rarely the result of a hideous lack of ability, skill or knowledge but more often a result of a hideous lack of relevance. Most examiners report that most papers they mark are hampered by the fact that the candidate, even if the paper is complete, has not responded to questions in their entirety and thus has made it impossible for the paper to access the upper range of marks available. To get full marks is unlikely, but to put yourself in the game and get a mark out of the full allocation must be a primary goal. In some scripts (this is examiner-speak for a candidate's examination answer book) the answers are so negligent of the questions that the final mark is low because only a third or even less of the question's scope has been addressed. Let's say this again: physically marking the paper makes this broader response to specific questions significantly more likely.

Looking for key words is part of your starting point, but even so it is vital to be aware that there are two sets of key words:

- Words that instruct, direct or govern (e.g. 'analyse', 'describe', 'state', 'evaluate', 'consider', 'compare')
- Subject-specific words (e.g. 'self-concept', 'feedback', 'semiotic').

If you can discover what it is you have to do and what is the precise focus of subject content of your examination, you are well on the way to success. Be careful you don't make the identification of key words your only goal – the next stage is necessary, too. Successfully identifying the key words of a question should always clarify the question but it may lead you to conclude that this is a question you should avoid.

Once the key words have been 'scored' they then should be 'exploded' into the margins of your question paper for note-form explanation. If the question addresses 'feedback', it is important that you should be able to write in your own words what 'feedback' is. Similarly, if the question asks you to consider the differences between high culture and popular, it is important that you are able to define each of these for yourself. Once you've dealt with the paper in this way, you're ready to offer your responses. Here the advice we offer must take account of the different kinds of questions that the new Communication and Culture exam favours. There are effectively three question styles here.

Three in one: the challenges of a Communication and Culture exam

1 The critic Dick Hebdige has suggested that 'Culture is a notoriously ambiguous concept', pointing out that 'the word has acquired a number of quite different meanings, often contradictory'. Choose **one** of the following definitions of culture and write about your own cultural experiences in the terms of your chosen definition.

EITHER

1(a) Culture is quite simply 'the best that has been thought and said in the world' (Arnold 1868).

OR

1(b) Culture is 'a particular way of life that expresses certain meanings and values' (Williams 1965).

OR

1(c) Culture consists of 'all the characteristic activities and interests of a people' (Eliot 1948).

(20 marks)

2 Which of the following statements best reflects your understanding of the relationship between verbal and non-verbal communication in personal communication? Use examples to support your example.

2a) Verbal communication dictates the meanings of personal communication.

2b) Verbal and non-verbal communication are entirely complementary: they work together to ensure effective communication.

2c) 'Actions speak louder than words'. Most social meanings are carried non-verbally.

(20 marks)

Given the obviously limited amount of time available to you for each of four compulsory questions (between 20 and 25 minutes per question), you should expect the tasks to be focused rather than open-ended. For the first two, as you can see in the samples overleaf, you will hopefully realize that this is being done in two ways:

- By a content focus on firstly culture, then communication
- By a format that requires you to support or explore answers to key questions rather than providing them for yourself

For example, question 1 asks you to consider one of three possible definitions of 'culture' and relate this to your own experiences and understandings. This reinforces a central platform of this course, the idea that most of the key issues are open to a variety of interpretations. Similarly the question on 'communication' addresses key cultural codes (verbal and non-verbal communication) in a way that allows you to choose which description of their relationship best fits your own understandings of this. You will be marked on the quality of your supporting arguments and evidence rather than your ability to 'back' the right answer!

By contrast task three is a little more familiar perhaps:

Task 3

Look at this RSPCA advert in Figure 9.6.

Figure 9.4 RSPCA advert

3(a) Give examples of potential barriers to communication in relation to this advert. *(4 marks)*

3(b) Identify the principal codes of communication working through this text. *(6 marks)*

3(c) What might a semiotic analysis of this advert reveal about the ways in which it communicates? *(10 marks)*

Task 4

The anthropologist Anthony Cohen wrote the following about how we learn to be part of the society and culture. Read the extract and answer the question that follows it.

Learning to be social is not like learning grammar or the Highway Code. It is not reducible to a body of rules. Of course, one can identify rule-like principles in culture. . . . These principles will sufficiently observed in practice that the contravention would identify the perpetrator as an outsider or as deviant.

Explore the argument that all cultural and subcultural groups have 'rule-like principles' which allow them to easily identify outsiders.

(20 marks)

Sample exam paper 2

1 People who criticise popular culture argue that it has little value; in fact some even claim it is a corrupting influence. Others argue for the importance of popular culture as an area of study. Choose **one** of the following justifications of the validity of popular culture and use examples to support your choice.

EITHER

1(a) Popular culture has value and is worthy of study because it comprises experiences which are in themselves sophisticated and complex.

OR

1(b) Popular culture has value and is worthy of study because it has a major role in defining people's identities.

OR

1(c) Popular culture has value and is worthy of study because it is demo-cratic and enjoyed by large numbers of people.

(20 marks)

2 Which of the following do you consider gives the best indication of our true identity? Explain your choice in a brief account.

■ Appearance
■ Idiolect
■ Body language

(20 marks)

3 This is an advert for Wonderbra, apparently created to cope with the restrictions on depictions of nudity imposed by Middle Eastern countries such as the United Arab Emirates.

Figure 9.5 Wonderbra – available soon in the United Arab Emirates

3(a) Comment on the woman's non-verbal communication.

(4 marks)

3(b) What is the status and function of the black patch obscuring the centre of the image?

(6 marks)

3(c) Explore the ways in which the words on this document influence the ways in which it is read.

(10 marks)

4   This is an imaginary letter to a problem page:

'Whenever I look at myself in the mirror, I can't believe that the person I see is really me. It's the same when my friends tell me what they think of me. Whether it's good or bad, I feel as if they are talking about a stranger.'

Analyse the views expressed in this letter using your knowledge of some or all of the following:

- self-image
- self-concept
- mirror self
- identity
- feedback
- self-disclosure.

As you can now see from two full sample papers each of the four questions has its own function and focus. Task 3 with its (even) shorter answers is a test of 'Toolkit' knowledge through a little application to a manageable text. Here more than anywhere, 'measuring' your response according to the marks allocated to each part is essential, with 3a) and 3b) only carrying together the same value as 3c). Note also that the a), b), c) here do not indicate options but rather essential parts of a compulsory question.

Task four completes the journey by continuing the theme of 'analysis' only this time you are analysing and responding to issues and situations whether these be concerned with the organization of sub-cultural groups or an individual's sense of their own identity. This task, along with the coursework, is the explicit meeting place between 'Communication' and 'Culture' and as such may range across the whole of the AS course. It is the most open of the four tasks since it is, with the presentation, the proper culmination of the AS work and a pointer to what is coming in A2. It will always have a stimulus text or an extract which you may or may not be required to use as a focus for the question.

GLOSSARY

Aberrant decoding 'reading' a text in any way other than as it is intended, usually because the receiver does not share a knowledge and understanding of the code or codes used by the sender.

Adapters almost unconscious gestures used to relieve stress or boredom; for example, drumming fingers on a desk or scratching the back of your head. Often, adapters signal nervousness or anxiety in situations such as giving a talk or being interviewed, so we do our best to control them.

Affective function refers to the important role non-verbal communication has to play in establishing and maintaining relationships.

Anchorage directing receivers towards one particular meaning from a range of possible meanings. A caption can anchor the meaning of a photograph.

Assertiveness training courses in assertiveness training seek to build confidence through the development of communication skills, which include the recognition and ability to resist manipulative non-verbal controls.

Bardic function bards were the poets and minstrels of their day. They translated the everyday cultural concerns of the Middle Ages into verse. In their book *Reading Television* (1990), Fiske and Hartley argue that television plays a similar role today. Television has its own specialised language and it helps to define reality for us, reinforcing the dominant myths of our culture. The idea of the bardic function stresses continuity; television is playing a role that has always been played.

Codes meaning systems consisting of signs. Signs are anything that has the potential to generate meaning, to signify. When a sign has generated meaning, it is said to have achieved signification. This is fundamental to the semiotic approach to the study of communication.

Code switching refers to the way in which we may change between languages or dialects depending on who we are talking to.

Convergence the way in which we adjust our language to make it more like the language style of the person we are addressing if we want to convey warmth, friendliness and empathy.

Cultural capital the idea that knowledge of certain topics can confer similar benefits to monetary wealth. People who possess lots of money and wealth have economic capital. Those who are able to converse knowledgeably about (say) philosophy, music, art or literature have cultural capital. We could also extend the concept to the realm of expert knowledge in subcultural groups: subcultural capital.

Divergence moving language style away from the other person's way of speaking can signal status or the desire to avoid intimacy.

Emblems gestures with the specific cultural meanings attached, often used as direct substitutes for words.

Entropy a communication that is high on new information and that is highly unpredictable is said to be entropic.

Gatekeeper someone who controls the selection of information to be offered to a given channel. Thus, for example, newspaper editors are significant gate-keepers, but we are all gatekeepers in an interpersonal sense, deciding as we do what we communicate and what we omit or hold back.

Genre this term describes the subdivisions of the output of a given medium (e.g. television, film, magazine publishing). A genre is a type, a particular version of a communication medium. For example, soap opera is a television genre, for it represents a particular approach to theme, style and form.

Haptics touching, physical contact such as holding, hitting, kissing, stroking, shaking hands, guiding.

Hegemony the Italian writer Antonio Gramsci explained why the majority of people in a culture do not adopt the values and beliefs of their own class. He argued that the dominant minority within cultures present the values and beliefs of their own class as somehow 'natural' and thus universal. In this way people end up promoting the values and beliefs of the dominant or ruling class rather than of their own class.

Illustrators these gestures reinforce the words of a speaker; for example, by pointing to something in a shop while saying 'I'll have one of those'.

Kinesics body movement such as gesture, facial expression, posture, nodding, orientation (where you put your self in relation to others).

Looking-glass-theory the idea that we base views of ourself on how we think others are perceiving us and judging us.

Mode of address this term describes the way in which a text 'speaks' to its audience. The text incorporates assumptions about its audience. If you can answer the question 'Who does this text think I am?', you are on the way to identifying its mode of address.

Motivation in addition to the everyday meaning of 'a force that drives us', motivation is a term used in semiotics to refer to the relationship between the physical form of a sign and the thing or idea it represents. A photograph of a cat is a highly motivated (or *iconic* sign) whilst the word 'cat' has low motivation (it is an *arbitrary* sign).

Narrative the way in which a text reveals information to the audience in order to create a 'story'.

Negotiation this concept is at the very heart of the semiotic approach to the study of communication, implying as it does that texts do not have meaning except through the process of negotiation between text and reader.

Non-verbal communication all communication other than that involving words and language.

Non-verbal leakage when messages 'slip out' in spite of our attempts to control them.

Occulesics eye movement, length and direction of gaze, changes in pupil size.

Olfactics smell, odour.

Paradigm a set of signs from which one might be chosen to contribute to a syntagm. Paradigms define their individual members with reference to all others in the set. To select from a paradigm is at that moment to reject all other signs in that set, just as by selecting something (or nothing) to cover your feet today, you have rejected all other possibilities; this choice from a paradigm of 'foot coverings' has contributed to the syntagms which constitute the things you are wearing today. When Peugeot's 'lion' went 'from strength to strength', it got its strength partly from the paradigm of 'elite animals' from which it was chosen and partly because that paradigm does not include 'weasel', 'frog' and 'sloth'.

Paralanguage consists of the non-verbal elements that accompany speech. It includes the way we speak (also known as prosodic features); volume; pitch; intonation; speed of delivery; articulation; rhythm; the sounds we make other than language; laughter; crying; lip smacking; yawning; sighing; screeching; coughing; filled pauses such as 'Mmmm', 'Ahhh', Errr', 'Ummm'; unfilled pauses.

Phatic communication aspects of language which serve to reinforce social relationships rather than to communicate information (e.g. 'Have a nice day').

Polysemy/Polysemic refers to the capacity of a text or part of a text to be read in several different ways. For example, a red rose might communicate love, a fondness for horticulture, a political allegiance or Lancashire.

Preferred reading the reading a text's producer would like receivers to make. The producer will compose the text in a way which ensures this occurs.

Proxemics the study of how we use space and distance including seating arrangements, queuing and territoriality.

Received pronunciation (RP) deals solely with the sounds of words (accent) and can be described as the prestigious speech of educated people. It is usually associated with London and the south-east and with the middle and upper classes. It is sometimes known as the Queen's English, Oxford English or BBC English.

Redundancy a communication that is low on new information and which is highly predictable is said to be redundant.

Reflexivity describes what it is to be self-conscious, to be self-aware and to reflect on who you are, what you're doing and how you present yourself in the world. It is a feature of much of contemporary communication that it is similarly conscious and aware. It is self-reflexive. In this way, for example, we are used to seeing films about the making of films, advertisements that play with the conventions of advertisements, and comedies that refer to the 'rules' of comedy.

Register is used to describe variations in the use of language associated with a particular context such as a job, an area of technical expertise or social setting. As a student, part of the task is to learn the register of your subject so that you are able to write and speak as, say, a historian or a geographer or a biologist.

Rubric these are the instructions that appear on the cover of the examination paper and at the head of each section of the examination paper. Typical rubrics are: 'Answer two questions' or 'Answer one question from each section'.

School of thought a set of beliefs or ideas held by a group of academics; a shared way of thinking about a particular issue.

Self-concept is the idea we have of ourselves as individuals.

Self-fulfilling prophecy refers to how our belief that something is true can cause it to be so. For example, if we believe we are confident, we act as if we are confident, and so become confident.

Signifier/signified according to Saussure, the basic unit of communication is the sign. The sign is composed of two elements – the signifier and the signified. The signifier is the physical form of the sign; for example, a written or spoken word or a photograph. The signified is the mental concept triggered by the signifier. When you see the signifier HORSE you think of a horse (the signified). Of course, neither one of these is a real horse. The first is a carefully designed but minuscule quantity of ink on the page; the second is an abstract idea. The signifier and the signified unite to form the sign, but the relationship between the two elements is an arbitrary one, that is, there is no logical or necessary relationship between them. That's why it's possible to change which signifier relates to which signified; there are no absolute rules connecting the signifier and the signified. If you had no knowledge of English or you could not read, then the signifier HORSE would not attach itself to a signified in your mind. If you speak French, you will recognise the signifier CHEVAL.

Stereotype a mould into which reality is poured, whatever its individual shape. A stereotype is a simplified and generalised image of a group of people, which is created out of the values, judgements and assumptions of its creators, in most cases society itself. A stereotype of men might suggest their machismo or manliness.

Style shifting this refers to the way in which we may modify our use of the same dialect within different situations. For example, we may use more formal language at an interview than we would use at home.

Syntagm a chain of signs, a unique combination of sign choices. Units may be visual, verbal or musical. The scale of the units and syntagms may range from the very large (the nine planned episodes of the *Star Wars* triple trilogy might constitute a syntagm) to the very small (as in the syntagm *I like noodles*, which consists of the signs 'I', 'like' and 'noodles'). The important point is that syntagms invite negotiation as a whole; they are bigger units of potential meaning. The signs which comprise a syntagm are organised in accordance with the 'rules' or conventions of the relevant code.

Transactional analysis an approach to understanding and ultimately improving interpersonal communication introduced by Eric Berne in his book *Games People Play* (1968). The essence of Eric Berne's theories of personality is that each of us at any one time has the option of adopting one of three ego states: 'the child', 'the parent' and 'the adult'. These are not stages of maturity, they are options within all of us; a 6-year-old can adopt a parent ego state in conversation with a 30-year-old in 'child' ego state.

Uses and gratifications theory this is an approach to understanding the role of mass communication in society. The basic premise runs as follows. We all have various needs and desires, such as needs for information, entertainment and social interaction which media texts (such as television programmes, video games, magazines and newspapers) help us to fulfil. Hence we use the mass media to gratify our needs.

Verbal communication communicating with words and language (as opposed to images, actions or behaviour).

INDEX

AS Media Studies: The Essential Introduction for AQA

Third edition

Philip Rayner and Peter Wall

AS Media Studies: The Essential Introduction for AQA is fully revised for the 2008 specification with full colour throughout, over 100 images, new case studies and examples. The authors introduce students step by step to the skills of reading media texts, and address key concepts such as genre, representation, media institutions and media audiences as well as taking students through the tasks expected of them to pass the AQA AS Media Studies exam. The book is supplemented with a companion website at www.asmediastudies.co.uk featuring additional activities and resources, further new case studies, clear instructions on producing different media, quizzes and tests.

Areas covered include:

- an introduction to studying the media

- the key concepts across print, broadcast and e-media

- media institutions

- audiences and the media

- case studies such as *Heroes*, *Nuts*, and the *Daily Mail*

- guided textual analysis of real media on the website and within the book

- research and how to do it

- a production guide and how to respond to a brief

AS Media Studies: The Essential Introduction for AQA clearly guides students through the course and gives them the tips they need to become proficient media producers as well as media analysts.

ISBN13: 978–0–415–32965–1 (hbk)
ISBN13: 978–0–415–32966–8 (pbk)

Available at all good bookshops
For ordering and further information please visit:
www.routledge.com

AS Film Studies: The Essential Introduction

Second edition

Sarah Casey Benyahia, Freddie Gaffney, John White

AS Film Studies: The Essential Introduction gives students the confidence to tackle every part of the WJEC AS level Film Studies course. The authors, who have wide-ranging experience as teachers, examiners and authors, introduce students step by step, to the skills involved in the study of film. The second edition follows the new WJEC syllabus for 2008 teaching onwards and has a companion website with additional chapters and resources for students and teachers that can be found at http://routledge.tandf.co.uk/textbooks/9780415454339/. Individual chapters address the following key areas, amongst others:

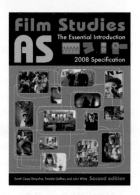

- British stars – Ewan McGregor
- Genre – Horror
- British Production – Working Title
- Social-Political Study – Living with Crime
- US Film – Westerns
- Film form
- Spectatorship
- The practical application of learning

Specifically designed to be user friendly, the second edition of *AS Film Studies: The Essential Introduction* has a new text design to make the book easy to follow, includes more than 100 colour photographs and is jam-packed with features such as:

- Case studies relevant to the 2008 specification
- Activities on films like *Little Miss Sunshine*, *Pirates of the Caribbean* and *The Descent*
- Key terms
- Example exam questions
- Suggestions for further reading and website resources

Matched to the new WJEC specification, *AS Film Studies: The Essential Introduction* covers everything students need to study as part of the course.

ISBN13: 978–0–415–45433–9 (pbk)

Available at all good bookshops
For ordering and further information please visit:
www.routledge.com

An Introduction to Language and Society

Second edition

Martin Montgomery

In this new edition of a classic textbook, Martin Montgomery explores some of the close connections between language and social life. He explores the ways in which children learn language in interaction with those around them, learning at the same time through language how to make sense of their world. He considers the social implications of accent and dialect as well as the broader interconnections of language with social class, ethnic group and subculture. He explores the role of language in shaping social relationships as part of everyday encounters and looks at the ways in which our habitual ways of interpreting the world may be shaped by the categories, systems and patterns of our language.

Despite the rapid development in new electronic technologies of communication, everyday language remains the most fundamental and pervasive communication technique. This book provides an ideal introduction to how language works in a modern society.

This new edition includes:

- a new chapter on gender and language
- new material on register, the speech community, language and subcultures and language and representation
- detailed suggestions for further reading and practical work.

ISBN13: 978–0–415–07238–7 (pbk)

Available at all good bookshops
For ordering and further information please visit:
www.routledge.com

The Media Student's Book

Fourth edition

Gill Branston and Roy Stafford

The Media Student's Book is a comprehensive introduction for students of media studies. It covers all the key topics and provides a detailed, lively and accessible guide to concepts and debates. This fourth edition, newly in colour, has been thoroughly revised, re-ordered and updated, with many very recent examples and expanded coverage of the most important issues currently facing media studies. It is structured in four main parts, addressing key concepts, media practices, media debates, and the resources available for individual research.

Individual chapters include: Interpreting media * Narratives * Genres and other classifications * Institutions * Questions of representation * Ideologies and power * Industries * Audiences * Advertising and branding * Research * Production organisation * Production techniques * Distribution * Documentary and 'reality TV' * Whose globalisation? * 'Free choices' in a 'free market'?

Chapters are supported by case studies which include: Ways of interpreting * *CSI: Miami* and crime fiction * J-horror and the *Ring* cycle * Television as institution * Images of migration * News * The media majors * The music industry, technology and synergy * Selling audiences * Celebrity, stardom and marketing * Researching mobile phone technologies * Contemporary British cinema.

The authors are experienced in writing, researching and teaching across different levels of pre-undergraduate and undergraduate study, with an awareness of the needs of those students. The book is specially designed to be easy and stimulating to use with:

- marginal terms, definitions, references (and even jokes), allied to a comprehensive glossary
- follow-up activities, suggestions for further reading, useful websites and resources plus a companion website to supporting the book at **www. routledge.com/textbooks/0415371430/**
- references and examples from a rich range of media forms, including advertising, television, films, radio, newspapers, magazines, photography and the internet.

ISBN 13: 978–0–415–37142–1 (hbk)
ISBN 13: 978–0–415–37143–8 (pbk)

Available at all good bookshops
For ordering and further information please visit: www.routledge.com

Cultural Studies: A Critical Introduction

Simon During

Cultural Studies: A Critical Introduction is a wide-ranging and stimulating introduction to the history and theory of Cultural Studies from Leavisism, through the era of the Centre for Contemporary Cultural Studies, to the global nature of contemporary Cultural Studies.

Cultural Studies: A Critical Introduction begins with an introduction to the field and its theoretical history and then presents a series of short essays on key areas of Cultural Studies, designed to provoke discussion and raise questions. Each thematic section examines and explains a key topic within Cultural Studies.

Sections include:

- the discipline
- time
- space
- media and the public sphere
- identity
- sexuality and gender
- value

Cultural Studies: A Critical Introduction will be very useful in classrooms but will also appeal to anyone with an interest in keeping up or familiarising themselves with cultural studies in its contemporary forms.

ISBN13: 978–0–415–24656–9 (hbk)
ISBN13: 978–0–415–24657–6 (pbk)
ISBN13: 978–0–203–01758–6 (ebk)

Media, Gender and Identity

An Introduction

David Gauntlett

David Gauntlett explores the gender landscape of contemporary media and draws on recent theories of identity negotiation to understand the place of popular media in people's lives. Discussing a range of examples from films such as *Charlie's Angels*, *What Women Want*, and *Tomb Raider*, men's and women's magazines from *FHM* and *Maxim* to *Cosmopolitan* and *Glamour*, primetime television programmes, and pop music, *Media, Gender and Identity* shows how the media are used in the shaping of individual self-identities.

Media, Gender and Identity includes:

- A comparison of gender representations in the past and today, with many examples drawn from 1998–2002
- An introduction to theorists such as Anthony Giddens, Michel Foucault and Judith Butler
- A discussion of queer theory and the idea of gender as performance
- A study of 'girl power' role models such as Destiny's Child and Britney Spears
- A website with extra articles, interviews and selected links, at www. theoryhead.com/gender

ISBN13: 978–0–415–18959–0 (hbk)
ISBN13: 978–0–415–18960–6 (pbk)

Available at all good bookshops
For ordering and further information please visit:
www.routledge.com